DON'T
EAT
THIS
BOOK

MORGAN SPURLOCK

G. P. PUTNAM'S SONS / NEW YORK

DON'T

FAST FOOD

EAT

AND THE SUPER SIZING

THIS

OF AMERICA

BOOK

IIP

G. P. PUTNAM'S SONS
Publishers Since 1838
Published by the Penguin Group
Penguin Group (USA) Inc., 375 Hudson Street, New York, New York 10014, USA •
Penguin Group (Canada), 10 Alcorn Avenue, Toronto, Ontario M4V 3B2, Canada (a
division of Pearson Penguin Canada Inc.) • Penguin Books Ltd, 80 Strand, London WC2R
0RL, England • Penguin Ireland, 25 St Stephen's Green, Dublin 2, Ireland (a division of
Penguin Books Ltd) • Penguin Group (Australia), 250 Camberwell Road, Camberwell,
Victoria 3124, Australia (a division of Pearson Australia Group Pty Ltd) • Penguin Books
India Pvt Ltd, 11 Community Centre, Panchsheel Park, New Delhi–110 017, India •
Penguin Group (NZ), Cnr Airborne and Rosedale Roads, Albany, Auckland 1310, New
Zealand (a division of Pearson New Zealand Ltd) • Penguin Books (South Africa) (Pty) Ltd,
24 Sturdee Avenue, Rosebank, Johannesburg 2196, South Africa

Penguin Books Ltd, Registered Offices:
80 Strand, London WC2R 0RL, England

Library of Congress Cataloging-in-Publication Data

Spurlock, Morgan, date.
Don't eat this book : fast food and the super sizing of America / Morgan Spurlock.
p. cm.
ISBN 0-399-15260-1
1. Junk food—United States. 2. Junk food—Humor. 3. Fast food restaurants—United
States. 4. Fast food restaurants—Humor. I. Title.
TX370.S68   2005   2005043196
614.5'9398—dc22

Printed in the United States of America
1   3   5   7   9   10   8   6   4   2

This book is printed on acid-free paper. ∞

Book design by Stephanie Huntwork

For Sasha, my love and my inspiration

CONTENTS

DON'T EAT THIS BOOK

ONE

DO YOU WANT LIES WITH THAT?

Don't do it. Please. I know this book looks delicious, with its lightweight pages sliced thin as prosciutto and swiss, stacked in a way that would make Dagwood salivate. The scent of freshly baked words wafting up with every turn of the page. *Mmmm*, page. But don't do it. Not yet. Don't eat this book.

We turn just about everything you can imagine into food. You can eat coins, toys, cigars, cigarettes, rings, necklaces, lips, cars, babies, teeth, cameras, film, even underwear (which come in a variety of scents, sizes, styles and flavors). Why not a book?

In fact, we put so many things in our mouths, we constantly have to be reminded what *not* to eat. Look at that little package of silicon gel that's inside your new pair of sneakers. It says DO NOT EAT for a reason. Somewhere, sometime, some genius bought a pair of sneakers and said, "Ooooh, look. They give you free mints with the shoes!"—soon followed, no doubt, by the lawsuit charging the manufacturer with negligence, something along the lines of, "Well, it didn't say *not* to eat those things."

And thus was born the "warning label." To avoid getting sued, corporate America now labels everything. Thank the genius who first decided to take a bath and blow-dry her hair at the same time. The Rhodes scholar who first reached down into a running garbage disposal. That one-armed guy down the street who felt around under his power mower while it was running.

Yes, thanks to them, blow-dryers now come with the label DO NOT SUBMERGE IN WATER WHILE PLUGGED IN. Power mowers warn KEEP HANDS AND FEET AWAY FROM MOVING BLADES. And curling irons bear tags that read FOR EXTERNAL USE ONLY.

And that's why I warn you—please!—do not eat this book. This book is FOR EXTERNAL USE ONLY. Except maybe as food for thought.

We live in a ridiculously litigious society. Opportunists know that a wet floor or a hot cup of coffee can put them on easy street. Like most of you, I find many of these lawsuits pointless and frivolous. No wonder the big corporations and the politicians they own have been pushing so hard for tort reform.

Fifty years ago it was a different story. Fifty years ago, adult human beings were presumed to have enough sense not to stick their fingers in whirring blades of steel. And if they did, that was their own fault.

Take smoking. For most of us, the idea that "smoking kills" is a given. My mom and dad know smoking is bad, but they don't stop. My grandfather smoked all the way up until his death at a grand old age, and my folks are just following in his footsteps—despite the terrifying warning on every pack.

They're not alone, of course. It's estimated that over a billion people in the world are smokers. Worldwide, roughly 5 million people died from smoking in 2000. Smoking kills 440,000 Americans every year. All despite that surgeon general's warning on every single pack.

What is going on here? It's too easy to write off all billion-plus smokers as idiots with a death wish. My parents aren't idiots. I don't think they want to die. (When I was younger, there were times when I wanted to kill them, but that's different.) We all know that tobacco is extremely addictive. And that the tobacco companies used to add chemicals to make cigarettes even more addictive, until they got nailed for it. And that for several generations—again, until they got busted for it—the big tobacco companies aimed their marketing and advertising at kids and young people. Big Tobacco spent billions of dollars to get people hooked as early as they could, and to keep them as "brand-loyal" slaves for the rest of their unnaturally shortened lives. Cigarettes were cool, cigarettes were hip, cigarettes were sexy. Smoking made you look like a cowboy or a movie starlet.

And it worked. When my parents were young, everybody smoked. Doctors smoked. Athletes smoked. Pregnant women smoked. Their kids came out of the womb looking around the delivery room for an ashtray to ash their Lucky Strikes. Everyone smoked.

The change began in 1964, when the first surgeon general's warning about smoking and cancer scared the bejesus out of everybody. In 1971, cigarette ads were banned from TV, and much later they disappeared from billboards. Little by little, smoking was restricted in airplanes and airports, in public and private workplaces, in restaurants and bars. Tobacco sponsorship of sporting events decreased. Tighter controls were placed on selling cigarettes to minors. Everyone didn't quit overnight, but overall rates of smoking began to decrease—from 42 percent of adults in 1965 to 23 percent in 2000, and from 36 percent of high school kids in 1997 to 29 percent in 2001. The number of adults who have never smoked more than doubled from 1965 to 2000.

Big tobacco companies knew it was a war they couldn't win, but they didn't give up without a fight. They threw billions and billions of more dollars into making smoking look cool, hip, sexy—and safe. They targeted new markets, like women, who increased their rate of smoking 400 percent *after* the surgeon general's report. Yeah, you've come a long way, baby—all the way from the kitchen to the cancer ward. They expanded their markets in the Third World and undeveloped nations, getting hundreds of millions of people hooked; it's estimated that more than four out of five current smokers are in developing countries. As if people without a regular source of drinking water didn't have enough to worry about already. Big Tobacco denied the health risks of smoking, lied about what they were putting into cigarettes and lobbied like hell against every government agency or legislative act aimed at curbing their deadly impact.

Which brings me back to those "frivolous" lawsuits. Back when people were first suing the tobacco companies for giving them cancer, a lot of folks scoffed. (And coughed. But they still scoffed.) Smokers knew the dangers of smoking, everyone said. If they decided to keep smoking for thirty, forty years and then got lung cancer, they couldn't blame the tobacco companies.

Then a funny thing happened. As the lawsuits progressed, it became more and more apparent that smokers did *not* know all the dangers of smoking. They couldn't know, because Big Tobacco was hiding the truth from them—lying to them about the health risks, and lying about the additives they were putting in cigarettes to make them more addictive. Marketing cigarettes to children, to get them hooked early and keep them puffing away almost literally from the cradle to the early grave, among other nefarious dealings.

In the mid-1990s, shouldering the crushing burden of soaring Medicare costs due to smoking-related illnesses, individual states began to imitate those "ambulance-chasers," bringing their own class-action lawsuits against Big Tobacco. In 1998, without ever explicitly admitting to any wrongdoing, the big tobacco companies agreed to a massive $246 billion settlement, to be paid to forty-fix states and five territories over twenty-five years. (The other four states had already settled in individual cases.)

Two hundred and forty-six billion dollars is a whole lot of frivolous, man.

What these lawsuits drove home was the relationship between personal responsibility and corporate responsibility. Suddenly it was apparent that sticking a cigarette in your mouth was not *quite* the same thing as sticking those sneaker mints in your mouth. No one spent billions and billions of dollars in marketing, advertising and promotions telling that guy those sneaker mints would make him cool, hip and sexy. Big Tobacco did exactly that to smokers.

Still, a lot of people were skeptical about those lawsuits. Are the big bad corporations with all their big bad money and big bad mind-altering advertising really so powerful that we as individuals cannot think for ourselves anymore? Are we really so easily swayed by the simplest of pleasant images that we'll jump at the chance to share in some of that glorious, spring-scented, new and improved, because-you-deserve-it goodness, without a thought about what's best for us anymore?

You tell me. Every waking moment of our lives, we swim in an ocean of advertising, all of it telling us the same thing: Consume. Consume. And then consume some more.

In 2003, the auto industry spent $18.2 billion telling us we needed a new car, more cars, bigger cars. Over the last twenty-five years, the number of household vehicles in the United States has doubled. The rate of increase in the number of cars, vans and SUVs for personal travel has been six times the rate of population increase. In fact, according to the Department of Transportation, there are now, for the first time in history, *more cars than drivers* in America. That's ridiculous!

Did we suddenly *need* so many more vehicles? Or were we sold the idea?

We drive everywhere now. Almost nine-tenths of our daily travel takes place in a personal vehicle. Walking, actually using the legs and feet God gave us, accounts for appallingly little of our day-to-day getting around. Even on trips of under one mile, according to the Department of Transportation, we walked only 24 percent of the time in 2001 (and rode a bike under 2 percent). Walking declined by almost half in the two decades between 1980 and 2000. In Los Angeles, you can get arrested for walking. The cops figure if you're not in a car you can't be up to any good. If you're not in a car, you're a vagrant. Same goes for the suburbs, where so many of us now live.

And what do you put inside that SUV, minivan or pickup truck you're driving everywhere, other than your kids? Well, lots of *stuff*, that's what. In 2002, the retail industry in this country spent $13.5 billion telling us what to buy, and we must have been listening, because in 2003 we spent nearly $8 *trillion* on all kinds of crap. That's right, trillion. How insane is that? We are the biggest consuming culture on the planet. We buy almost twice as much crap as our nearest competitor, Japan. We spend more on ourselves than the entire gross national product of any nation in the world.

And all that shopping—whew, has it made us hungry. Every year, the food industry spends around $33 billion convincing us that we're famished. So we all climb back into our giant vehicle filled with all our stuff from Wal-Mart, and we cruise to the nearest fast-food joint. If not McDonald's or Burger King or Taco Bell, then a "fast casual" restaurant like Outback Steakhouse or TGI Friday's or the Olive Garden, where they serve us portions larger than our smallest kid, with the calories to match.

What does all that consumption do for us? Does it make us happy? You tell me. If we were all so happy, would we be on so many drugs? Antidepressant use in the U.S. nearly *tripled* in the past decade. We've got drugs in America we can take for anything: if we're feeling too bad, too good, too skinny, too fat, too sleepy, too wide awake, too unmanly. We've got drugs to counteract the disastrous health effects of all our overconsumption—diet drugs, heart drugs, liver drugs, drugs to make our hair grow back and our willies stiff. In 2003, we Americans spent $227 billion on medications. That's a whole lot of drugs!

This is the power of advertising at work, of billions of hooks that've been cast into our heads in the last thirty years, billions of messages telling us what we want, what we need and what we should do to feel happy. We all buy into it to some degree, because none of us is as young as we'd like to be, or as thin, or as strong.

Yet none of the stuff we consume—no matter how much bigger our SUV is than our neighbor's, no matter how many Whoppers we wolf down, no matter how many DVDs we own or how much Zoloft we take—makes us feel full, or satisfied or happy.

So we consume some more.

And the line between personal responsibility and corporate responsibility gets finer and more blurred. Yes, you're still responsible for your own life, your own health, your own happiness. But your *desires*, the things you *want*, the things you think you *need*—that's all manipulated by corporate advertising and marketing that now whisper and shout and wink at you from every corner of your life—at home, at work, at school, at play.

Consume. Consume. Still not happy? Then you obviously haven't consumed enough.

Like this book, the epidemic of overconsumption that's plaguing the nation begins with the things we put in our mouths. Since the 1960s, everyone has known that smoking kills, but it's only been in the last few years that we've become hip to a new killer, one that now rivals smoking as the leading cause of preventable deaths in America and, if current trends continue, will soon be the leading cause: overeating.

Americans are eating themselves to death.

TWO

GIRTH
OF A
NATION

The United States is the fattest nation on earth. Sixty-five percent of American adults are overweight; 30 percent are obese. According to the American Obesity Association, 127 million Americans are overweight, 60 million Americans are obese and 9 million are "severely obese." In the decade between 1991 and 2001, obesity figures ballooned along with our own figures: from 12 percent of us being obese in 1991 to 21 percent in 2001. Almost double. In ten years.

> Over 20 percent of the adults in forty-one states and Washington, D.C., are obese. As of fall 2004, obesity is highest in Alabama (28.4 percent) and lowest in Colorado (16 percent). All that mountain climbing and hiking really must be good for you.

We've added so much weight in the last couple of decades that even the airline industry has to struggle to haul us around. In November 2004, the Associated Press reported:

America's growing waistlines are hurting the bottom lines of airline companies as the extra pounds on passengers are causing a drag on planes. Heavier fliers have created heftier fuel costs, according to [a] government study.

Through the 1990s, the average weight of Americans increased by 10 pounds, according to the Centers for Disease Control and Prevention. The extra weight caused airlines to spend $275 million to burn 350 million more gallons of fuel in 2000 just to carry the additional weight of Americans, the federal agency estimated in a recent issue of the American Journal of Preventive Medicine. . . .

The extra fuel burned also had an environmental impact, as an estimated 3.8 million extra tons of carbon dioxide were released into the air, according to the study.

So many of us are obese that we've created a market for a whole industry supplying us with extra-large and reinforced car seats, giant chairs, super-heavy-duty bathroom scales, "toilets rated to 1,500 pounds, beds built to hold 1,100 pounds, even something called a 'trapeze' that helps people who weigh 1,000 pounds turn over in bed," the AP reports. Even our military forces are fat: 16 percent of active-duty troops are obese. (Well, they always said an army moves on its stomach.)

This was posted on my blog at www.supersizeme.com in December 2004:

I am in the USMC in Iraq. . . . Not only is the Marine Corps experiencing drastic problems with obesity (yes, obesity) but they're also running into more cases of severe depression, bipolarity disorders and severe hormone imbalances. In addition, the average MRE (meal-ready-to-eat) contains 1,400 calories (and that's one of the modest ones) and hundreds of different preservatives, high fructose corn syrup and large quantities of

salt. I guess if you're starving in the trenches, then it's not so much a problem, but the grand majority of us aren't.

Who supplies a lot of the food products that go into MREs, and our hot
chows from Sodexho [the food service company contracted by the mili-
tary]? You guessed it. Kraft, Mars, Hershey's, etc. Theoretically (and we've
gone through the nutritional information on our side), in order to eat health-
ily from the chow hall for three meals a day, you would have to completely
skip over the hot meal section (you know, the cafeteria portion where they
serve you fried beef patties and potatoes) and go straight to the salad bar,
and even then, you would be minus major nutrients like protein, calcium
and essential fats (unlike unessential grease and butterfat). So, yeah. Obesity is even hitting the Marine Corps.

We've taught our kids how to be fat, too. Obesity rates in children
remained stable up through the 1960s. They began to climb in the
1970s, and in the last twenty years, the rate of obesity has doubled in
children and *tripled* in adolescents and teens.

Sixteen percent of American kids are now overweight or obese. As
of September 2004, *nine million* American kids between the ages of six
and eighteen were obese. Kids are starting to clock in as obese as early
as the age of two.

The obesity epidemic is truly nationwide, cutting across class, race,
ethnicity and gender. But like so many health issues in this country
(smoking, for one example), it has the worst impact among poor Americans, especially African Americans and Hispanic Americans. The *Journal of the American Medical Association* says that 77 percent of African
American women and 61 percent of African American men are overweight or obese. The National Women's Health Information Center
says that Mexican American women are 1.5 times more likely to be
obese than the general female population. The *Seattle Post-Intelligencer*

says that in the Seattle area, "nearly 22% of adults living in households with incomes of less than $15,000 a year are obese, compared with almost 15% in homes pulling in $50,000 a year or more."

There are many interlocking factors that probably contribute. Some of it may be genetic: Blacks and Hispanics seem to be genetically more at risk for some diseases, like diabetes, than whites, and may be genetically more prone to obesity as well. But many factors are social, economic and environmental. For one thing, obesity rates decline as the level of education increases:

- Less than high school: 27.4 percent
- High school degree: 23.2 percent
- Some college: 21 percent
- College or above: 15.7 percent

Obviously, lower-income folks don't have the access to health education and information that people of higher incomes do, just as a matter of course.

Maybe more critically, they also don't have access to health-promoting facilities or institutions. There are far fewer supermarkets in low-income urban neighborhoods than in better-off suburbs—and even if they can get to a supermarket, they may well find junkier, less nutritious foods more affordable than healthier items like lean meat and fresh veggies. The USDA reports that the cost of vegetables and fruit rose 120 percent between 1985 and 2000, while the price of junk like sodas and sweets went up less than 50 percent on average.

What the lower-income neighborhoods do have is an overabundance of predatory fast-food joints, bad takeout and small corner grocery stores stocked with nothing good. For example, go to the McDonald's website and look at its location map for a major metropolitan area—say, Los Angeles. You'll see so many Golden Arches in lower-income areas like South-Central and East L.A. that they overlap on the map. Now look at Beverly Hills. How many Golden Arches do you see?

You don't see many Bally's Total Fitness or Crunch gyms in low-income areas, either. Also, most diet plans and programs are priced for and marketed to people of middle income and above. Adam Drewnowski, director of the Center for Public Health Nutrition at the University of Washington, says that sticking to the Atkins diet (not that I'm advocating that) costs about $15 per person per day, whereas low-income families spend more like $3.57 per person per day on food.

Being poor discourages healthy eating habits in lots of ways. Many lower-income kids depend on the federally funded National School Lunch Program for their primary hot meal of the day—and get basically the same high-fat, low-nutrition food dumped on them there as they'd get at a fast-food joint. Then, too, according to *The Baltimore Sun*, families who rely on government assistance have a tendency to splurge when the monthly check or food stamps arrive (which I think is human nature), then find the cupboard bare toward the end of the month. Nutritionists say that kind of cyclical feast-or-famine diet unbalances your metabolism, so it's easy to store fat and hard to get rid of it.

Being overweight doesn't just mean you get called names by other kids. Fat is *deadly*. Obesity-related illnesses will kill around 400,000 Americans this year—almost the same as smoking. "The epidemic of childhood obesity is only the latest grim chapter of a burgeoning American tragedy," *The Washington Monthly* has declared. Obesity brings on a whole host of health problems, including high cholesterol, high blood pressure, heart disease, colon cancer, gout (which I thought went out with Henry VIII), arthritis, menstrual abnormalities, sleep apnea and diabetes. The United States spends about $117 billion annually on treating these illnesses.

The prevalence of diabetes has skyrocketed among American kids in the last twenty years—right along with their blood pressure. There are basically two types of diabetes. Type 1 diabetes develops when the body's immune system destroys the cells that make insulin, and is generally thought to be caused by genetic, autoimmune or environmental factors. Type 2 diabetes is the kind you can develop through bad diet and excess weight. It used to take years to develop type 2 diabetes—that's why it was called "adult-onset" diabetes. Now, so many kids have type 2 diabetes that we have to stop calling it by that old name. New cases of type 2 diabetes in adolescents increased by a factor of ten between 1982 and 1994.

You want a really sad and scary statistic? In 2003, the Centers for Disease Control and Prevention reported that one out of three kids born in America in the year 2000 will develop type 2 diabetes. Among African American and Hispanic kids, it's almost one out of two.

One out of two! When I was a kid, type 2 diabetes was something your classmate's neighbor's overweight Uncle Joe might get. Now *every other* kid in your class might get it.

If you have diabetes or know someone who does—and the chances are growing that you do—you know it's no joke. Diabetes can lead to heart attacks, strokes, blindness (in 12,000 to 24,000 Americans a year), kidney failure (in 38,000 per year) and nerve damage in the lower legs, which may result in amputation (in 82,000 per year). Diabetes-related chronic kidney failure doubled in America in just the years from 1990 to 2001. Diabetes also makes you more susceptible to death from flu and pneumonia. Diabetes is currently the sixth-highest cause of death in America, but that's obviously going to increase a lot as today's kids grow up and we become a nation where one-third to half of us are diabetic.

And then there's the Big C.

Larry Axmaker of Vanderbilt University's Online Wellness Center writes: "According to studies conducted by the American Cancer Society . . . more than 20 percent of all cancer deaths in women and 14 percent in men are linked directly to being overweight. Another 33 percent of cancer deaths are linked to poor diet and physical inactivity. . . . That's a lot of people dying needlessly."

Specifically, diet and obesity have been linked to increased risk for breast, colon, endometrial, esophageal, and kidney cancer. Diets rich in plant-based fibers—whole grains, vegetables, fruits and beans— apparently reduce risks for these types of cancer. Diets high in animal fat seem to promote cancer and inhibit recovery from things like breast and colon cancer.

Where do people eat high-fiber, plant-based diets? The nonindustrial world, that's where. Where do people eat too much meat and fat? Guess.

In 2004, the American Cancer Society reported, "Because up to 60 percent of cancers may be prevented through healthy lifestyle behaviors that often begin in childhood, children and youth are an important audience for cancer prevention." Instead, overweight parents are teaching their kids not to exercise and to go to Mickey D's for Happy Meals.

Then again, it's less likely that very overweight people will have children in the first place. Very overweight women are less able to become pregnant, even when embryos are fertilized in the lab. Very overweight males are likely to have poor sperm quality, possibly because they often have too much estrogen, which is produced by fat cells.

You want to know how truly, sadly ridiculous things have gotten? Pet experts now say that we're even training our pets to be fat. One in four cats and dogs in America is now obese. No wonder they won't come when you call them.

And in the last few years we've been spreading this epidemic of obesity around the world. As we export American values, the American lifestyle and especially American fast food to other cultures around the world, we have sparked a global obesity crisis.

Way to go, America. Making the world safe for diabetes.

. . .

The sudden obesity epidemic that has erupted over the last thirty years invites the obvious question: What has changed in America during the last three decades? If your answer is that we've become more genetically predisposed to be fat, *tzzzzzzt!* Sorry, wrong answer. But don't worry—your parting gift is a lovely, extra-large toaster oven, where you can heat up a whole box of Pop-Tarts at one time.

It's true, there does *seem* to be some sort of genetic predisposition to obesity. It's thought to be one reason obesity is especially prevalent among African Americans and Hispanic Americans. In 2001, the BBC reported that a French team of scientists had pinpointed an "obesity gene"—but, they went on to note, "the majority of people in Europe carry the gene—so it is only one piece in the jigsaw of reasons why obesity develops."

The point is that our genes haven't changed over the last thirty years, just the waist size of our jeans.

So what *has* changed in the last thirty years? Experts cite a complex list of social factors that have contributed to the epidemic, but when you de-jargonize the language, it's really simple:

- We are eating more food than ever before—way more.
- We are eating more food that's bad for us—way worse.
- And we are getting less physical exercise—way less.

Between 1971 and 2000, the daily caloric intake of the average adult American woman went up from 1,542 calories to 1,877. For the average adult male it rose from 2,450 to 2,618. The government recommends women take in around 1,600 daily calories and men around 2,200, so the average

American adult is now overeating by a few hundred calories a day. For kids, it's gone up anywhere from 80 to 230 extra calories a day.

Ah, but what's a few hundred extra calories a day between friends, right?

Wrong. Here's the math:

An extra 10 calories a day translates to the addition of one extra pound of fat a year. If the average American is overeating by about 200 calories a day, that's a whopping twenty pounds of flab every year.

Everybody in the world, in every culture, has known that overeating was bad for you. From the ancient Greeks to the modern age, we have been told to be moderate in our eating. In the Judeo-Christian tradition on which our society was supposedly founded and to which we Americans give so much lip service (pardon the pun), overeating wasn't just bad for you, it was *bad*, period. As in morally wrong. They even made it one of the seven deadly sins—gluttony. In Dante's *Inferno*, gluttons are tormented for all eternity in the third circle of Hell, where the three-headed dog-monster Cerberus entertains himself by tearing them limb from limb and flaying their skins off. And no one ever tells them, "You deserve a break today!"

In just the last thirty years, we've trashed those thousands of years of civilized tradition. In our new consume-consume-and-consume-some-more culture, gluttony isn't a sin, it's a virtue. We're encouraged to eat, and eat more, and eat a big dessert on top of that. Everywhere we look, there are all-you-can-eat-buffets and super jumbo value packs of candy, and chocolate chip cookies the size of footballs, and hot-dog-eating contests, and bored teens behind fast-food counters telling us that for just a few pennies more we can double the size of that burger, those fries, that Coke or Pepsi.

How did this happen? In his book *Fat Land,* Greg Critser cites a couple of things that got us started on our national binge. Once again, your government at work for you, looking out for your best interests. No, wait, I mean your government at work *against* you, looking out for your *worst* interests.

To start with, in the early to mid-seventies, the American economy was stuck in a long, grinding recession. It was the era of long gas lines, longer lines at the unemployment office, war debt, "stagflation" and the economic collapse of the big cities (as in the infamous *New York Daily News* headline, FORD TO CITY: DROP DEAD). Two groups who felt the pinch the worst were American farmers and American families. On the farm, inflation was driving food-production costs into the stratosphere. At the grocery store, this translated into sky-high prices on basic items like hamburger, sugar, cheese, coffee and margarine. Everyone was unhappy. Farmers went to Washington to complain to their congressmen. Families actually held protest rallies inside grocery stores.

I remember during this time how great my mother was at stretching a dollar and making food last. She would roast a chicken for dinner on Sunday, and on Monday, we'd have chicken sandwiches, chicken soup on Tuesday, chicken salad on Wednesday, chicken pot pie on Thursday, and on Friday I would crawl into the kitchen, pleading with my mother, "Please tell me there's no more chicken."

"Nope," she'd say. "Chicken is all gone. Tonight we're having roast beef!" And the cycle would continue.

So the federal government tried to appease both families and farmers. It did a bunch of things to stimulate farm production, and at the same time did a bunch of other things to bring prices back down at the grocery store. The result was that by the 1980s American farms were producing an overabundance of food, and it was affordable again. In fact, there was more food, and cheaper food, than ever before in human history. Americans responded the way you'd expect us to—by buying more and eating more.

The other, and I think much more influential, factor in the fattening up of America was the rise of the fast-food industry. It's no coincidence that the explosion of obesity in this country happened at exactly the same time as the explosive growth of the fast-food industry. Before 1970, a "fast-food joint" was a burger or hot dog stand out on the highway somewhere. Now we're literally surrounded by fast food, everywhere we go—in every city and town, in every mall and shopping center, in airports and on airplanes, even in our schools and hospitals. As I've traveled around the country, I've been to a lot of places where fast food was the only kind of food available "on the go."

> In 1970, there were around 70,000 fast-food establishments in the country. In 2001, there were 186,000.
>
> In 1968, McDonald's operated about 1,000 restaurants. Today it has about 31,000 worldwide—almost 14,000 of them in the United States.

In 1970, Americans spent $6.2 billion at fast-food joints. In 2004, it was $124 billion. Twenty times as much! The *American Journal of Preventive Medicine* published a study in 2004 showing that the percentage of fast-food calories in the American diet has increased from 3 percent to 12 percent over the last twenty years.

The fast-food industry has been pretty relentless in encouraging us to eat. Critser explains that during those recession years of the mid-1970s, Americans cut way back on what they spent at the movies, in restaurants and at fast-food joints. The problem for the fast-food industry was how to convince them to eat and spend more.

A McDonald's exec named David Wallerstein came up with the answer. He'd faced the same problem in the movie theater business. Movie theaters make tons of money on popcorn and the other crap they push on us. It's what they call a "high markup" item—it doesn't cost them much, so there's a big profit margin on it. Wallerstein wanted to get people to eat more popcorn. He tried two-for-one specials, but they didn't work—no one wanted to be caught scarfing down two boxes of popcorn. "So Wallerstein flipped the equation around," Critser writes. "Perhaps he could get more people to spend just a little more on popcorn if he made the boxes bigger and increased the price only a little. The results after the first week were astounding. Not only were individual sales of popcorn increasing; with them rose individual sales of that other high-profit item, Coca-Cola."

Call it the Birth of the Super-Size Nation. The fast-food industry took the idea and ran with it in the mid-seventies. Instead of trying to get people to buy two burgers, they put a bigger patty on one sandwich, called it a Whopper and charged you a little extra for it. Instead of two Cokes, they started offering larger cups. Who could forget the birth of the Big Gulp at 7-Eleven? That giant quart tub of cola that cost only a fraction more than what you used to spend for half as much soda! People got to eat more, and they felt like they were getting a good deal. They were even called "value meals." Sales skyrocketed. Everybody in the fast-food industry started doing it—Taco Bell, Burger King, Pizza Hut and of course Mickey D's. By the mid-nineties, one out of four meals sold at fast-food joints was a value meal, a special combo or a super-size meal.

"Fast casual" and "family" restaurants also started increasing the size of their portions—and even the plates they served them on. Since food only represents about one-fifth of a restaurant's expenses, they can pile a lot more on your plate and charge you just a little more for it. You'll feel like you got to stuff yourself at a good price, so you'll come back.

Outback Steakhouse, with its "Aussie-size" portions, is a particularly grievous offender. (Outback is not really an Australian company, by the way. It's based in Tampa, Florida.) When I called Outback to ask, they told me that one order of its Bloomin' Onion rings wallops you with up to 2,500 calories—that's what the average adult male is supposed to eat in an entire day. And that's an appetizer. Throw on, say, a Drover's Platter of ribs and chicken, a salad drenched in cheese and fatty dressing, and finish off with one of their mountainous Sydney's Sinful Sundaes, and you've packed in as many calories as you should be taking in over several days. In one meal.

"The portions that are served are so enormous that to finish a portion is like you've eaten enough food for a week," *New York Times* restaurant reviewer Eric Asimov told me. "People . . . feel they're disobeying their mothers if they don't clean their plate." At the same time, he says, "I can't tell you how many people complain to me about the small portions in more expensive restaurants, or when they travel in Italy or France or Japan. They get much less food than they're used to, and they feel cheated."

Believe me, I understand. I come from a long line of eaters. Every family function I go to is centered around food. And I grew up in a house where "value" was very important, as I'm sure a lot of you did. So when we see ALL YOU CAN EAT, TWO FOR ONE, SUPER-SIZE or MORE FOR LESS, those messages go straight to a very basic instinct that has been banged into our craniums since birth: *Get your money's worth.*

Lisa Young, a New York University professor of nutrition, food studies and public health, explained to me how the portions grew. When fast-food places first opened, they tended to offer one size of fries, for example. At McDonald's, that size, which contained about 200 calories, eventually became the "small order." Then they added "medium," "large," and "super size." A super size order of fries, which came in a cardboard bucket the size of a small child's head, packed over 600 calories. A Big Mac Combo delivers a hefty 1,140 calories. Until 2004, you could super size it and get 1,460 calories for just pennies more! The average meal at McDonald's, according to Critser, expanded from 590 calories to a jumbo 1,550 calories. By the end of the century, Del Taco was offering a "Macho" meal that weighed *four pounds.*

Young helped conduct an NYU study that compared the portion sizes of what's served at fast-food joints and family restaurants to what the FDA and USDA call "a portion." They found muffins that were three times what the USDA calls a portion, restaurants that served five times the pasta, and cookies that were 700 percent of a USDA portion! That's a big-ass cookie! Even the portion sizes in diet food like Lean Cuisine and Weight Watchers have increased over the years.

In the early days, a soda at Burger King was 12 ounces. That's now called a "small" soda. A medium is 20 ounces, and a large is 32. A super size soda at McDonald's was 42 ounces. The Double Gulp at your local 7-Eleven comes in a bucket the size of a wastepaper basket, which holds 64 ounces of soda—half a gallon! Depending on how much ice you put in it, that's 600 to 800 calories. And it contains the equivalent of 48 teaspoons of sugar. It's liquid diabetes! Who needs to drink a half-gallon of soda at one time? Nobody, that's who. But we buy it—because the offer seems like a great deal.

One nutritionist has said that your average fast-food meal isn't one meal, it's more like three, and a Cornell professor has proved it. Each year, he sends his students to McDonald's with an assignment: figure out how to satisfy—but not exceed—your daily nutritional requirements eating only McFood, for the least amount of money. He arms them with the McDonald's nutritional chart and the government's Recommended Dietary Allowance information and nutrition guidelines. For a healthy young adult male, the best they could come up with, ringing in at a price of $6.70, was:

- ⅓ of a regular hamburger
- a little more than one side salad, without dressing
- four butter garlic croutons
- a little more than one hotcake with margarine and syrup
- three nuts (from a sundae)
- ⅓ of a baked apple pie
- nearly all of a 32-ounce Chocolate Triple Thick Shake
- about 3 ounces of orange juice

In other words, it was totally impractical.

I had to laugh when *Playboy* magazine published its "Women of McDonald's" pictorial in November 2004. It was pretty obvious to me that none of these young ladies ate much of the McFood they were serving up.

These joints have influenced us to eat more at home, too. A recent study showed that the average American dinner at home has also been super-sized over the last twenty years. Portion sizes have increased dramatically at home. They've also increased in the snacks we munch on, often when we're not even thinking about it. Now we don't just go through half a bag of the Cheez Doodles while watching Monday Night Football, we wolf down the whole bag.

Have we all become compulsive eaters? Are we all gluttons? Are we actually, physically hungrier than we used to be? Or will we simply eat more if you put it in front of us, whether we're really hungry or not?

A study done at Penn State suggests the latter. Volunteers were served a series of lunches that kept increasing in size and "as portions increased, all participants ate increasingly larger amounts," no matter how hungry they were. A University of Illinois study found that if you hand the average person a one-pound bag of M&Ms, he'll eat 80 pieces; hand him a two-pound bag, and he'll eat 112 in the same period of time.

If you put it there, we will eat it. Just keep your hands away from our mouths.

John Robbins, author of *Diet for a New America* and *The Food Revolution*, offers a wise, and I think true, explanation. "The quality of food that we're eating is degrading so rapidly," he told me. "We're eating more of it, because it's advertised so massively and it's so convenient. . . . So we're always wanting to eat more and more and more, because there's something inside us that's saying we're not getting what we need and want. . . . We lose touch with that inner compass by which we can sense what's good for us. Instead, we give up control over what we eat to the corporations and the fast-food companies."

The evidence is clear, America. We don't really need to eat more. We're not really hungrier than we were thirty years ago, and God knows we're not more physically active. No, friends, we've been *trained* to eat more. Conditioned to do it. Have you seen that commercial where the pizza guy rings the doorbell and the guys in the house go running like Pavlov's dogs, literally salivating and slobbering all over themselves? It was played for laughs, but I saw that commercial and thought, "What the hell is *funny* about that?" That's what we've become—lab rats for the junk-food industry!

We're not only eating more food, we're eating more food that's bad for us, that doesn't satisfy us and that makes us hungry for more soon after. Fast food is terrible for you. It shouldn't even be called "food." It should be called more like what it is: a highly efficient delivery system for fats, carboyhdrates, sugars and other bad things. Most of those extra calories we're putting on come in the form of carbohydrates. Especially fries. The average American now wolfs down 30 pounds of french fries annually—up from only 3.5 pounds in 1960. And don't forget sodas. Soft-drink consumption in the United States increased 135 percent between about 1977 and 2001. It's highest, not surprisingly, among kids: American kids now drink twice as much soda as they did twenty-five years ago.

In the late 1970s, the USDA reports, boys consumed more than twice as much milk as soft drinks, and girls consumed 50 percent more milk than soft drinks. By 1996, both boys and girls consumed twice as much soda as milk. One-fifth of American kids are now drinking sodas at the ages of one and two.

The average American teen drinks two or more 12-ounce sodas a day. How much sugar is in a single 12-ounce soda? Ten teaspoons. *That kid is consuming the equivalent of twenty teaspoons of sugar every day.* Just in soda. Throw in all the other sugar the average kid consumes in fast food, junk food and snacks. Then ask me again why we're seeing an epidemic of type 2 diabetes in America's children.

Soda is also bad for the teeth and bones, especially for teenagers. Between 40 and 60 percent of peak bone mass is built during the teen years. But the phosphoric acid in sodas prompts the body to pull calcium and other minerals *out* of the bones to counteract the acidity, which can lead to osteoporosis down the line.

There ain't a nutritionist or physician on the planet who'd tell you that sucking down that much daily sugar—not to mention the caffeine—is good for a teenager. In fact, they'd tell you what health researcher David Ludwig of Children's Hospital in Boston says—that "for every additional serving per day of soft drink consumed, the risk of becoming obese increased by about 50 percent." But try getting Coke or Pepsi to admit they're harming our kids and they just howl that you're un-American, a pinko Commie and definitely a "food Nazi." Meanwhile they've got that kid so surrounded with their product, and so inundated with their message, that trying to get him or her to stop drinking soda is worse than trying to get an alkie off the sauce.

THREE

THE LIGHT AT THE END OF THE TACO

It would be one thing if we needed all those extra carbs because we'd all become more physically active. If the adults were all out chopping wood, building houses, pushing lawn mowers, hanging wet laundry and hauling groceries, and the kids were all out climbing trees, running, swimming and jumping, then it would make sense.

But you know the truth—the exact opposite has happened. Physical activity has declined across the board at the same time that our caloric intake has increased. Studies show that almost 60 percent of Americans exercise rarely or never. That figure pretty exactly correlates with the number of overweight and obese Americans. An amazing coincidence, right?

We don't walk, run or ride bikes, we drive. Even golfers don't walk anymore, they ride. We roll our groceries from the store to the SUV. We ride our lawn mowers. Who hangs wet laundry anymore? Who chops wood? Who does windows? (You do? Could you come over and do mine?)

Physical activity declined 13 percent among adolescents between 1980 and 2000.

Kids used to walk or ride their bikes to school. Now Mom or Dad drives them. Kids used to run around for an hour of recess every day. Many schools have eliminated that. Kids used to have to take phys ed each day in school. Now, more and more schools have severely reduced or eliminated that, too. After school, kids used to run, walk or ride their bikes to the playground, the baseball diamond or, if they were city kids, just out to the back alley. They'd chase each other around, play ball, shoot some hoops. If they tried to sneak into the house and lie around watching cartoons on TV, their moms would force them back outside to run and play. Now kids are driven home after school and plunk themselves down with the Xbox, where the only parts of their bodies that get any exercise are their thumbs.

Adults used to get at least some exercise at work, but that's changed now, too. We drive to work, take an elevator to our floor and sit down all day in front of a computer. As America switched from a manufacturing and farming economy to a service and high-tech one, more and more of us have jobs that don't require anything in the way of physical activity. We sit in cubicles and answer phones. We stand behind a counter pushing value meals on customers. And we're all working longer hours, too. By the time the workday is done, we know we should get to the gym, but it's so late, we're so tired and we're so hungry.

And the weight sneaks up on us. "[I]f a person drives instead of walks for only 20 minutes every day for a year he will store about 26,000 calories, thus gaining about five pounds," *The Washington Monthly* notes. "Researchers at the University of Minnesota estimated that over a year, those who spend only five minutes each workday sending e-mails to coworkers instead of visiting their offices will gain an extra pound. Most of us gain weight this way, a few grams a day, a few pounds a year—but enough to shorten our lives."

Believe me, I know all the excuses for not exercising. I've used them all.

I'm too busy.

I'm too tired.

I ran out of time today.

I look terrible in my gym shorts.

Besides, you've been to the gym. You know what it's like. It sucks. You get all sweaty and tired. When you're done punishing yourself, you get to walk into the stinky locker room and avoid looking at a whole lot of people you'd really rather not see naked. No wonder it's so easy to come up with excuses for not going.

I spend an average of ten hours a day at work, occupied by something that I have to do to further my career in a way that makes me happy. With that comes sacrifice—less time spent with friends, less time with my girlfriend, less time spent taking care of myself. Usually it's the taking care of myself that gets thrown out the window first. Alex (my girlfriend) and my friends come before going to the gym.

Take today. Today I flew into Los Angeles and promised myself that as soon as I got to my hotel I would go to the gym. I had been cramped up in an airplane with two hundred smelly strangers for hours. There was nothing I wanted more than to get to my room, change clothes and go exercise.

When I get to the hotel, I unpack. And what do I do next? I get on my computer and start working.

Working. Immediately. I haven't even gone to the bathroom yet! E-mails, news, research, some quick thoughts on this book . . . It's two hours before I look up. I smell like plane. I decide to take a shower, *then* hit the gym.

Well, you know how that is. You get out of the shower, now you're squeaky clean and the steam has made you all soft and lazy. Last thing you want to do is hit the gym and work out and get smelly again.

Besides, it occurs to me I'm starving. All I've eaten so far was the "snack" on the plane. A Lorna Doone, a handful of really salty nuts, and a little plastic cup of lukewarm water that tasted, I don't know, *old*. Like used water.

No, you can't work out on an empty stomach. Let's order some lunch first, then we'll go.

I eat a good, healthy lunch—salad with goat cheese and balsamic dressing, some bread. Should I go to the gym now? Nah, can't exercise right after eating. It's like swimming. Need to wait a while. So I stretch out on the bed and grab the remote. I love TV. Nobody can waste more time in front of the TV than me. The Home Shopping Network? *Love* that knife show. VH1? I watch all the recap shows. Does this hotel have movie channels? Oh man, now it's guaranteed I'm gonna get sucked in for the next two to six hours.

At some point much later, I rouse myself from my TV-induced stupor. The light is fading from the sky out my window. Jesus, where'd my day go? Couldn't I have watched the director's cut of *American Wedding* some other time?

Now I face an ethical dilemma: How best to atone for wasting the whole afternoon? Should I go to the gym, or get some work done on this chapter? Finish this chapter, I tell myself sternly, and *then* you can go.

So I sit down and stare at this page, the flashing cursor, trying to find the next path to inspiration. When I look up again, it's 9 p.m. Too late to work out now. If I do, I'll never get up and go to the gym in the morning. Might as well order some dinner and watch another movie. Hmm, *Terminator 3* is on. I wave to my laptop. "I'll be back," I tell it. . . .

That's my daily battle, so you can't lie to me—I know this is how a lot of us live, searching through the minutes of our days for the quickest escape routes from all our best-laid plans. Believe me, I am as bad as the next guy. But I'm changing, though it ain't easy. Especially when you're a stubborn thirty-four-year-old who doesn't like to be told what to do.

But hey, wait a minute! What have I been thinking? I just remembered something! (I'd slap my forehead, but that's too much exertion.) I don't have to spend time in a smelly old gym to work off those extra carbs! All I have to do is . . .

Diet!

Yes, the All-American Diet. Another consumer's dream. Today's American diet plan is to overeating what the charge card is to overspending: a handy-dandy, painless way to make it *easy*.

In the bad old days, dieting was hard. A diet was a "strict regimen." It required willpower and self-discipline. Dieting meant you had to *deny* yourself. *Eeeewww!*

Ah, but don't worry, America. Over the last thirty years, dieting has been completely transformed to bring it more into line with our effortless, consumerist lifestyle. The folks who design diet plans now realize that moderation and discipline are hopelessly old-fashioned concepts that went out with the corset and the high-button shoe. The modern diet plan makes you exactly the opposite promise: Now you can lose weight without changing your habits one bit. Now you can shed those ugly extra pounds of flab without lifting a finger. It's so easy, you can even do it in your sleep.

The lovely and talented Suzanne Somers coos that you can *Get Skinny on Fabulous Food* and *Somersize Desserts* and *Eat, Cheat, and Melt the Fat Away*. The late, great, and suspiciously overweight Dr. Atkins declared, "Fighting the scale armed only with will-power and determination works, at best, for only five low-fat dieters out of a hundred." But by applying his breakthroughs in nutritional science, he offers a way to lose weight and still "eat as much as you want, as often as you want," eat "like a king or queen," and eat "luxuriously." *The Zone* and *Protein*

Power make similar promises. And you wonder why these books were best sellers. But no one beats *The Abs Diet,* which helpfully explains that "the best way to maintain a fit physique is to eat *more* food, not *less.*" This diet "lets you enjoy the foods you crave. It's not low-carb, low-fat, or low-anything-else. It's just a smart, sensible, healthy plan that will give you the body you want in weeks. And you'll never feel hungry, restricted, or deprived."

Yeah, baby! Sign me up! I want to eat all I want, turn my abs into a six-pack, look like Brad Pitt and lie on the couch all day! These guys have found the cure for world hunger and world peace at the same time! Give them the Nobel!

One guy swears, "My 'formula for living' lets you eat: hamburgers, hot dogs, fries, steak, ice cream, sausage, bacon, eggs and cheeses! And STILL LOSE WEIGHT!"

Another croons, "Eat any mouthwatering food you want, and still blast away dress sizes and belt notches lightning fast."

There are even creams on the market that you can supposedly just rub on your fat and it will magically disappear. And, of course, there are pills. It wouldn't be modern America if there weren't pills. Some of them are old-fashioned "appetite suppressants"—conventionally known on the street as "speed." Then there are the new "fat-blockers." One declares, "Super Fat-Fighting Formula guarantees rapid weight loss. Shortly after ingesting small amounts of the component, it dissolves into a gel that absorbs and surrounds excess fat and calories, preventing them from forming body fat."

If you believe that, I'd try to sell you the Brooklyn Bridge—if you didn't already hold the deed.

The Federal Trade Commission is the government agency that's supposed to act as watchdog for false advertising—and every once in a while, it does seem to get around to doing that. It has a brochure for its agents called "Red Flag: Bogus Weight Loss Claims," with guidelines for what they should be looking for in diet ads. Here's what it says:

If the claim looks too good to be true, it probably is.

Despite claims to the contrary, there are no magic bullets or effortless ways to burn off fat. *The only way to lose weight is to lower caloric intake and/or increase physical activity. Claims for diet products or programs that promise weight loss without sacrifice or effort are bogus.* And some can even be dangerous.

Oh, darn. Guess it's back to the gym.
Tomorrow.
I swear.

Okay. That's the bad news.

So what do we do now?

It's not like we don't know there's a problem. There are even reality TV shows about obesity now. On *The Biggest Loser*, people competed to lose weight; whoever dropped the most won $250,000. In the UK, they put an entire street in Birmingham on a diet on the show *Fat Nation*. And the rest of us sink back on the couch and watch.

It's sort of the new American Way.

Or we could wake up. Fight back. Get off our butts and do something. You know, the *old-fashioned* American Way.

Because there is light at the end of the taco. Trust me. Remember, we've only become aware of the obesity epidemic in the last few years. The government's actually getting involved now. Some extremely dedicated health experts and nutritionists have defined the problems and are pointing to solutions. This being America, some folks are taking the food industry to court. Books and movies have alerted millions of folks to the issues, and in the past few years we've definitely spooked the fast-food industry into making at least some changes in the way they do business.

There are things we can all do to take back the responsibility for our own health and our families'. We've spotted the iceberg, and we're beginning to make course corrections that might actually turn this *Titanic* around.

The key is, we can't keep saying the iceberg isn't there.

I remember when you would see President Clinton get up in the morning and go for a jog with his Secret Service guards to McDonald's. *Advertising Age* said his infamous morning jogs were worth millions of dollars in free publicity for the company. He would eat so much fast food that he joked, "When my daughter started preschool and she was asked what her father did, she said that he works at McDonald's." He also had Domino's pizza delivered to the White House. An intern named Monica Lewinsky was given the task of ferrying it to the Oval Office. As *The New York Times* later joked, that was one "fateful pizza."

In 1992, concerned schoolkids sent him a petition asking him to give up junk food. In a quintessential display of Clintonian logic, *The New York Times* says, he felt he already had, saying: "I don't necessarily consider McDonald's junk food, you know. I eat at McDonald's and Burger King and these other fast-food places. A lot of them have very nutritious food. You know, they have chicken sandwiches, they have salads, they got all kind of things."

He must not have read the fine print about all the sodium, saturated fat and sugar contained in all those "healthy" options—because in September 2004, former President Clinton was rushed to the hospital for quadruple-bypass surgery. He claimed to have a genetic predisposition for heart trouble, but he readily admitted that his lifelong fast-food diet probably contributed.

Then take Jim Cantalupo, former CEO of the McDonald's Corporation. He was with McDonald's for nearly thirty years and twice served as its CEO. Then, on April 19, 2004, four months before Clinton was rushed to the hospital, he keeled over and died of a heart attack while at a global McDonald's conference in Florida. He was only sixty years old.

The man who instantly replaced Cantalupo was Charlie Bell, an Australian, the first non-American to run the company. Bell was a McDonald's legend. A McGenius of sorts, he started working for the company slinging burgers and cleaning toilets in Sydney, Australia, at age fifteen. By nineteen, he was managing his own location, one of the youngest managers ever. At twenty-nine, he was elected to McDonald's Australian board of directors. At forty-three, he was named the new CEO, the youngest CEO ever to run the company. Impressive, right?

Well, a week later he held a press conference to announce to the world that he had colorectal cancer and would begin treatment immediately.

A reporter at the press conference asked, and I'm paraphrasing, whether Bell thought all the McFood had any impact on his cancer and Cantalupo's death. Was it more than just a coincidence?

Bell scoffed. "These are isolated, totally unrelated acts of God," he declared.

When I told that story to a journalist in Perth, Australia, he screamed, "Crikey!" (because they say funny things like that in Australia). "Sounds like God doesn't like McDonald's."

In November of 2004, only seven months after taking over, Bell stepped down as CEO to fight his cancer full-time. His condition worsened, and two months later he passed away. A new CEO, Jim Skinner, was named.

Let's hope he packs a lunch.

FOUR

A
REALLY GREAT
BAD IDEA

It was Thanksgiving 2002. I was sitting on the couch in my mother's living room in Beckley, West Virginia, my stomach stuffed like the turkey I had just helped devour. I grew up in a house with two older brothers, where I graduated from the Eat It *Fast* school of etiquette. At our dinner table, if you didn't eat fast you didn't get seconds—you barely got firsts.

So there I lay, sunk into my mom's couch in a tryptophan daze, hand inserted into the top of my pants, pulling a total Al Bundy, just like tens of millions of other American males at that moment, when a story came on CNN. It was about a couple of teens in the Bronx who'd hired a fancy New York City lawyer, Samuel Hirsch, to sue McDonald's. You know the story. The girls claimed they'd become obese and sick from eating McFood. Ashley Pelman was fourteen years old, four-foot-ten and weighed 170 pounds. Jazlen Bradley was eighteen, five-foot-six and weighed a whopping 270 pounds. Their obesity had led to diabetes, heart disease, high blood pressure and elevated cholesterol. Ashley said she ate a Happy Meal three or four times a week. Jazlen said she liked a McMuffin for breakfast and a Big Mac for dinner.

When I'd first read about this case a couple of months earlier, my reaction was like a lot of people's—get out of here! This thing had "frivolous lawsuit" written all over it. The kid ballooned to 270 pounds before she realized she had a weight problem? What the hell were her parents doing while this kid bloated up like that? She's been gorging on McMuffins and Big Macs and now wants to blame Ronald McDonald because she's overweight and a diabetic? That's like a suicide's relatives suing Smith & Wesson because the gun worked. Or that case from the nineties, where some genius spilled hot coffee in her lap and sued McDonald's because the coffee was . . . hot. Isn't coffee *supposed* to be hot?

When is hot coffee just too frickin' hot?

Like most folks, I was disgusted when a woman in Albuquerque, New Mexico, who'd spilled a cup of McDonald's coffee in her lap, won her $2.9 million lawsuit against the company in 1994. Then I looked into the details.

Turned out that Mickey D's was serving its coffee at 180 degrees Fahrenheit, an average of 20 degrees hotter than most any other food establishment. Hot enough to give this poor woman gruesome third-degree burns of the groin, inner thighs and buttocks, requiring skin grafts and a week in the hospital. She was eighty-one years old and had never brought a lawsuit against anybody in her life. She only sued McDonald's after they offered her a measly $800 toward her medical bills.

It also turned out that during the decade before this case, McDonald's had received no fewer than *700 complaints* about burns from its coffee, from mild ones to third-degree scaldings, and had paid some $500,000 in out-of-court settlements. In other words, the company ignored more than ample evidence that it was serving its coffee dangerously hot.

How's that for a caring corporate citizen?

I was even more skeptical when I learned that the same lawyer representing these two girls suing McDonald's was also representing a guy named Caesar Barber. Barber is a middle-aged maintenance man who'd lived on fast food for years and was suing McDonald's, Burger King, KFC and Wendy's because he'd had two heart attacks.

But then I started to put the case in some context. The cases of Ashley and Jazlen, and of Caesar Barber, were just the latest installments in a long line of stories detailing what was being portrayed as a growing problem in America. In 2002, you couldn't turn on the TV, open a newspaper or magazine or listen to the radio without hearing a report on the "Obesity Epidemic in America!" (Cue scary thriller music here.) We had just broken free from all the 9/11 news, Osama was still running around and there was no big war in Iraq going on yet, so we needed a new villain, and fat fit the bill. It was killing us, we supposedly knew it and we weren't doing anything about it. It had all the makings of a war story, without the actual war. Hey, it's not called the battle of the bulge for nothing.

Maybe it interested me because my mom raised me at a dinner table eating good, home-cooked meals. Or because my girlfriend Alex, who happens to be a vegan, has taught me a lot about eating healthy. Vegans are like super-sized vegetarians. They not only don't eat meat, but they also avoid a lot of other foods, like dairy and eggs. Alex is a vegan chef. I know, you think that's funny. Well, so did my family. In fact, when my grandmother first met her, she said, learning across the table and whispering to me, "Morgan, how can she be a chef? She doesn't eat anything."

Now, I'm not a vegan. Not by a long shot. I'm not even a vegetarian. I still love to eat the occasional cheeseburger, juicy rib eye, slice of sugar-cured ham or fresh tuna steak. I just don't eat a lot of red meat anymore—not because we all know it's bad for us to eat too much of it, but just because of how sluggish I feel after eating it. Maybe twice a month I'll have that burger or steak. But no one on this planet loves the swine more than I do. *Mmmm*, pork. To put it simply, I would make one terrible Jew and an even worse Muslim, but I make one hell of an infidel. Just ask McDonald's.

Mostly I eat fish, a little chicken, pork, pasta and of course lots of fresh vegetables. If Alex is cooking, we eat vegan. But if you want to take my Thanksgiving turkey drumstick away from me, you'll have to pry it from my cold, dead fingers. I love to eat.

Hirsch's argument was not that selling unhealthy food should be illegal. It was that McDonald's fails to give consumers adequate information about the ingredients and possible health risks of its food and in fact falsely advertises it as "nutritious." He also accused the corporation of marketing a "physically and psychologically addictive" product to kids.

McDonald's responded the way you'd expect them to. Good old Ronald McDonald, friend of every kid in the whole wide world, wasn't shedding a single tear for these two girls. If these kids were fat and ill, it was their own fault. And their parents'. Ronald McDonald didn't put a gun to their heads, march them into the nearest Mickey D's, and force them to gorge on Big Macs and super size fries. He didn't prevent them from eating a balanced diet or getting any exercise. They did it themselves, of their own free will.

As I lolled on the couch, a McDonald's spokesman appeared on the screen and said (I'm paraphrasing), Listen, you can't link our food to these girls being sick. You can't link our food to these girls being obese. Our food is healthy and nutritious. It's good for you.

That got me to sit up. It is? Egg McMuffins and Big Macs are healthy and nutritious? They're *good* for me? Really?

Well, if it's that good for me, shouldn't I be able to eat it every day, with no side effects? Shouldn't I be able to eat it for breakfast, lunch, dinner, snacks, desserts, the works, and be fine?

The light bulb switched on.

I turned to Alex.

"I've got a great idea for a movie!" I said.

She looked very dubious.

I told her my idea—to use myself as the guinea pig and see what would happen if I dove into a typical American lifestyle of overeating and underexercising for thirty days. And I'd film myself doing it.

"I'll tell you what'll happen," she said. "You'll kill yourself."

By this point, I was already running through my mom's house like a kid who just beat his older brother in basketball for the first time ever. I grabbed the phone and called Scott Ambrozy, a longtime friend and director of photography. He was at his parents' house in Jersey, flopped on the couch in his own gobbler haze. I told him the plan.

"I'm gonna eat nothing but McDonald's food for thirty days straight to see what happens, and you're going to film me doing it."

When he finished laughing, he said, "Wow. That's a really great bad idea."

Little did we know how great and how bad. That phrase soon became our running mantra throughout the production of the film.

So that was the birth of *Super Size Me*, my first feature film. I'd always said I wanted my first movie to be something different. Something that would catch people's attention about an important issue. Something that might do some good in the world.

I never said I wanted to risk my health making my first movie, but what the hey? Everybody suffers for their art, right? Van Gogh lost an ear. Kurt Cobain lost his life. Poor Britney twisted her knee and had to cancel her summer 2004 tour. These things happen.

Still, since the movie came out in 2004, lots of people have asked me how an apparently sane person in evidently great health would want to do something so crazy and potentially dangerous as living solely on McDonald's meals for thirty days. The answer is rooted in lessons I've learned from three women in my life—it's all their fault that I became so interested in issues surrounding what and how we eat.

It started with Mom. No, it's not that she didn't love me or that she locked me in a closet and beat me with her shoe (much). It's that this terrible woman, for as long as I can remember, loved being a cook and took great pride in teaching her kids about food. When I picture my mother, it's a struggle for me to imagine her anywhere but in the kitchen, either wearing an apron or with a towel draped over her shoulder, cooking up a storm and listening to NPR on the radio. She cooked dinner for me and my brothers almost every single day. It was at her dinner table that my food education began.

"This is good for you and this isn't."

"You should eat this food this many times a week, but not this."

"This is a treat."

She wasn't a stay-at-home mom, either. She worked her ass off all day as an English teacher, ran us kids around all afternoon as we did kid things, then came home and made dinner. Every day. Why? Because it was important to her. Almost as important as making sure I never left any participles dangling (the downside of having an English teacher for a mother). She instilled in me many great habits for everyday life: opening doors for people, saying please and thank you, respecting my elders and, most important, what good, fresh food is.

Every summer my mother would plant a garden, and I would be put to work watering the plants, pulling weeds, hoeing, harvesting vegetables. Under the boiling summer sun I'd curse her name, but when I look back, I am so thankful this evil woman made her lazy son get off the couch and do some work. Hindsight is 20/20.

It's not like I was eating only greens and eggplant sandwiches, either. My mother was the farthest thing from a tree-hugging green queen. (No offense to the tree-hugging green queens. I myself am in love with one.) I grew up in West Virginia, where if it's not fried, it's not food. Meals in my house usually featured all of the following: something fried, some dead animal, a tall glass of vitamin D–fortified whole milk, iceberg lettuce salad with Thousand Island dressing, and Jell-O. To this day I cannot stand Thousand Island dressing, and to this day, if you walk in my mom's house, I guarantee you will find some sort of fruit floating in a pan of Jell-O in the fridge. I drank more milk growing up than many a calf, and we had meat at every meal: bacon, sausage, cream beef, ham (*mmmm*, ham), fried chicken, you name it. But no fish. Never any fish, unless it was fried, and that was still a rarity. My mom hated fish, so under her influence, so did I.

Everything we ate in my house was fresh, from the store or from our garden, rarely frozen or from a box. To ask my mom to take us out to eat was to get laughed out of the kitchen. We didn't have a lot of money when I was growing up, so when we did eat out, it was a treat, a special occurrence. Maybe once a month we'd go to Pizza Inn or Burger Chef or Tiki Garden, the local Asian flavor in Beckley, West Virginia. The rest of the month we ate at the dinner table.

There was never a TV on during dinner, either. We talked. Yes, we actually spoke to one another. Crazy, right? Dinner was a great time in my house, a time to share stories about the day, a time to reconnect with the people you love, no distractions, a time to nourish your spirit as well as your body.

Yep, first I blame my mom for making me a twisted, food-loving freak.

Then there's my ex-wife. Yeah, I was married. So what? And now I'm divorced, like more than half of American adults. Another staggering statistic in a world filled with staggering statistics. I was young, stupid and in love. We've all been there.

My ex-wife was (and still is) a beautiful force of nature. A forest fire trapped in the body of a six-foot-tall model from Columbus, Ohio. We met right after I graduated from New York University. She'd just moved to Manhattan, and we were immediately drawn to each other. She was working as a model, I was taking jobs as a production assistant on any movie, TV show or commercial that'd have me.

She would get up in the morning, fill a glass with six or seven different liquid vitamins and call that breakfast. Then off she would go to start another day of appointments and fashion shoots and meetings and emotional overload. From the instant she left the house, her entire day would be filled with criticism about how she looked, dressed and moved. If her agents, bookers or photographers saw what they considered the tiniest flaw, they attacked it, like flies on an open wound.

The result was a person who couldn't help but have food issues. A gorgeous young woman who loved to eat but was forced to obsess over her eating habits, trying to maintain her weight and her sanity in a business that pushes image and perception. Add the strain of being in a relationship with the difficult guy I was at the time, and you've got an explosive mix.

But I really felt for her. She lived in a world that exerted an incredibly warping influence on her sense of self. When I was a kid, women were shaped like women. In her world, if you weren't shaped like a ten-year-old boy there was something wrong with you. It put tremendous stress on our relationship in the early years, but at the same time I have huge admiration for the way she eventually triumphed, finding pride in who she is, and a balance in her life in maintaining a healthy weight.

She also opened my eyes to the world of food beyond the standard American grub I'd grown up eating. When I first met her at the age of twenty-four, she'd already traveled to more countries and had more experiences than most of us do in a lifetime, and she introduced me to all sorts of cuisines—Moroccan, Thai, Indian, Japanese—things this boy from West Virginia had never ventured to try. She was the first person to turn my mind and my palate on to the power of a "taste explosion"—that's what she called it when something so new and exciting hit your mouth that you felt as if your head might explode. I always liked that.

And last but not least, of course, is Alex. From the moment I met her (she picked me up in a bar) she's been a beacon of inspiration.

Alex is not one of those nutty far-left PETA vegans who throw paint at people in minks, protest Siegfried & Roy and refuse to wear leather belts. Her influence is far more subtle than that. If my mother began my food education, and my ex-wife opened the door to new taste experiences, then Alex showed me the way through it. I've tried more new things in the four years I've known her than I did in my first eighteen years of life, things I never would have eaten had I not been with her.

I mean, who in their right mind eats seaweed, right? I do now, thanks to her. Alex also turned me on to quinoa (KEEN-wah), artichokes, spelt, polenta, rice syrup, cane juice, seitan (SAY-tan), bulgar, edamame (ed-ih-MAH-may), jicama (HICK-uh-muh), tofu and a slew of other tasty delectables. Half that shit I couldn't even pronounce before I met her. Now look at me learning new things! You *can* teach an old redneck new tricks.

Don't worry, I'm still no vegan. I just love quality food now. Alex showed me that we really are what we eat. If you eat a lot of fat, sugary food, there's a good chance you're going to end up a fat diabetic; if you eat a healthy, balanced diet, then you can live a healthy, balanced life. Easy.

Since meeting Alex, I eat very little fast food (in fact, I haven't eaten "food" from any major chain since completing the film). I rarely drink soda—maybe one 12-ounce can a month. And I read more labels and pay more attention to what I'm shoveling into my mouth than ever before.

Yeah, the women in my life.

It's all their fault.

. . .

As long as I'm dealing with issues raised in response to the film, let's stroll over to the McCritics' Corner and deal with a few more before we move on.

The instant *Super Size Me* got such a great response at the Sundance Film Festival—before it had even been released in theaters—the fast-food industry was attacking me and the film, claiming that what I'd done was nothing but a "stunt."

My answer to that is: Of course it was a stunt. But it was a stunt with a very serious message behind it. Sometimes that's the only way to cut through the impenetrable fog of media and marketing, to grab people's attention and alert them to an issue the big corporations don't want them to think about. (God forbid the masses start thinking!) When people were first suing Big Tobacco in the mid-1980s, that industry's spokesmen said that was all just a stunt, too. Just greedy lawyers looking to grab a lot of headlines and make a lot of money exploiting their clients' tragedies.

Baloney. I'm not so naive that I think all those lawyers' motives were pure. I may be from West Virginia, but I didn't roll into the big city yesterday on the back of my Uncle Tom's manure-spreader. I know some of those lawyers looked at Big Tobacco and saw Big Dollar Signs. My point is, so what? Whatever their motives were, the results were spectacular. You can't deny that the documents Big Tobacco were forced to cough up in court painted a terribly revealing picture of an industry-wide conspiracy to conceal all sorts of facts and truths from the smokers they were killing with their product. Finally, we could all see Big Tobacco for the evil empire it really is, and the government had new ammunition, both to punish the industry financially and to end or severely restrict some of its most insidious practices.

We're now at a point where obesity is rivaling smoking as a killer, and a lot of people are beginning to see parallels between Big Tobacco and Big Food. Years ago, no one thought smoking was that bad, and the companies denied that it was dangerous to your health. Then they had to admit it was unhealthy, and they paid the price for misleading consumers.

Dr. Erik Steele, a physician and hospital administrator in Maine, recently wrote,

> In the debates over how to fight the obesity epidemic in America, the food industry is acting a lot like the tobacco industry did in the tobacco wars. The parallels between the two industries are striking. Both spend billions of dollars trying to get us to use more of their products and then deny any responsibility for any ill effects caused by the use or overuse of their products. Both have spent billions advertising directly to children, then denied responsibility for our children eating too much high fat and high sugar foods, or smoking. The two industries have said it is our job to be smart about what we put in our mouths, and then resisted efforts to get us the information we need to be smart.

For years, we've been hearing from the fast-food companies either that the food they push on us is "part of a healthy, nutritious diet" or that "everybody knows this food is bad for you." But do we really know that? Do most people know exactly *how* bad a diet heavy in this type of food can be? I mean, is it bad enough to cause some weight gain? Bad enough to give you a little tummy ache? Or is it bad enough to cause heart disease, liver disease, diabetes or cancer? I don't believe that most of us know exactly *how* bad a diet of high-fat, high-sugar, high-sodium and high-caffeine food can truly be on the body. We don't make that connection, and it's certainly not something the food companies do much talking about.

So I decided to talk about it for them. To use myself as a guinea pig.

Hey, what are friends for, right? I mean, Ronald has been saying he's my pal for years. I just thought I'd repay the favor. And to be heard against the tens and tens of billions of dollars the junk food industry spends shouting at us about its junk, I figured I'd better talk *really loud*. One McCritic said my movie was like a "science project conducted by the class clown." Perfect. Two clowns, mano a white-gloved mano. Bring it on, Ronny Boy.

Let's see, what other complaints have I gotten about the film? Oh yeah, the "extreme" diet I put myself on. To try to keep some semblance of structure to my very unbalanced diet, I set myself some ground rules. I would eat McFood and only McFood for thirty days straight. If they didn't sell it, I couldn't eat it. If the kid behind the counter asked me if I wanted to super size the meal, I had to say yes. And I would limit my physical activity to 5,000 steps per day, or 2.5 miles. (The average American walks about 1.5 miles per day.) Over the course of the diet, this last one would turn out to be the one rule that I couldn't consistently maintain. On average, I walked more than three miles a day, no matter how hard I tried to limit it.

"No one eats fast food that often!" the food industry cried. "No one eats that much!"

Really? Look at McDonalds' own numbers. Seventy-two percent of McDonald's patrons—nearly three out of four—are what the industry calls "Heavy Users." Kind of a Freudian slip of the corporate tongue, don't you think? *Users?* Makes us sound like a bunch of junkies, doesn't it? If that doesn't give you a clue that the McCrack Shack is open for business, I don't know what will. Anyway, these three out of four patrons go to the Golden Arches at least once a week. Another 22 percent, which pretty much means everybody else, are called "Super Heavy Users": They eat there three, four, five times a week and up. That's right—you're *Super* Heavy Users, because you're so darn good. You're super!

Now let me tell you something: If you're eating at McDonald's four or five times a week, I'd bet the organic farm that you're not going home and eating veggie tofu stir-fry at your other meals. You're not eating sprout and hummus sandwiches and going to yoga. No, you're eating junk *all* the time and you're probably doing a super job of it.

No, it's Taco Bell one day, Domino's the next, etc. I've got a friend who will eat McDonald's for breakfast, Taco Bell for lunch and order Domino's pizza for dinner. All three food groups in one day!

So when you think about it that way, my diet wasn't so extreme or that far from how way too many Americans consistently eat. And if I did exaggerate it a bit, it is still very representative of what can happen to your body over years of eating this type of food. I only did it for thirty days.

One of the funniest and lamest charges the fast-food attack dogs lobbed at me was that "Morgan Spurlock is not a physician or nutritionist." Oh man, you got me with that one! Guilty. I'm not a doctor. I don't even play one on TV. That's why both the film and this book were informed by an array of physicians, nutritionists, obesity experts, educators, psychologists, law professionals and other experts in related areas. People with impeccable credentials and the highest respect in their fields. Plus a few small, insignificant outfits like the Centers for Disease Control and Prevention and the World Health Organization.

Of course, some of these great folks have been slandered by the food industry as "food police," "cookie cops" and "the grease Gestapo." But that's a tactic as old as time: When you don't have the facts on your side, try ridiculing your opponent. Just like they tried on me.

Before we leave the McCritics Corner, let's look at who some of them were, and what their motives were.

Big corporations are careful not to attack their critics too openly or viciously in public. They're happy to haul them into court—which can backfire, as in the McLibel case (more on that later)—but in the court of public opinion, corporations try not to besmirch their carefully maintained images.

So they farm out their efforts to squash, vilify and destroy their critics through a network of hired guns and paid attack dogs who operate under the guise of lobby groups, think tanks, and even fake grassroots organizations, known as "astroturf" organizations (a ploy perfected by Big Tobacco in the 1990s). These corporate fronts have benign-sounding names, often with something pseudoacademic like "institute" or "foundation" in them, and just as often the words "citizens" or "consumer." But they're really just public-relations and lobbying outfits, and on every issue pitting the interests of their corporate sponsors against the well-being of citizens and consumers, they're in there fighting for the corporate side.

McDonald's said very little directly to attack me or my movie when it came out. My favorite line was, "We see no reason to respond to Morgan Spurlock when so many other experts have already spoken out on the film's distortions and irresponsibility. . . ."

Right. The experts. Like the experts at Tech Central Station, among my most rabid McCritics. TCS looks like a think tank and puts out a right-wing Internet magazine that's gung-ho on technology, uniformly procorporate and antiregulation. It has published a slew of articles taking Big Food's side on obesity and trashing many in the health professions, government or media who say Big Food is part of the problem.

An article in the December 2003 *Washington Monthly* noted that unlike most think tanks, which tend to be nonprofit organizations, TCS is a for-profit limited partnership. It doesn't have to make its funding sources public, but on its own website it says ". . . we are grateful to AT&T, Avue Technologies, The Coca-Cola Company, ExxonMobil,

General Motors Corporation, Intel, McDonald's, Merck, Microsoft, Nasdaq, PhRMA, and Qualcomm for their support."

What a coincidence, right?

Another hotbed of anti–*Super Size Me* sentiment was the Competitive Enterprise Institute (CEI). It calls itself "a non-profit, non-partisan public policy group dedicated to the principles of free enterprise and limited government." It's another front that looks like a think tank but operates as a corporate shill, pro–Big Food, pro-biotechnology and genetically modified foods, anti–nutritional labeling, antiregulation and very anti-me. CEI's "non-partisan" activities include lobbying against the Kyoto global warming negotiations, auto-emissions reductions and pretty much any other sound environmental policy you could name. They even sued the Clinton White House Office of Science and Technology for publishing a report on global warming it called "junk science" and a "$14 million compilation of global warming scare stories."

While lobbying on behalf of pro-smoking, pro-tobacco legislation, a CEI analyst stated in a report that the government's efforts to discourage smoking "may further the cause of health," then concluded that "there are things more valuable than health." That should give you an idea of where these people are coming from and where their loyalties lie.

CEI's big anti–*Super Size Me* idea was to promote a woman named Soso Whaley, a CEI "adjunct fellow" and anti-PETA propagandist, who started her own all-McDonald's diet in 2004 to "debunk" my movie.

It was hilarious. This woman went to McDonald's for thirty days, then another thirty; she limited herself to 1,800 calories a day, exercised regularly, lost weight and said she proved my movie was "junk science." Amazing how that happened, considering she did the two things no one in America does: *She ate less and exercised.*

She should be thanking me. My movie probably added a few years to her life.

The Center for Media & Democracy's *Disinfopedia.com* notes that while "CEI does not publish a list of its institutional donors," companies and foundations "known to have given $10,000 or more" include the Amoco Foundation, Inc., Coca-Cola Company, ExxonMobil, CSX Corporation, the Ford Motor Company Fund, Philip Morris Companies, Inc., Pfizer Inc., the ultra-conservative Scaife Foundations, and Texaco, Inc.. Additional "known sponsors" include the American Petroleum Institute, ARCO Foundation, Armstrong Foundation, Burlington Northern Railroad Co., Cigna Corporation, Dow Chemical, General Motors and IBM. Sounds like a bunch of people who have your best interests in mind, right?

And then there's Richard—or as I prefer to think of him, Dick—Berman, and his Center for Consumer Freedom (CCF), which, despite the "consumer" in its name, is really a front for the food, alcohol and restaurant industries. As *PR Watch* has pointed out several times, Berman's publicity firm, Berman & Co., has a long history of creating phony "institutes" and "centers" to lobby for his corporate clients' interests. He's an especially vicious attack dog of anyone who speaks out against his clients, and even calls his technique "shooting the messenger." In the 1990s he was a big advocate of "smokers' rights."

Berman's fronts do not reveal their funding sources, but *PR Watch* claims to have documents revealing that the major funding behind his prosmoking efforts came from Philip Morris. His "Employment Policies Institute" lobbied against increasing the minimum wage for restaurant employees. Both CCF and his "American Beverage Institute" rabidly attack Mothers Against Drunk Driving and lobby against any and every effort to regulate alcohol consumption, lumping it all under the rubric of "neo-prohibition." CCF has taken out full-page ads in places like Newsweek to oppose Greenpeace, PETA, and "professional activists spreading fear and hysteria" about foodborne diseases like Mad Cow. It rants against all environmental causes and is pro-biotechnology, pro-pesticide, and pro-genetically modified foods. (*Mmmm*, GM foods.) On the issue of obesity, Dick's one of the loudest critics of the "food police" and "the nanny culture." In fall 2004, CCF put out a press release claiming that the entire obesity epidemic was a scam created by the diet-pill makers!

Ultimately, as *PR Watch* notes, "Anyone who criticizes tobacco, alcohol, fatty foods or soda pop is likely to come under attack from Berman's front groups. His enemies list has included such diverse groups and individuals as the Alliance of American Insurers; the American Academy of Orthopedic Surgeons; the American Medical Association; the Arthritis Foundation; the Consumer Federation of America; New York Mayor Rudy Giuliani; the Harvard School of Public Health; the Marin Institute for the Prevention of Alcohol and Other Drug Problems; the National Association of High School Principals; the National Safety Council; the National Transportation Safety Board; the Office of Highway Safety for the state of Georgia; Ralph Nader's group, Public Citizen; the U.S. Centers for Disease Control and Prevention (CDC); and the U.S. Department of Transportation." And me.

If being in the company of all those folks makes me a bad guy, then I don't want to be good. That's a helluva list to be added to. I'll take it. Thanks, Dick.

It's amazing how often I'll see journalists quoting Dick, or citing a position taken by another one of these fronts, without mentioning one word about who and what they really are, or where their funding comes from. A lot of reporters seem to be naive enough to take the word of a lawyer with no formal nutritional education at face value. They'll run a quote from someone real and reputable—a government scientist, a Harvard Medical School physician, someone like that—then follow it with one from "Richard Berman, director of the Center for Consumer Freedom," as though he were somehow just as credible. What it should say is "Dick Berman, paid public relations flack for the food and alcohol industry."

. . .

While I'm on this subject, I should mention that you also have to be careful about organizations like the American Dietetic Association (ADA), the American Heart Association (AHA), the American Cancer Society (ACS) and others of that type. You see their opinions and recommendations quoted all the time in the media. You think of them as organized to watch out for your health, to keep an eye on what Big Food and the pharmaceutical industry are up to, things like that. But actually, they all take money from Big Food and/or Big Drugs, and they all have conflicts of interest that color the advice they offer you. They've got their donors' and board members' interests in mind at least as much as, and maybe more than, yours.

The American Dietetic Association, for example, calls itself "the nation's largest organization of food and nutrition professionals," and says it serves the public by promoting optimal nutrition, health and well-being."

But really, the ADA serves its corporate sponsors and, as the Center for Media & Democracy notes,

> hauls in large sums of money advocating for the food industry. Its stated mission is to "improve the health of the public," but with 15 percent of its budget, more than $3 million, coming from food companies and trade groups, it has learned not to bite the hand that feeds it. "They never criticize the food industry," says Joan Gussow, a former head of the nutrition education program at Teachers College at Columbia University. The ADA's website even contains a series of "fact sheets" about various food products, sponsored by the same corporations that make them (Monsanto for biotechnology; Procter & Gamble for olestra; Ajinomoto for MSG; the National Association of Margarine Manufacturers for fats and oils).

How messed up is that?

Big American Dietetic Association funders (100,000 plus) have included Kellogg, Kraft Foods, Weight Watchers International, Campbell Soup, the National Dairy Council, Nestlé USA, Ross Products Division of Abbott Labs, Sandoz, Coca-Cola, Florida Department of Citrus, General Mills, Nabisco, Uncle Ben's and Wyeth-Ayerst Labs. The ADA's 2004 donor report lists other interesting Big Food names like ConAgra, Goya, Sunkist, the Cattlemen's Beef Board and Sodexho (who run school-lunch programs as well as prisons—a nice combo for your kids, don't you think?).

Similarly, there are good reasons the American Cancer Society seems to focus all its energies on promoting cancer drugs and treatments, then falls almost silent when it comes to identifying potential carcinogens in our food, air and water, and is downright quiet about strategies for cancer prevention. The ACS recruits board members and receives huge donations from the very pharmaceutical, chemical, food and biotech companies that sell cancer drugs, manufacture pesticides, experiment with genetic modification, peddle foods that are bad for us and pollute our environment.

According to its own 2002 annual report, the American Cancer Society's major donors that year included 3M Foundation, Abbott Laboratories, Amgen, Avon Products, Inc., BFI Waste Systems, Bristol-Myers Squibb Company, Colgate-Palmolive, Dr Pepper, DuPont, the Eli Lilly & Company Foundation, Genentech, GlaxoSmithKline, IDEC Pharmaceuticals, International Flavors & Fragrances, Johnson & Johnson, Merck & Company, Nissan, Novartis Pharmaceuticals, Ortho Biotech, Pfizer, Procter & Gamble, SmithKline Beecham Consumer Healthcare, Unilever/Bestfoods, Warner Lambert, Wendy's and Winn Dixie.

Now, whose interests do you think they have at heart?

And speaking of hearts, don't even get me started on the American Heart Association. I'll give my two cents on them later.

The point is: When it comes to your health, and your family's, you need to be extremely careful whose advice you trust. Some groups may look and sound like your friends, but they're often bought and sold by the very corporate interests who are killing you. At the very least, they're trying to balance your interests with those of their multimillion-dollar donors.

These groups all seem to believe that I'm some sort of food communist, a propagandist who wants to take away all your freedoms and rights and have the government save you from the big bad corporations. Well, that couldn't be further from the truth—because, believe me, the government isn't looking out for you, either! What I want is exactly the opposite. I want to overwhelm you with personal freedoms: freedom of information, freedom from deception and the freedom to make a truly educated decision. God forbid we all actually become educated consumers. That's what these companies fear most.

In February 2003, New York District Court Judge Robert Sweet ruled against Ashley Pelman and Jazlen Bradley, saying that Hirsch, their lawyer, had failed to make his case against McDonald's on any count. In a sixty-five-page ruling, Judge Sweet noted that:

> The issue of determining the breadth of personal responsibility underlies much of the law: where should the line be drawn between an individual's own responsibility to take care of herself, and society's responsibility to ensure that others shield her? . . .
>
> If a person knows or should know that eating copious orders of supersized McDonalds' products is unhealthy and may result in weight

gain (and its concomitant problems) because of the high levels of cho-
lesterol, fat, salt and sugar, it is not the place of the law to protect them
from their own excesses. Nobody is forced to eat at McDonald's. . . .
Even more pertinent, nobody is forced to supersize their meal or choose
less healthy options on the menu.

As long as a consumer exercises free choice with appropriate
knowledge, *liability for negligence will not attach to a manufacturer.*
It is only when that free choice becomes but a chimera—for instance,
by the masking of information necessary to make the choice,
such as the knowledge that eating McDonald's with a certain fre-
quency would irrefragably cause harm—that manufacturers should be
held accountable. Plaintiffs have failed to allege in the Complaint that
their decisions to eat at McDonald's several times a week were any-
thing but a choice freely made and which now may not be pinned on
McDonald's. (My emphases.)

Although he dismissed the suit, Judge Sweet not only held the
door open for Hirsch to submit an amended case, he pretty much
drew him a step-by-step map for walking through it. In particular, he
noted that the average teenager and her parents might not know
that "Chicken McNuggets, rather than being merely chicken fried
in a pan, are a McFrankenstein creation of various elements not
utilized by the home cook," packed with "twice the fat per ounce as
a hamburger." After noting that McDonald's fries could also be char-
acterized as Frankenfries, he went on to suggest that "if plaintiffs
were able to flesh out this argument in an amended complaint, it
may establish that the dangers of McDonalds' products were not
commonly well known and thus that McDonald's had a duty toward
its customers."

Judge Sweet also said that if it could be shown that a diet of McFood
alone, without other contributing factors like a genetic or social pre-

disposition to obesity, can make you fat, then maybe Mickey D's could be accused of negligence.

What a coincidence! February 2003, when this ruling was delivered, was the very McMonth that I put my health on the line to show just that.

FIVE

IT'S A MAD, MAD, MAD, MAD McWORLD

I know what you're thinking: Why pick on poor little McDonald's? Aren't all the other fast-food chains just as bad?

Well, yes, they mostly are. But they're not McDonald's. For one thing, it was that lawsuit against McDonald's that gave me the idea. But on a larger level, McDonald's is the peak, the pinnacle, the Everest of fast-food joints. It's been the industry leader for fifty years, and the Golden Arches have been the gold standard against which all other crappy food chains are judged.

Could I have made the movie eating Burger King, Pizza Hut, KFC or White Castle? Yes, I could. (Then again, I might be dead if I'd gone to White Castle. Well, maybe not dead, but definitely reeking of those little minced onions . . . and probably killing all my friends with my Vidalia halitosis.) But it wouldn't have been the same. These companies don't stand for the entire industry the way McDonald's does, nor do they have the influence over the industry that the Arches have. Whatever McDonald's does, their competitors follow suit, from jumbo sizes to value meals to Chicken McNuggets. I picked the company that I truly

believed could change the way the entire industry functions . . . if they
wanted to.

> McDonald's now operates around 31,000 restaurants worldwide, "serving"
> 46 million people a day. That's more than the entire population of Spain. Al-
> most half of McDonalds' daily global patronage is in the United States alone.
> Every day, one in four Americans eats fast food, about 43 percent of them
> at a McDonald's. Which translates into one out of every ten fast-food pur-
> chases in America being made at the Golden Arches.

The first McDonald's arrived in New York City in 1973; now there
are over eighty of them in Manhattan alone! That includes the country's largest, the mega Mickey D's at 42nd and Broadway in the heart
of Times Square. It's 17,500 square feet, has a full-size Broadway-style
marquee, twenty-seven 15-inch TV monitors and eighteen 42-inch
plasma screens to entertain customers. Yes, millions and millions of
tourists flock to Manhattan from all over the world to take in the
wonders of the Empire State Building, the Statue of Liberty, the
Chrysler Building, the Great White Way . . . and a really big-ass
McDonald's.

By the way, in the summer of 2004, city health-code inspectors found
one or multiple violations in sixty-eight out of seventy-three of those
NYC locations, for which information was provided. Although all but
one passed their inspections, ranging from employees' inadequate personal cleanliness to mice and insects to unclean food-handling surfaces
and utensils. Yeah, I know, lots of food places get slapped with these
kinds of violations, but still, that's a *lot* of violations!

McDonald's is literally everywhere, on every continent except
Antarctica. And I'm sure someday soon intrepid explorers will tramp
across the miles of frozen wasteland there to find the Golden Arches

shining like a beacon of hope at the South Pole. Home of the Seal Burger and Penguin Nuggets.

At travel destinations around the globe, Ronald is there to greet tourists. There's a Mickey D's at the Eiffel Tower, there are Golden Arches standing next to the Great Pyramids in Egypt, and there's a McDonald's drive-through marring the view near the Taj Mahal. One of the first things the United States occupying forces did after invading Afghanistan was to welcome a McDonald's. *Hey, Mr. Taliban, tally me some french fries!*

There's even a McDonald's situated strategically near the Dachau concentration camp. I couldn't make that up if I tried. They built a McDonald's where more than 30,000 people were exterminated during World War II. When this store first opened in 1996, visitors to one of history's most horrific sites emerged to find this note under their windshield wipers:

Dear Visitor,
Welcome to Dachau, welcome to McDonald's. Our restaurant's got 120 seats, about 40 outdoor seats and for our young guests an Indoor and Outdoor Playland. How to find us? Really simple. Just follow the picture! We're happy for your visit!
Your McDonald's Restaurant, Dachau

Good old Ronald. He may sell food, but no one ever said he had taste.

McDonald's opened its first restaurant in South Africa in November 1995, and quickly opened thirty more in under two years. Today there are ninety restaurants there. It's one of the most successful markets in McDonalds' international history. Nutritionists there say the fast spread of fast food is contributing to drastic changes in the eating habits of South Africans, from traditional plant-based foods to high-fat, high-sugar, energy-dense, low-fiber foods. In short, McCrap. And obesity is spreading there rapidly. The World Health Organization says 29 percent of men and no less than 56 percent of women in South Africa are overweight, with the highest rates in the areas with the largest number of fast-food joints. Go figure.

There are now over 600 McDonald's in China, and the company plans to open another 400 by 2008, just in time for the Beijing Olympics, where McDonald's will proudly serve its healthy burgers and fries as the "official restaurant." McDonald's is now spreading all over Asia, from Japan (of course) to the Indian subcontinent, teaching people who for thousands of years have eaten a sensible, balanced diet based on fish, rice and vegetables how to gorge like Americans.

Surprise—they're getting fat from it.

In November 2004, the News Target Network reported on the rapid spread of obesity in China, saying

that importing the typical American diet, high in red meat, dairy, processed food, soda, fried snacks, and white flour has increased diabetes, heart disease, cancer and obesity in just a few years. . . .

• China's rising incomes are expanding its waistlines, the health ministry has found: 200 million citizens are now judged overweight.

• More than 160 million have high blood pressure and 20 million have diabetes, the ministry says.

• Other conditions linked to obesity are also rising in number.

• The weight has piled on as the country has shifted to more sedentary work in the past twenty years, been freed from famine, and switched to a fattier diet.

• The report released this week says that since 1992, the proportion of adults who are overweight has risen by a third, to 23 percent, and the number considered clinically obese has nearly doubled to 60 million, according to the official news agency Xinhua.

Take India. "As India struggles to eliminate malnutrition among the rural poor, wealthy urbanites are packing on extra pounds due to sedentary lifestyles and the growing abundance of sugary, high-fat foods," the Associated Press reports. One in three adults in the cities are either overweight or obese; 10 percent of New Delhi residents aged fourteen to twenty-four are obese, and 5 percent have high blood pressure. Men are having heart attacks at age forty-five, ten years younger than in the United States. Granted, Indian food, with all its white rice and sweets, has never been what you'd call slimming, and Indian culture has always promoted chubbiness as a sign of prosperity. Still, physicians there attribute the rise of obesity in the cities to the spread of fast food and the adoption of a Western sedentary lifestyle.

Japan and other Asian countries are reporting similar problems.

"American-style fast food was unknown in the Philippines until the 1970s, when Jollibee, the Filipino version of McDonald's, opened its doors," reports World Watch magazine. "Now, thanks to fast food giants like McDonald's, Kentucky Fried Chicken, Burger King, and others, the traditional diet of rice, vegetables, and a little meat or fish is changing—and so are rates of heart disease, diabetes, and stroke, which have risen to numbers similar to those in the United States and other western nations."

Can a single corporation reshape an entire culture? Change its eating habits? Well, here's a small but telling example: In China, there used to be no such thing as birthdays, at least not the way we celebrate them in the West. Traditionally, Chinese people didn't make a big deal of birthdays until you hit sixty, when I think we can all agree you've earned it. Parents' children served them a bowl of "long-life noodles" and peaches, and that's it. Then they only celebrated every ten years after that. They didn't even pay attention to the actual date of your birth; everybody just added a year to their age at the Chinese New Year.

Guess what? Chinese parents are bringing their kids to McDonald's for Happy Meal birthday parties now. Yeah, they're singing "Happy

Birthday" in Chinese and everything. Ronald is training a whole generation of Chinese kids how to whine for presents, toys and a trip to Mickey D's just like their American cousins! (*Mmmm*, tastes like freedom to me.)

Outside of the United States, the opening of a McDonald's is quite a huge event. We're jaded. In the United States, we have more McDonald's than public libraries (a little over 9,000) or hospitals (around 5,800). But open a McDonald's in a place like Singapore or Budapest or Lima or Mumbai and huge crowds form and all the major media attend. On opening day in Kuwait City in 1994, the line for the first McDonald's drivethrough was 10 kilometers long. Yes America, that's why the Gulf War was fought: We were making the world safe for McDonald's.

The opening of the first McDonald's in Moscow's Pushkin Square in 1990, still the largest and busiest McDonald's in the world with no fewer than twenty-seven cash registers, drew world media and customers who lined up for blocks and blocks, just like they used to line up for bread or eggs in the bad old days. Funny how the "true end of Communism" and "birth of a new age of democratic consumerism" in Russia still involved standing in line for food. There are now 103 McDonald's in Russia, and counting.

People outside the United States can always tell you about the day the first McDonald's opened in his or her country. They remember it the way Americans remember 9/11, JFK's assassination or O.J.'s white Bronco. It's an indelible memory. For many, it was their first solid link with the American culture they'd always heard and dreamed about. For them, the taste of freedom is forever associated with the taste of fries. Others remember it as a black day in their country's history, the day their heritage began to be encroached on by those goddamn Americans. For them, the Golden Arches are an eyesore.

When I was in Berlin, people kept telling me about the day the Wall came down, the overpowering feeling that they'd accomplished something many of them thought could never happen. The day they freed themselves from the yoke of Soviet Communism. Just days later, the first trucks carrying goods started crossing into East Berlin, and none crossed faster than the ones bringing McDonald's and Coke. The flavors of America. The taste of freedom. "Is this what we've been missing?" East Berliners wondered, as more trucks filled with the American way of life rolled into their part of the city, trucks carrying Nike shoes, Budweiser, Pizza Hut and Levi's. Some were quite excited at the prospect of being able to taste that Big Mac they'd been hearing about for decades. Others, though happy to have the freedom to come and go as they please, questioned the Pandora's box that had been opened. Some of them even say they miss the old days. They call it "Ostalgia"—nostalgia for the way things were in East (*Ost* in German) Berlin before the Wall came down.

A young couple in Poland wrote to me: "We remember there were hundreds of people in front of the first branches to open [in 1993], mainly in big cities. Later on when another McDonald's was opening it wasn't such a big deal and people stopped being so excited to rush to the counter to order anything and say, 'I've had a hamburger at McDonald's.' "

A friend in Turkey wrote to me about when the "first restaurant opened at Taksim Square in Istanbul in 1986. At that time I was in university. At first, people were queuing up to get into the restaurant. Now there are plenty of them but not crowded at all. Some of them shut down, even. People around me generally hate McDonald's not because they represent 'American Imperialism.' People dislike McDonald's because the food is so unhealthy." There was even a huge protest rally by Turkish university students in 1998 when McDonald's opened a new outlet on their campus. And a bomb went off in front of a Turkish McDonald's in October 2004. (Maybe the bomber had tried a Filet-O-Fish. Those things are nasty.)

Right now, I'm planning a trip to Cuba. I want to experience the country and its people before that Pandora's box is opened there. Because you know the day after Fidel dies, the shipments of American consumer crap will come flooding in. Within a few weeks you won't be able to throw a dead communist in Havana without hitting a Wal-Mart, Starbucks, Burger King or Mac Shack.

Now you tell me, is it just a coincidence that the WHO has identified a global obesity epidemic happening at the same time as the global expansion of fast-food chains? I mean, McDonald's alone feeds nearly 17 *billion* people a year, most of whom are presumably Heavy Users. Add in all the other chains worldwide, and you have the makings of a health crisis showdown with the Good, the Bad and the Hungry.

More than a billion adults worldwide are now overweight—and at least 300 million of them are clinically obese. Childhood obesity is already epidemic in some areas and on the rise in others. Worldwide, an estimated 17.6 million children under five are said to be overweight.

"The global epidemic of obesity is completely out of control," the BBC noted, reporting from the first international obesity conference in 2004. "Obesity rates are escalating everywhere. . . . Doctors at the meeting are warning that unless something is done, health care services in both the developed and developing world will not be able to cope with treating people with diseases linked to obesity."

The report went on to note that "about 25% of the people living in the Middle East are obese or overweight, while obesity has risen by 100% among Japanese men since 1982." In Africa, some doctors now consider obesity a major disease on par with AIDS and, ironically, malnutrition.

As more and more people live like Americans, work like us, laze around like us and eat junk like us, they're getting fat like us.

Take England. No country in the world embraced Ronald and his pals more warmly than the English, at first. Since the first Mac Shack opened there in 1974, they've spread all over the country like poison toadstools. There are over 1,200 of them now—that's twice as many as in China (in case you haven't looked at a map lately, England is way smaller than China).

Guess what? Obesity levels in England have tripled in the past twenty years. Around 50 percent (24 million) of adults in the UK are overweight or obese, and levels are still rising. In the past ten years, mirroring the United States, obesity in children has doubled (to 8.5 percent), and it's tripled among teens (to 15 percent). Type 2 diabetes is now on the rise in British kids, as well. The British rock star Morrissey once sighed, "Everything went downhill from the moment the McDonald's chain was allowed to invade England." No kidding.

But while many Brits have been indulging, others have been fighting back. Charles, the Prince of Wales, is famously opposed to fast food and is a huge supporter of the "Slow Food" movement, which started, of course, in Italy, where good, healthy food is central to the culture. "Slow Food" means old-fashioned cooking, with real, fresh ingredients grown and raised in environmentally sound ways. The movement started in 1986 in reaction to the opening of the first McDonald's in Rome. Now it's spread to forty-five countries, including the United States. In October 2004, Prince Charles was the guest of honor at the movement's first annual conference and food fair in Italy.

But nobody in England, or most anywhere else, has stood up to Ronald like London Greenpeace has. In 1990, McDonald's took advantage of England's ridiculous libel laws (basically, all you have to do in England is call someone an ass to get your own ass sued off) to sue London Greenpeace for distributing a leaflet called "What's Wrong with McDonald's?" It was a helluva document, accusing McDonald's of everything from destroying the rainforest and causing starvation in the Third World to exploiting children, lying to them in false advertising and feeding them food that could kill them.

Since London Greenpeace was not incorporated, McDonald's had to pick individual members to sue. So it infiltrated the organization with spies. One of them even had an affair with a member—that's what they call due diligence in legalspeak. McDonald's named five individuals in its suit. Three of them dropped out, leaving Dave Morris and Helen Steele as the two Davids who stood up to McGoliath.

The case dragged on for years. In fact, it became the longest-running trial in British history. It was a war of attrition, with McDonald's spending tens of millions of dollars in the hopes that Morris and Steele would go bankrupt or give up out of sheer exhaustion. Dumb move. Along the way, the trial got tons and tons of international publicity, most of it bad for McDonald's.

In 1997, the judge ruled that since Morris and Steele had failed to prove their allegations against McDonald's about the rainforest and Third World starvation, they were guilty of libel. But then he dropped a bombshell, declaring that they *had* proven that McDonald's exploits children, uses false advertising and threatens the health of long-term customers. The judge drastically reduced the damages they were to pay McDonald's, but it didn't matter, because they refused to pay one pence anyway. And they immediately filed an appeal.

Although McDonald's technically won its case in court, it was a disastrous loss in the court of public opinion. It ain't no coincidence that right about the time the judge was reading his verdict in court, the president of McDonald's Corporation was being fired by his board of directors.

October 16 has been designated United Nations Food Day. In England, it's also World Anti-McDonald's Day. For twenty years now, protesters have gathered in London on this day to hand out anti-McDonald's leaflets demanding that Ronald stop manipulating the kids of the world with his brainwashing and his fat, sugary foods.

The results of all this bad publicity have been devastating for McDonald's in England. McDonalds' pretax profits there plummeted from £83.8 million in 2002 to £23.6 million in 2003. That's a huge drop. Who says good old street-level activism can't get the big corporations' attention?

Some other countries have resisted McDonald's total domination of their cultures as well. In 2004, the Scottish government urged the company to drop its "Go Large" menu, the local version of super sizing. McDonald's also began offering a new trial breakfast item it thought would appeal to Scots: porridge. Italy, not surprisingly, has been slow to embrace Ronald; there are McDonald's in all the big cities, but not nearly as many as you see in other countries. There are only four locations in all of Rome, four in Naples, two in Venice. I think it's gonna be a long, long time before you see the Golden Arches rise inside the Vatican. (Maybe if they ever get an American pope they'll get the Passion of the Ronald.)

The Swedes have done a lot to get McDonald's to act like a responsible corporate citizen. McDonald's represents something like 75 percent of the fast-food market in Sweden. The company has initiated all sorts of ecoconscious programs there, from using hydropower to building with recycled materials to filtering the exhaust from fry stations. Swedish McDonald's outlets offer things like organic milk and beef. The results have been the opposite of what the company has seen in England: lots of great publicity and healthy sales.

Margareta, a young mother in Sweden, writes:

I remember the first and second McDonald's in Stockholm. The second was close by to where we lived when I was a child, and it was on rare occasions that my one-year-older brother and I were allowed to go there. My parents didn't like the idea of the American fast-food lifestyle. I think my generation, although much more in acceptance than our parents were, have had a rather clear view on what is healthy, both for us and for the environment.

Now, the next generation is another thing. My nine-year-old son is bugging me to take him there. Sometimes I indulge, because it's practical, fast and not too expensive, for example, when we are on the road or coming late from football practice and so on. I try to keep the visits not so frequent and use it as a special treat, one that he really appreciates.

Since the first Mac Shack opened in France in 1979, the French attitude toward Mickey D's has been, well, French. A love-hate thing. McDonald's opens thirty to forty new restaurants every year in France. It has over a thousand now, more per head than most of its European neighbors, and not far behind England. A million people a day now eat at a French "McDo" (as they call it). The French now drink an average of seventy-four pints of soda a year. It's been said that traditional French cuisine has been terribly eroded—that only 20 percent of the population has stuck to the old ways, and the rest have succumbed to *restauration rapide*. I have a feeling that's a scare statistic, but there's no doubting that the American style of eating has had a huge impact.

McDonald's success in France has met with a lot of resistance from those who see the spread of le Big Mac in their country as another symptom of the Americanization and Disneyfication of their culture. Not every French person is shouting, *"C'est tout ce que j'aime"* (I'm lovin' it). McDonald's actually had to drop lovable ol' Ronald as its mascot there, replacing him with a familiar French cartoon character, Asterix.

A friend of mine named Guillaume remembers growing up in the French countryside of Saumur in the 1980s, before McDo had spread itself throughout the nation. "Some people knew about McDonald's," he recalls. "Its name, the brand, its products. But only a few large cities were lucky to have gotten one. We thought of it back then as a privilege! Funny enough. Although my parents never took me to any McDonald's restaurant in France, I found out about one, on my own, when I turned eighteen. Healthy, traditional cuisine is well-rooted in the French countryside. But kids have always been made curious by looking at the restaurants' façades and Christmas-looking food."

Guillaume never tasted a burger until a trip to America. But he watched as France really discovered the mass consumption of hamburgers with McDonald's in the nineties, when the company "was opening a branch every two days or so." The French found themselves getting an appetite for what they thought was a new, modern concept: fast foods. "For young people in Paris, the nearest Mac Shack became the hip new hangout. For the youngsters, it replaced the traditional cafés."

Still, not everyone in France was happy. Not by a long shot. Guillaume recalls the outcry when the McDonald's at the Eiffel Tower opened. "What a symbol. The local press went mad. 'What's next?' some said. 'A branch inside Le Louvre?' People thought the company had no respect for historic sites like this one. Parisians also believed McDonald's just wanted to gain from the monument, both in cash and respectability."

In 1999, a French farmer named Jose Bove led a group of farmers and activists in attacking a local McDonald's in the process of being constructed in his hometown of Millau, tearing the building down with his tractor. Needless to say, he is now a national hero in France.

In another move that could only happen in France, chef Dominique Valadier abandoned his career in fancy five-star restaurants to run the students' and teachers' canteen at a school near Marseilles. He serves the teens and their delighted teachers gourmet meals like bull stew and polenta, squid-ink pasta, and salmon, washed down with glasses of Côte du Rhône—and does it for about the same price as a crap meal at McDo. As a result, the McDo outlet right across the street from the school is now empty at mealtimes. Kids are now enrolling in the school just to get to eat there!

But the most spectacular reaction to McDonald's has been in India. In the late 1980s, McDonald's took tremendous flak from vegetarians in the United States when it was revealed that the company was cooking its fries in beef tallow (lard). In 1990, it switched to vegetable oil. But the fries didn't taste as good as before, so the company quietly put a tiny amount of beef flavoring back into them. After reading about this in Eric Schlosser's book *Fast Food Nation*, Indians in the United States, who were of the Hindu and Jainist faiths, freaked out. Hindus revere cows as sacred and would never let beef touch their lips. Jains do not eat or wear any animal products. Here they'd been eating McDonald's fries all these years, thinking it was all right, and now they were pissed!

A Hindu in Seattle brought a class-action lawsuit against the company for having lied to its customers. McDonald's eventually settled for $12.5 million, most of which went to charities, and posted an apology on its website. Back home in India, meanwhile, folks chose to show their dismay in a more direct way: Angry crowds trashed a couple of McDonald's outlets in Bombay. The funny thing about this story is that the fifty-six McDonald's outlets in India had already adjusted the company's formulas and did not use beef or pork in any of their items.

Oops! Maybe along with the rest of the relentless self-promoting, the company should have let its customers in India know that.

On McDonald's website there's a disclaimer that runs in very small print at the bottom of its nutrition information page (which is already filled with small print to begin with): No products are certified as vegetarian; all products may contain trace amounts of ingredients derived from animals. *All products!* They can't guarantee you that a single item has no meat in it. They can't guarantee you that there won't be meat in your Sprite? Your salad? Your fries? What the heck is going on in that kitchen?

John Robbins, author of *Diet for a New America*, had some interesting things to say about fast food when I spoke to him. Robbins, for those of you who don't know, was the heir to the Baskin-Robbins empire when, at eighteen, he opted out. He walked away from all the money and the ice cream to find a better, healthier way of life. He'd grown up in a kid's paradise, eating ice cream whenever he wanted it, and it had made him sick. He watched his father's partner and brother-in-law, Bert Baskin, die of a heart attack at the young age of fifty-one. He has intimate, firsthand knowledge of what the typical All-American diet can do to a person's health, and he's alarmed to see us spreading this diet around the globe.

"The fast-food companies are starting to take over the world," he told me. "I mean, Baskin-Robbins now has more stores in Tokyo than it does in Los Angeles, where it originated. This is true about KFC, about Taco Bell, about McDonald's. They're always opening up more franchises worldwide. They're globalizing the American way of eating, which is a way of death, really.

"Now, the World Health Organization tells us that there are about a billion people on the planet who are suffering from diseases that are caused from inadequate nutrition. They don't have enough to eat. They're suffering and dying from malnutrition. This is a terrible tragedy. Meanwhile, the World Health Organization is also telling us that, coincidentally and at the same time, there are another billion people on the planet suffering from diseases caused by too many calories, by eating too much. There's something grotesque about this symmetry."

SIX

McD-DAY

In preparation for my monthlong diet of McFood, I recruited a small team of physicians and health experts to give me their counseling and to monitor my physical condition before, during and after. I made sure that they didn't know one another and would each provide opinions and monitoring independent of the others.

The first to sign on was Dr. Lisa Ganjhu, a gastroenterologist and hematologist from St. Luke's–Roosevelt Hospital Center. I met her through a friend of mine who is a surgeon at the hospital. From the minute I began telling Dr. Ganjhu about the film, she was excited about what I was trying to accomplish.

I contacted my alma mater, New York University, to see if they could recommend a doc from their medical school. Since I now had a liver and blood specialist, I thought a cardiologist would probably be a good idea. They pointed me to Dr. Stephen Siegel, and he signed up immediately.

The last doc was the big question. What type of specialist should I get? What insight could he or she bring to the story that may be missing? Walking back to my office, I passed the Mercer Street Medical

Center, a small clinic near my building. Inside, I found one ear, nose, and throat specialist, one gynecologist, and an internist named Dr. Daryl Isaacs. Isaacs turned out to be a busy, affable, flustered man in a jacket spotted with remnants of that day's lunch. My first impression was that *he* needed a doctor. Dr. Isaacs has one of the largest practices in New York City, seeing forty to fifty patients a day, more than 12,000 a year. "The only way you can survive in this HMO world today," he sighed.

He laughed when I told him about the movie—they all laughed—but then went on, "It's a great idea. A great idea. Never been done before. Never been done . . . Fantastic. Could be great. Could be really great."

Along with my three physicians, I wanted to enlist the advice of a nutritionist, someone who could talk about the health aspects of the food I'd be eating. Alex suggested Bridget Bennet. She and Bridget had met at Haelth, a shmancy SoHo wellness center with exercise classes, nutrition classes and an overall focus on one's well-being. The place was pretty swank, even though they couldn't spell "health."

Bridget laughed like all the others when I told her about my idea. She asked if I planned to have my head examined as part of a full physical.

The results of my physical and blood work were what I'd expected. Weight 185.5 pounds, everything normal, blood pressure excellent, liver function excellent, general health outstanding. And no STDs! Woo hoo! Wait till I tell Alex!

January 31, 2003. My McDiet was about to begin. I had stopped exercising two weeks earlier, to slow my metabolism down. I was trying to get "normal," or as normal as I thought normal could be, to prepare for the month ahead.

That night, Alex cooked me my Last Supper. My last healthy meal for a month. I looked at that fresh tossed salad, the vegetable tart, the quinoa and roasted red pepper salad, and bid fresh greens and veggies a fond adieu.

I love vegetables. As a kid the only vegetable I liked was green beans—you know how kids are—but today, the greener the better for me. As I sat there putting away that tasty red pepper, it sunk in that for the next month I would be eating no red peppers. No green beans. No broccoli. No lima beans. No okra. No asparagus. No peas. No spinach. No Brussels sprouts. No celery. No cucumbers. Also no squash, cauliflower or eggplant. And no onions—or at least no fresh onions (McFatty's does put those delightful dehydrated ones on its burgers—M*mmm*, dehydrated onions.)

And no fruit. No apples (except the ones they love to compare to Granny Smiths that they put in their sugar pies). No oranges. No limes. No kiwis. No grapefruit. No lemons. No pineapples. No cantaloupe. No watermelon. No bananas. No pears. No plums. No peaches. No nectarines or tangerines, or even tangelos for that matter! No cranberries or blackberries or raspberries or snozberries. And definitely no cherries.

No, I was on a straight downhill slide to culinary boredom and intestinal suicide.

Still, somewhere deep down inside, I have to admit I was excited on the night of McD's Eve. I have this suspicion that part of what brings us back to fast food and junk food, completely apart from the sugar rush and our evolutionary addiction to fat, is a perverse little psychological thrill we get from doing something we know is bad for us, something we know we shouldn't do. In his book *Cigarettes Are Sublime*, Richard Klein theorizes that this little thrill of danger is part of what smokers are hooked on. Maybe the same applies to the way we eat. I mean, most of us now are at least vaguely aware that fast food is not good food. Maybe part of why we like it is that little thrill of doing something bad. It's almost like it's naughty to eat at a McDonald's. Everyone enjoys being naughty once in a while, don't they?

So that night, I heard the voice of my mother in my head, talking to me like she used to when I asked if we could go to McDonald's. "We just ate there last week. I'm not taking you again. We have better food at home." I could see her shaking her head at me, disappointed that I was about to do everything that she'd raised me not to do when it comes to diet. I was about to be the worst son ever, the worst role model for any kid, the poster boy of how we should not eat. But sometimes even Mom is no match for the Big Mac.

But all that was just in my head. In real life, I had Alex to contend with, too. Alex made sure to put her two cents in. She was just as much against this project on January 31 as she'd been when it first popped into my head on Thanksgiving Day. We ended up cutting a deal: She'd go along with my making the movie and eating this "food" for one month, but the second it was over, my diet was hers. We shook on it. Thirty days later, true to our bargain, she put me on a strict but delicious detox diet to flush out what I'd shoved into my body during the month.

On the morning of McD-day I sprung from bed feeling like a ten-year-old on the last day of school. Charlie Bucket with that golden ticket. A sumo wrestler at an all-you-can-eat buffet.

The McDonald's on 14th Street and First Avenue, my home-base Mac Shack, was packed for breakfast that morning. Kids on their way to school, homeless people who bought a cup of coffee to get out of the cold, policemen taking a McBreak from their patrol. It would stay like this all day, busy from open to close, due to its proximity to the stop for the uptown M1 bus and the L train subway entrance—an urban cross-roads of sorts, and Ronald was there to feed the weary traveler.

Already on this first morning I encountered what would continue to be a bedeviling problem for the entire month. Just walking from my place to McDonald's, I had used up more than half a mile. It was only 9 a.m.

At lunchtime, that frustration was offset by a delightful discovery: By pure happenstance, I'd chosen to start my McDiet in the middle of the Big Mac's Thirty-fifth Birthday Celebration. Hurrah! For the next few weeks, if you bought a Big Mac, you could get an additional one for only 35 cents. What a deal! Who could say no? In fact, since I'd made it a rule to accept any upsizing of any meal or add-ons that were offered to me during the filming, I just had to say yes, didn't I? Carrying my tray away from the counter, I passed table after table of other customers who'd also found that second Big Mac irresistible.

The ones who were still smiling obviously hadn't eaten them both yet.

Have you ever eaten two Big Macs in one sitting? Well, it ain't easy. A bloat, a sensation of complete, greasy, glassy-eyed satiation sets in. Your limbs weaken. It becomes a real effort to keep lifting that second sandwich to your mouth and biting into it. And yet, all around me, folks were struggling heroically to finish off that second Mac, because we'd paid for it and, like Mom always said, "Waste not, want not." It had been such a bargain. A graphic lesson in the super-sizing of American eating habits, and it was only our first day of filming.

Later that afternoon, all the sugar I'd ingested in just two McDonald's meals—we calculated it at about half a pound's worth—plus the caffeine had me all jumpy and jittery. My body wasn't used to that much of either substance. I felt all cracked out, with weird, electrical buzzing sensations pulsing in my arms.

And that very first night, I began to feel the first effects of what I now think are the addictive properties of the food. Within three hours of dinner (two cheeseburgers, medium fries, medium Coke, three soft-baked Sugar Cookies, plus three bottles of water I'd bought to be drunk whenever), I was hungry again. It was like Chinese food, only worse.

After lunch on the very next day, sitting at the wheel of the car in the parking lot of the McDonald's at 34th Street and Tenth Avenue, I threw up in the middle of my first super size meal. One of the more colorful scenes in *Super Size Me*. I knew my body was revolted, and revolting—trying to tell me something in the clearest way it could. My body was rejecting McDonald's the way some bodies reject organ transplants. It was screaming at me, *What are you doing to me, pal?!? What are you feeding me? C'mon, let's stop this craziness right now. Let's go get some broccoli and a colonic. My treat.*

But no, I did not listen. I had a mission. I had a film to make. And twenty-eight more days of eating this crap. Yippee.

Alex was not a happy camper.

In a perfect world, every American would have three doctors and a nutritionist around to monitor their diet and health like mine were. Maybe then we'd all be better educated about what we're doing to ourselves.

The typical American gobbles three burgers and four orders of fries every week. Toss in the pizzas, the popcorn, the sugary breakfast cereals, the sodas, the snack cakes, candy bars, ice cream and everything else we eat in lieu of real food in this society, and your body is like an eighteen-wheeler roaring down a high-fat highway straight to obesity and an early grave.

Fast food is bad food. It's loaded with bad stuff like fat and sugar and sodium. It's packed with chemicals that are in there to make it taste and smell and feel like it's real food. What it lacks is vitamins, minerals, fiber, all the stuff you really need.

To start with, let's just talk about fat. The USDA recommends that no more than 35 percent of your calories should come from fat, and that no more than 10 percent should come from saturated fat, the worst kind. If your diet is too heavy in fat calories, your body is going to store those extra calories as fat; you're going to gain weight, and you're putting yourself at risk for heart disease, diabetes, all those other problems associated with obesity, and maybe cancer. So if you eat something that gives you 50 percent of its calories in fat, that's a "fatty" food item. If a lot of those calories are from saturated fat, that's a really fatty food, one that you should eat in very limited quantities and balance with a lot of other foods that are high in protein and fiber—you know, the good stuff.

The problem with the typical American diet is that it's loaded with fatty items: burgers, french fries, fried chicken, pizza, shakes, ice cream, cookies—they all provide too many calories from fat, and especially from saturated fat.

For example, let's take the Big Mac and do the math. A Big Mac contains 30 grams of fat. Each gram of fat contains 9 calories. $9 \times 30 =$ 270 calories from fat. Since a Big Mac packs 560 calories total, that means that nearly 50 percent of the calories in it are fat calories. That's 20 percent more than recommended. Some 16 percent come from saturated fat, so that's well over the recommended max, too.

That's a superfatty food item.

How do I know that? I looked it up online. Fast-food joints aren't in the habit of posting big nutrition charts to catch your eye and scare you away as you walk in the door. If they have one posted in the store at all, it's almost always in some inconspicuous spot where nine out of ten customers wouldn't see it even if they were looking. And there's no cigarette-style label on the Big Mac box that says WARNING: THIS BIG MAC CONTAINS 560 CALORIES, 50 PERCENT OF WHICH ARE FROM FAT. THAT'S 20 PERCENT OVER THE USDA RECOMMENDED MAXIMUM. A REGULAR DIET INCLUDING TOO MANY FATTY FOODS LIKE THIS CAN LEAD TO SERIOUS HEALTH PROBLEMS. Some people say there should be, but it hasn't happened yet. (Not in the United States, anyway. Late in 2004, England decided to start putting highly simplified color-coded labels— in effect, warning labels—on packaged foods.)

If you do get to see their nutrition charts, you see it's kind of hard to eat a meal at a joint like McDonald's or Burger King or KFC that does not overload you with too many fat calories. Eating a "balanced" meal at a fast-food joint ain't easy.

Some of the fast-food companies now post—or maybe the more accurate word would be "hide" or "obscure"—nutrition charts on their websites. (At least Outback is up-front about it: "Outback Steakhouse does not make nutritional claims about our menu items. Accordingly, we have not conducted a detailed nutritional analysis of our menu items. . . .") At the time of this writing, based on the company websites:

- A Burger King Whopper with cheese packs a massive 800 calories—55 percent of them from fat, 20 percent from saturated fat—roughly *double* the USDA recommended maximums. A large order of fries adds 500 more calories, 44 percent of them from fat. Have a small vanilla shake with it. That's another 400 calories, 33 percent of them from fat.
- A Quarter Pounder with cheese (McDonald's #1 burger) loads you up with *510* calories, *44.1 percent* of them from fat, and a budget-busting *21.1 percent* of them from saturated fat. Large fries will run you another 520 calories—*43 percent* from fat, *8 percent* of it from saturated fat. Dessert? Even the cookies are fatty: A Sugar Cookie provides another *150* calories, *36 percent* of them from fat. Ever wonder how Grimace got the way he is? Well, now you know.
- In the mood for fried chicken instead? A KFC extra crispy chicken thigh contains 360 total calories, 230 of which come from fat. So 64 percent of its calories come from fat. That's more than twice what the USDA recommends. (In fact, nearly every piece of chicken you buy from KFC hits you with 50 percent or more of its calories from fat.)

But let's say you already knew that burgers, wings, fries and shakes were superfatty. What about the more "healthy" items on the menu, like the salads?

In May 2004, Cathy Kapica, formerly a spokesperson with Quaker

Oats and the American Dietetic Association, and the newly hired "director of global nutrition" for McDonald's was interviewed on the radio about the "healthy" choices McDonald's customers make. (Let's note that Kapica's job never existed before Ashley and Jazlen sued the company.) "Our customers make healthy choices every single day," she said to the radio host. "In fact, last year we sold 150 million salads."

You hear that and you're like, "Damn, that's a lot of salads!" But then I started thinking about it. Let me put it in perspective for you: McDonald's feeds 46 million people a day. That's almost 17 billion people a year. So what does 150 million salads mean? That means *less than 1 percent,* not even 1 out of every 100 people who go there, make this "healthy" choice!

When I was on my McDiet, I made it a personal rule to try to eat one salad every ten meals. I'd watched people order their lunches at McDonald's. At one, I watched for over an hour as about one in every fifteen customers ordered a salad. At another, it was only one in about every twenty-five. At still another, about one in forty. So, to be more than fair in my approximation of the typical American fast-food diet, I tried to eat one salad with every tenth meal—way beyond what the average McCustomer does. Almost ten times as much!

But I'll play along. Let's belly up to the salad bar for a "healthy" choice, but first, know this:

- Wendy's Taco Supremo Salad with all the fixin's hits you with 670 calories, 43 percent of them from fat, 18 percent from saturated fat. Wendy's Chicken BLT Salad with honey-mustard dressing and garlic croutons has two and a half times the fat calories of a Wendy's Classic Single burger.
- McDonald's Fiesta Salad with sour cream and salsa brings 450 calories—56 percent from fat, 26 percent from saturated fat—

a higher percentage of saturated fat than a Double Cheeseburger.

Yeah, those are the healthy choices. I guess you've gotta give
Wendy's credit for one thing: They don't even try to bullshit you that
something called a Chicken BLT Salad is good for you.

The math is inescapable: *Fast food is fat food.*

And it's the same story for sugar, and cholesterol and sodium at these
places: too much, too much, too much.

Why does all fast food, even the "healthy" salad choices, have so
much fat, sugar and salt in it? Because it tastes great! And we can't
seem to get enough of it, so we keep coming back for more, like lab rats
keep pushing that lever that delivers them the food pellets. Our bodies
crave fats, salt and sweet. For millions of years they were hard to come
by. Now everything we eat is bursting with them, dripping with them,
caked in them. But our bodies still think it's the bad old days, and they
can't get enough.

Some scientists believe that high-fat, high-sugar food is actually
physiologically addictive, like a form of drug. The data are still incon-
clusive, but it's possible that a meal high in fat may dull the hormonal
signals your body usually sends itself to let you know you're full, so you
keep eating long after you should have put that Whopper down.

In its February 1, 2003 issue, the British magazine *New Scientist* reported that there's evidence that suggests that if you have too much fat
in your system, or just ingest too much too suddenly in one fatty meal,
your hypothalamus grows less reactive to leptin and other weight-
regulating hormones. In effect, your brain gets too fat and lazy to do its
job of telling you to drop the chalupa.

There's also some worry, *New Scientist* went on, that "early exposure
to fatty food could reconfigure children's bodies so that they always
choose fatty foods." You hear that? Parents, teachers, schools, get your
act in gear now!

A message posted on my site that should be filed under "Why I'll Never Eat McDonald's Food Again" Stories:

I used to work in a funeral home, and one night I was down in the morgue when I was summoned to the crematorium. When I got there, I saw the embalmer standing in the door of the crematorium holding a fire extinguisher. As soon as he saw me, he told me to run back downstairs and grab some sheets or hospital gowns. So as I'm heading downstairs I feel strangely hungry, which is not a feeling you usually get working in a funeral home. I grab a stack of hospital gowns and run back to the crematorium.

What happened was that this morbidly obese gentleman was so big that his fat was melting off faster than the machine could burn it up. Having worked in the funeral home for a while, I have smelled some hellacious things and know it helps to not pay attention to what I am smelling. But this actually smelled . . . familiar, and slightly appetizing. As I was walking out of the crematorium, I realized exactly what it smelled like: all that melted human fat smelled exactly like the inside of a McDonald's.

You want something else to worry about? Go to McDonalds.com and check out how many of the chemical formulas—I mean, lists of ingredients—contain the words "partially hydrogenated vegetable oils." That's bad. Real bad. So bad that it's being banned in some countries in Europe.

Why? Because partially hydrogenated vegetable oils, also called trans-fatty acids, or trans fats, are now widely thought to be a leading cause of heart attacks. In fact, Harvard Medical School nutritionists report that, "by our most conservative estimate, replacement of partially hydrogenated fat in the U.S. diet with natural unhydrogenated vegetable oils would prevent approximately 30,000 premature coronary deaths per year, and epidemiologic evidence suggests this number is closer to 100,000 premature deaths annually."

Quick chemistry—I mean, nutrition—lesson. There are four kinds of fats: monounsaturated fat, polyunsaturated fat, saturated fat, and trans fat. The first two are "good" fats, saturated fat is bad fat and trans fat is by far the worst. Trans fats severely lower your HDL cholesterol (the good kind) and drastically increase your LDL (bad) cholesterol, which hardens and clogs your arteries, which leads to heart attacks. Oh, and it promotes diabetes, as well.

The food industry uses partially hydrogenated oils in literally thousands of products. Check the label of your favorite foodstuffs—odds are high that they will be loaded with partially hydrogenated oils. Yeah, it extends the shelf-life of those indestructible processed foods you eat, but it can drastically shorten *your* shelf-life. They're in lots of commercial baked goods like cookies and cakes. They're even in many diet and so-called "health" foods. At their peak use, they were ingredients in almost 40 percent of the prepared foods you bought, but that will be going down now, as the controversy over their use goads manufacturers to stop using them.

In the last couple of years, Canadian and European governments have been on the move to ban or sharply reduce food companies' use of partially hydrogenated oils, while here in the good ol' U.S. of A., your friends at the Food and Drug Administration have been dragging their feet. The FDA has stated that "intake of trans fats should be as low as possible" but, as I write this, has taken no real action to make sure the food industry stops using them.

In Europe, food makers have been busy figuring out how to change the oils they use to remove the trans fat risk. In the United States, they've mostly been stonewalling and bullshitting us about it. Dr. Walter Willett, chairman of the Department of Nutrition at the Harvard School of Public Health, put it this way: "In Europe [food companies] hired chemists and took trans fats out. . . . In the United States, they hired lawyers and public relations people. No one doubted trans fats have adverse effects on health, and still companies were not taking it out."

When it became clear how bad trans fats were, the big food companies in the United States said they would do everything in their power to stop using partially hydrogenated oils as soon as they could. "Trust us." They smiled. "We're as concerned about your health as you are. Our scientists are working day and night, experimenting with different oils. We'll have those bad oils outta here in no time. (Oh, and by the way: You're on your own in the meantime. Don't blame us if you get a heart attack or your kid's arteries clog up like a rusty drainpipe. You're responsible for your own health. It's not our fault for loading up our food with chemicals and not telling you about it! Blah blah blah.)"

The following is from the press release McDonald's issued with a lot of hoopla and fanfare in September 2002:

McDonald's USA Announces Significant Reduction of Trans Fatty Acids with Improved Cooking Oil

REDUCTION IS MAJOR STEP TOWARD GOAL OF
ELIMINATING TRANS FATS FROM COOKING OIL

OAK BROOK, *Illinois. McDonald's USA announced today a significant reduction of trans fatty acids (TFAs) in its fried menu items with the introduction of improved cooking oil in all of its 13,000 restaurants—a major step toward McDonald's goal of eliminating TFAs from its cooking oil. The new oil will reduce French fry TFA levels by 48%, reduce saturated fat by 16% and dramatically increase polyunsaturated fat by 167%. While the total fat content in the fries remains unchanged, health experts agree that reducing TFAs and saturates while increasing polyunsaturates is beneficial to heart health.*

"It's a win-win for our customers because they are getting the same great French fry taste along with an even healthier nutrition profile," said Mike Roberts, President of McDonald's USA. "This leadership

initiative is all about giving our customers a wide range of wholesome choices, the highest quality ingredients and the same great taste that they have come to expect from McDonald's. America's favorite French fries are about to get even better."

With this nutrition initiative, McDonald's becomes the first national QSR company to set a goal of eliminating TFAs in cooking oil. The national rollout of the improved cooking oil begins in October 2002 and will be completed by February 2003, according to Roberts. The company plans to use the new oil to prepare McDonald's French fries, Chicken McNuggets, Filet-O-Fish, Hash Browns and crispy chicken sandwiches."

Yippee! Hurray! Let's all go to Mickey D's right now to celebrate!

Yeah, well, February 2003 came and went, and those partially hydrogenated oils are still in McDonald's foods. Turns out it was harder to figure out how to replace them than they'd thought. If European food makers could figure it out, why couldn't the mighty McD's? What, they don't have phones in Oak Brook? Couldn't drop a dime and just ask their colleagues in Denmark how *they* had managed it?

Fortune magazine, on August 9, 2004, had the answer:

[T]he company ran smack up against two basic facts. First, most unsaturated oils are unable to reproduce the crispy texture, savory taste, and pleasing "mouth feel" of a McDonald's fry. Achieving the right flavor is critical for McDonald's, whose beloved fries were once deemed "sacrosanct" by founder Ray Kroc.

Second, the bad-for-you oil is cheaper than the better-for-you kind. . . . Filling a typical fast-food fryer with 35 pounds of partially hydrogenated vegetable oil costs about $13; filling it instead with a reduced-trans-fat soybean oil might cost about $20. When you factor in fry life, the cost difference becomes even more dramatic. Hydrogenated oils are much more stable than less saturated oils; they stand *up better to the 350-degree heat of a fryer. According to one oil supplier, partially hydrogenated oils last about twice as long in a fryer as trans-fat-reduced ones. Because a restaurant typically goes through 500 pounds of oil a week, switching to the healthier oil would cost more than $19,000 a year. Multiply that by the 13,000 McDonald's stores in the U.S., and you have an added cost of about a quarter of a billion dollars annually.*

McDonald's quietly released a teensy, two-paragraph press release on the very last day of February 2003, muttering that it needed to "extend the timeframe" of the switch. As I'm sure McDonald's hoped, the news slid under the media's radar, leaving millions and millions of trusting customers to think they were now eating safer McFood.

Unfortunately for Ronald, some consumer groups noticed that he'd fallen asleep on the job. And they woke him up the American Way: *They sued the bastard!*

Hey, it worked against Big Tobacco.

A California-based nonprofit group called Ban Trans Fats filed a class-action lawsuit against McDonald's, "asking the court to order that McDonald's take effective steps to inform its customers about its failure to make the change. BTF is also asking that McDonald's make the change to the new cooking oil as soon as possible, just as it promised and represented to the public."

Another group, the Washington, D.C.–based Center for Science in the Public Interest (CSPI), took the matter to the court of public opinion. They ran a full-page ad in *The New York Times*, an open letter to McDonald's CEO Mike Roberts, the guy who'd made us the promise about the oils back in 2002:

Dear Mr. Roberts:

McDonald's has done a lot of things right. You've recently added some healthier menu items, and you've stopped supersizing fries and sodas. But you broke an important promise you made in 2002 to your customers, a promise to eliminate trans fat from your cooking oil. You still fry in partially hydrogenated vegetable oil, making all of McDonald's fried foods unnecessarily high in trans fat, a potent promoter of heart disease. . . .

The Institute of Medicine says that any amount of trans fat increases the risk of heart disease and should be kept to a minimum. Some of your European restaurants have already switched to trans-free cooking oils. But your broken promise puts your American customers at greater risk for heart attacks and early death. Please keep your promise.

Can pesky, "frivolous" lawsuits do the trick? In February 2005, McDonald's agreed to settle the case brought against them by Ban Trans Fat by paying out $8.5 million dollars. Seven million dollars of that money will go to the American Heart Association to help educate consumers on how dangerous trans fat is to our bodies. McDonald's agreed that it will use the other $1.5 million to publish notices to enlighten us patrons about the fact that it has not yet followed through on its 2002 pledge. I can't wait for that press release.

Here's one example: In May 2003, Ban Trans Fats sued the giant Kraft Foods, asking the court to ban the marketing and sale of Oreo cookies to children. Oreos are heavy in trans fats. The suit didn't ask for money. Not one penny. It just asked that Kraft stop clogging kids' arteries. It was a great example of using the court system to do the job the FDA wasn't.

And it worked. Sort of. Kraft sent out a detailed press release in which it promised to

- limit portion sizes of single-serve packages,
- reduce the fat and sugar content of some foods,

- provide nutritional labeling in all countries, even those that don't require it, and
- eliminate marketing in schools.

It has kept a couple of those promises. In 2004, Kraft debuted a new and improved Reduced Fat Oreo, a new Golden Oreo Original and the Golden Uh Oh! Oreo, all with no trans fat. They replaced the partially hydrogenated soybean oil with palm fruit oil or sunflower oil. As of this writing, Kraft still hasn't gotten rid of the trans fat in regular Oreos, but they swear they're working on it. Kraft also agreed to stop all in-school marketing. Kraft has cleaned up some of its other brands, too, like low-fat Fig Newtons (*mmmm*, Fig Newtons), Triscuits and SnackWell's Cracked Pepper crackers.

Even though it took a lawsuit and lots of bad publicity to goose Kraft into making these changes, there are still a lot of people out there who say these kinds of suits are a misuse of the judicial branch of government to do the job the legislative and executive branches should be doing.

I asked John Banzhaf III, a law professor at George Washington University, about this. For thirty years he spearheaded the move to drag Big Tobacco into court, and now he's a leading advocate of doing the same to Big Food. Instead of going to court, I asked him, shouldn't we be asking our duly elected political representatives to be passing laws that regulate the food industry?

"The problem of passing legislation over the objections of a very powerful industry with a big pocketbook is exactly what we faced with Big Tobacco and smoking," he replied. "That's why litigation has led the way. . . . I and every one of the attorneys and public health experts I'm working with would much rather see this go through legislation then litigation. Our motto is, 'If the legislators don't legislate, then the litigators will litigate.' "

Kraft Foods is a giant corporation, the umbrella for dozens of familiar brand names like Ritz, Nabisco, Planter's, Maxwell House, Kool-Aid, Jell-O, DiGiorno, Cream of Wheat, Good Seasons, Claussen's pickles, Oscar Mayer's wieners, Milk-Bone, Cool Whip, Minute Rice, and a couple dozen breakfast cereals. Not many politicians or bureaucrats are going to go up against a Foodzilla like Kraft, or McDonald's, unless they're sure they've got the people behind them. When a guy can sue McD's for a $12.5 million settlement and a public apology, and a lawsuit can make Kraft Foods hop, it sends a message.

It's also worth noting that Kraft is itself owned by Philip Morris (yep, the tobacco giant), a corporation that knows a thing or two about litigation. (See Appendix 3 of this book for a list of the foods you eat that are manufactured by tobacco companies—you won't believe it.)

Even so, Foodzilla still found a way of weaseling out of its responsibilities to its customers. According to the *Chicago Tribune*, as of June 2004, Kraft had reduced trans fat in only "about 5% of its North American product volume."

Now that you know more than you ever wanted to know about fat, especially trans fats, let's look at sugar. Did you know that McDonald's only has four items on its menu that contain no sugar whatsoever? (Those are the unsweetened iced tea, coffee, diet soda and sausage.) There's even sugar in the french fries! And the hash browns! (I got it wrong in the movie when I said these items don't contain sugar—both do contain dextrose.)

Some scientists believe that those ten teaspoons of sugar you slurp down in a 12-ounce Coke or Pepsi may stimulate the same part of your brain, the "reward circuits," that cocaine and nicotine do. "Eating energy-dense food, for example, triggers the release of endorphins and enkephalins," *New Scientist* explains. "Exactly how this generates a feeling of reward isn't understood, but it is clear that addictive substances provide a short cut to it. . . . Repeated use of addictive substances is thought to alter the circuitry in as yet unknown ways."

I asked Neal Barnard, MD, of the Physicians Committee for Responsible Medicine, his opinion about food addiction.

"For many people food does seem to be addictive," he said. In his book *Breaking the Food Seduction*, he writes that "sugar triggers the release of natural opiates within the brain, just as chocolate does. . . . [T]he result is a pleasant 'feel-good' effect, and whatever physical or psychological troubles might have been bothering you are toned down a bit."

From *Breaking the Food Seduction:*

Researchers at the Johns Hopkins University in Baltimore tested sugar's effects in an unusual way. Their test subjects were babies who were just one to three days old. Needless to say, none of these tiny infants had ever tasted a doughnut, seen a television commercial for sugary cereals, or made a trip to a convenience store. But they had a very noticeable reaction to sugar. The researchers first placed the infants in their bassinets for five minutes, and, naturally, some began to whimper a bit during this time. Then they gave each baby either a tiny amount of sugar in water or else just plain water, dribbling the fluid into the baby's mouth with a plastic syringe. The effect was almost immediate. Sugar water stopped them from crying. Water alone did nothing.

A pacifier can do that, too, but there is a critical difference: if the pacifier is removed, crying can ensue immediately; but sugar's effect lingers for several minutes, even after the taste is gone. The reason is that sugar causes opiates to be released in the infant's brain, and these naturally calming compounds stay on after the sugar is gone.

Infants whose mothers were narcotic addicts during pregnancy react very differently. Sugar is useless. They cry whether they get sugar or not. The fact is, these babies were exposed to narcotic opiates in the womb, and their natural opiate circuitry no longer responds normally; they are resistant to its effects.

Well-known nutrition expert Marion Nestle (pronounced NESS-uhl, like "wrestle", and no relation to the chocolate family) put it to me more cautiously: "I would say the evidence is suggestive, not proven. Some components of food stimulate the same parts of the brain as opiate receptors, but to a much, much smaller extent."

So it remains to be proven whether fast food can truly be called addictive. From my personal experience, I'm thinking it is. I well remember nights during my month of eating only McJunk when I'd get these inexplicable feelings of hunger, even though I was stuffed from McMuffins and Big Macs and Chicken McNuggets. I knew I couldn't really be hungry, but I sure felt like I was. In less than a month, I'd become a junk-food junkie.

As Greg Critser points out in *Fat Land*, there's sugar in everything. Sugar is the number-one food additive in the United States. Refined sugar is the predominantly used sweetener, but it's gradually being replaced by high-fructose corn syrup (HFCS).

Humans have been cultivating sugar cane and sugar beets for thousands of years, but it was only after Columbus brought the plant to the New World that sugar cane started to become a major crop. The production and transport of sugar and molasses were a major drive behind the Atlantic slave trade. In the 1700s, Europe developed a mad sweet tooth for jams, candies, cocoa and sweetened tea and coffee, promoting the spread of vast sugar plantations throughout the Caribbean and South America.

In the last century and a half, the refinement of white, granulated sugar, the sugar we all have on our tables at home and in every restaurant, became a profit-making mass-production business. As refined-sugar production became a giant industry, supported and subsidized by the United States and other countries, a superabundance of sugar poured into the foods we all eat. In my month of eating at McDonald's, I took in nearly a pound of sugar a day. People were shocked. Well, don't be—you may be taking in almost that much without even realizing it.

Every year, the typical American consumes between 120 and 150 pounds of refined sugar. That translates to over a third of a pound a day, packing over 600 calories.

Even if you don't eat sweets, the amount of refined sugar you may be consuming would shock you. Mostly it's hidden in things like french fries . . . and breads, soups, cereals, hot dogs, lunch meat, salad dressings, spaghetti sauce, crackers, mayonnaise, peanut butter, pickles, pizza, canned fruits and vegetables, tomato juice and . . . well, the list is endless.

Writing in the journal *Wholife,* Canadian nutrition consultant Paulette Millis notes that

excessive sugar consumption is believed to be involved in many common health problems: hypoglycemia, diabetes, heart disease, high cholesterol, obesity, indigestion, myopia, seborrheic dermatitis, gout, hyperactivity, lack of concentration, depression, anxiety, and more. Sugar is rapidly converted in the blood to fat (triglycerides), which increase obesity, risk of heart disease, and diabetes. Sugar greatly increases the risk of dental decay. It is devoid of vitamins, minerals, or fibre; it is an empty food. The lack of fibre in sugar causes a tendency to overeat.

And then there's high-fructose corn syrup, refined sugar's upstart rival. Corn syrup has been around as a sweetener and something to pour on pancakes since the 1800s, but it was only in the 1950s and '60s that the technology was developed for significantly upping the fructose levels to create HFCS. HFCS first appeared in the American market in 1967, and now the average American gobbles 63 *pounds a year!* And sodas aren't the only thing sweetened with HFCS. Go to the McDonald's website and check out the ingredients: HFCS is used to sweeten the ketchup, all the sauces you dip your McNuggets in, all the buns, the Big Mac sauce, the croutons you put on your "healthy" salad and more.

When I was growing up, my mother would make herself, as a treat, a Karo syrup and peanut butter sandwich. Corn syrup, peanut butter and bread. I tried it once and that was enough for me. I'll stick to blueberry jam.

According to the McDonald's website, all of the following items include HFCS:

Big Mac Bun	Warm Cinnamon Roll
Big Mac Sauce	Biscuit
Ketchup	Hotcakes
Regular Bun	Strawberry Sundae

Sesame Seed Bun	Hot Caramel Sundae
Barbeque Sauce	McDonaldland Cookies
Hot Mustard Sauce	Oreo McFlurry
Sweet 'N Sour Sauce	Chocolate Triple Thick Shake
Honey Mustard Sauce	Strawberry Triple Thick Shake
Butter Garlic Croutons	Coke
Newman's Own Cobb Dressing	Sprite
English Muffin	Hi-C Orange Lavaburst

Some critics believe HFCS is a major player in the obesity epidemic. Because your body processes it differently from old-fashioned sugar, HFCS screws with the way your metabolic-regulating hormones function. It also forces your liver to kick more fat out into the bloodstream. The result is a double-whammy of obesity: Your body is tricked into wanting to eat more at the same time that it's storing more fat.

Because high-fructose corn syrup mixes easily, extends shelf-life and can be as much as 20 percent cheaper than other sources of sugar, Big Food manufacturers love it. It can help prevent freezer burn, so you'll find it on the labels of many frozen foods. Take a walk through the frozen-food aisle and see for yourself. It also helps breads brown and keeps them soft, which is why hot dog buns and even English muffins have it.

While we're on the subject, let's consider artificial sweeteners. They've been around for a long time, too: Saccharin was discovered in 1878, and its benefits as a low-calorie replacement for sugar were being heavily promoted—by none other than Monsanto—by the 1900s. But it was with the various low-calorie diet crazes of the 1950s that artificial sweeteners really took off, and packets of the saccharin product we all know as Sweet'N Low began to appear next to the sugar in every restaurant and diner in the land. Cyclamate, discovered in 1937, goes by the brand name Sucaryl, and is used in SugarTwin. Aspartame, introduced in the mid-sixties, is in NutraSweet and Equal, and also in lots of diet sodas and cereals. Acesulfame K, also from the sixties, is marketed as Sunette. Sucralose, a chlorinated sucrose derivative, has become all the rage in recent years as Splenda.

All of these things are tremendously sweeter than natural sugar: Saccharin is 300 times sweeter, aspartame and acesulfame 200 times, cyclamate 30 times and sucralose an incredible 600 times. You don't need to be a nutritionist to realize the damage all these turbocharged sweeteners have done to our natural taste for sweets. Many of us can hardly even taste the natural sweetness in cane sugar, honey or fruit anymore. I was sitting on a train in Penn Station once behind a tall brunette who walked in carrying a "Venti" coffee from Starbucks. She proceeded to shake and dump no less than thirty (*thirty!!!*) packets of Equal into her coffee. Can you even imagine what's happening inside her body?

The potential health risks of artificial sweeteners have been debated for a long time. In 1970, cyclamate was banned in the United States as a possible carcinogen, and the FDA proposed a ban on saccharin due to cancer concerns raised by lab experiments; though the ban was not enacted, saccharin came with a warning label until Congress had it removed in 2000. (Once again, the fine folks in Congress were working with your best, I mean worst, interests in mind.) Studies have also shown potential cancer-promoting properties in acesulfame. The FDA has said aspartame may be linked to some uncommon but troubling side effects, including headaches, hallucinations, panic attacks, dizziness and mood swings. There were far more troubling studies possibly linking aspartame to birth defects and brain tumors, one conducted by the FDA itself as early as 1981, but they were overlooked in the rush to get NutraSweet approved and marketed. In large-dose lab testing, sucralose has been linked in animal studies to shrinkage of the thymus glands and enlargement of the liver and kidneys. But, as with NutraSweet, Splenda made it to the market before any large-scale, long-term population studies could prove or disprove those results.

The huge growth in the use of both HFCS and artificial sweeteners has thrown the refined sugar industry into a panic. We interviewed Andy Briscoe, president and CEO of the Sugar Association, the D.C. lobby for the massive sugar industry. In the interview, Briscoe went to great lengths to distance refined sugar from HFCS and the artificial stuff, especially in terms of health and obesity concerns.

"Everything we've seen from a scientific standpoint has exonerated sugar from being a cause of diseases, obesity, diabetes," he kept repeating. He also insisted that "the consumption of white sugar, the granules, has not increased, at all, since the 1960s. It's basically maintained an even consumption. So from our perspective we shouldn't be getting a bad rap. We certainly don't feel like we're a contribution to obesity or the cause of any other disease, as science shows."

SEVEN

IS IT CHEMICAL SOUP YET?

So now you know all about fat and sugar. Believe me, all that will sound downright natural and healthy when you hear about food processing, from meat production to pesticide use in cultivation to chemical additives. (*Mmmm*, chemical additives.)

We eat a stupendous amount of meat in this country. The USDA says we eat 1 million animals an hour. One million an hour! That's mostly chickens, but it's also cows, pigs, lambs, what have you. That's around 10 billion a year. Just here in the United States. Globally, it's around 50 billion. That's right, we're 4.6 percent of the global population, and we eat 20 percent of the meat consumed on the entire planet.

Now, think about the enormous industry that has grown up around the process of growing, feeding, housing, slaughtering, butchering and shipping all that meat. Take the cattle industry, which, *The Christian Science Monitor* reports, is "the largest single segment of U.S. agriculture, generating more than $30 billion a year in direct economic output plus three times that in related economic output." In short, raising cattle ain't what it used to be in the day of the cowboy, pardner. Now it's corporatized and centralized into four main companies, like ConAgra in

Colorado, where as many as 200,000 cows at a time stand around in a swamp of their own feces, getting pumped full of grains, anabolic steroids and bovine growth hormone. It's because of the BGH that countries in the European Union won't let us export beef to them anymore; BGH has been linked to mad-cow disease.

"Mad-cow disease" is the popular name for bovine spongiform encephalopathy (BSE), a degeneration of the central nervous system of cattle. Originally discovered in the UK in 1986, the first case of mad cow in the United States wasn't documented until 2004 (in a cow raised in Canada and slaughtered in Washington state). It is widely thought that if humans eat the meat of cows suffering from BSE, they can contract the fatal brain disorder known as variant Creutzfeldt-Jakob disease. By the end of 2003, 143 official cases had been counted in the UK, six in France, one each in Canada, Ireland, and Italy, and two in the United States—most recently, a Florida woman died of it in 2004, apparently after having eaten bad beef in the UK.

In 1996, sales of beef and burgers plummeted after Oprah Winfrey did a show on mad cow, which she said "has just stopped me cold from eating another burger." Her guest on the show, Howard Lyman, was a former cattleman who'd become a passionate opponent of the dangerous ways the corporate cattle industry was handling meat. He was known as the "Mad Cowboy."

"A hundred thousand cows per year in the United States are fine at night, dead in the morning," he told Oprah. "The majority of those cows are rounded up, ground up, fed back to other cows. If only one of them has mad cow disease, it has the potential to affect thousands."

A group of Texas cattlemen sued them both for libel and "disparagement." In 1998, a jury found in favor of Oprah and Lyman. The Texans appealed twice and were twice turned down.

Beef factories are models of waste-not-want-not efficiency. Filthy, disgusting and disease-ridden, maybe, but terribly efficient. Very little of one of these cows is discarded. Leftover bits and pieces are scooped up, ground together and fed back to the cows. And then those cows are ground up and fed to you.

A pound of ground beef used to come from one or two cows. But in the late 1990s the USDA found that a pound of ground beef could be made from leftover scraps collected from a dozen, a few dozen, or as many as 400 cows, all smashed together.

Interviewed for PBS's *Frontline* in 2002, Dr. Robert Tauxe, chief of the food-borne and diarrheal diseases branch of the CDC, went much farther than that when he said, "I suspect there are hundreds *or even thousands of animals* that have contributed to a single hamburger" (my emphasis). They could be from different states, even different countries. In a single patty. A juicy, tasty little United Nations of Burger.

It's been estimated that as much as 78 percent of ground beef contains microbes that are spread primarily by fecal matter. It's all that shit the cows produce and then stand around in. Kind of gives a whole new meaning to the old curse "Eat shit and die." It's like the food industry is saying that to all of us: *Eat shit and die, America.*

And it's not just beef. Hogs are raised in giant, shitty feedlots, too. In North Carolina, according to *World Watch* magazine, feedlot production has grown

from 2 million hogs per year in 1987 to 10 million hogs per year [in 2003]. Those hogs produce more than 19 million tons of manure each year and most of it gets stored in lagoons, or large uncovered containment pits. Many of those lagoons flooded and burst when Hurricane Floyd swept through the region in 1999. Hundreds of acres of land and miles of waterway were flooded with excrement, resulting in massive fish kills and millions of dollars in cleanup costs. The lagoons' contents are also known to leak out and seep into groundwater.

Meanwhile, the vast majority of the roughly 9 *billion* chickens alive in this country at any point are born, raised and slaughtered in what are called "factory farms." They spend their entire lives in enormous sheds, never seeing natural daylight—or much dark, either. To keep them active and productive, they get only one hour of dark in every twenty-four.

Something like 20 million of them are slaughtered every day. Some are ground up alive. Egg-laying hens live their entire lives in small wire cages, stacked on top of one another like prison cells, up to 80,000 of them in one windowless building. They don't walk, fly, perch, preen, nest, peck, dust-bathe or scratch for food. They just squat there and crank out eggs. The terrible conditions drive them nuts, so they'll scratch and peck one another's eyes out, and even turn cannibal. To prevent that, they often have their beaks and toes cut off.

Because of all the stress, their immune systems shut down, so they're pumped full of antibiotics—which, of course, are passed on to us every time we eat chicken. Which is helping to spread new, drug-resistant bacteria through the human population. For instance, there's a new superstrain of salmonella out there that's resistant to Cipro, one of the most powerful antibiotics known. Other antibiotics like penicillin, bacitracin, erythromycin and tetracycline are also losing their potency against the new "supergerms." You don't even have to eat meat for this to affect you—testing has found evidence of antibiotics and antibiotic-resistant bacteria in many of the country's waterways.

The E. coli scare of a few years ago was a warning signal. E. coli 0157:H7 is only one of hundreds of strains of E. coli bacteria sometimes present in the beef used in burgers, fast-food tacos, etc. While most are harmless, this one produces a toxin that can trigger bloody diarrhea, abdominal cramps, vomiting, fever and sometimes even kidney failure. The CDC estimates that more than 73,000 Americans are infected with E. coli 0157:H7 each year, and at least 60 die.

The spread of E. coli and mad-cow disease are just two of more than a dozen examples of foodborne pathogens that have been linked to beef. One of the more harebrained methods that meatpackers have been testing to kill the bacteria in tainted meat is to hit the meat with bursts of low-level radiation, which screws with the bacteria's DNA. Watch for glow-in-the-dark burgers at your neighborhood McDonald's and schools.

In an amazing display of collective insanity, the meat producers of this country are feeding all sorts of animals to the animals they feed to us. Dead pigs and dead horses are ground up for cattle feed, and so are dead chickens. A lot of chicken manure gets mixed up into the feed in the process, so the cows are not only eating chicken, but chicken shit, which can spread salmonella, tapeworms and chemicals like arsenic. Not only are cows fed dead chickens, but chickens are fed dead cows. (Cue "The Circle of Life" from *The Lion King*.)

You want to hear something really disgusting? The cattle industry buys millions of dead cats and dogs from animal shelters every year, then feeds them to the cattle who end up in your burger.

Yeeecccchhhh!!

Remember how sad you were the day you took poor ol' Scruffy to the pound to be put down? Well, don't worry. You'll be reunited with him again. At your local burger joint.

Oh, and they do the same with roadkill.

Is your mouth watering now?

This is not only disgusting, it's utter madness. It's the new, insane version of the old "circle of life." It passes new types of diseases around and around the food chain. And at every pass, we make some of those strains of disease stronger and stronger, because we keep bombing them with antibiotics that kill off some of them but only make the survivors and their offspring more resistant. And then they pass through the whole cycle again.

The FDA has regulated some of this and issued recommendations on certain points, but the basic facts are as I just told you.

Still think my girlfriend is nuts for being a vegan?

And, like everything else, we've spread the mass production and consumption of meat around the rest of the world. Hedging their bets against increased environmental and food-safety regulations in the United States and Europe, the giant meat corporations have been expanding their operations in less developed regions of the world, where the laws are looser and the ability to enforce them is often nil. One result is that more cultures around the world are increasing their meat consumption.

"Despite the fact that many health-conscious people in developed nations are choosing to eat less meat, worldwide meat consumption continues to rise," *World Watch* reports. "Consumption is growing fastest in the developing countries. Two-thirds of the gains in meat consumption in 2002 were in the developing world, where urbanization, rising incomes, and globalized trade are changing diets and fueling appetites for meat and animal products . . .

"Feedlots are responsible for 43 percent of the world's beef, and more than half of the world's pork and poultry are raised in factory farms. Industrialized countries dominate production, but developing countries are rapidly expanding and intensifying their production systems."

Here's another reason the food we eat today is bad for us: It's not food, at least not like food used to be. We've gone from old-fashioned farming, ranching, chicken-raising, food handling and food preparation—in short, the real ways to make real food—to mass-produced, mass-marketed, chemically enhanced processed food. Today, Americans spend about 90 percent of their food budget on processed foods. And processed food isn't really food, it's chemicals. It's like a huge science experiment.

You ever see that Charlton Heston sci-fi movie *Soylent Green?* Set in a toxic future where there are massive food shortages, and the government hands out these little crackerlike squares of nutrients, called Soylent, the way it hands out surplus cheese today? The kicker is that Soylent Green turns out to be made from processed human corpses. "Soylent Green is people!" the hero screams at the movie's climax. The ultimate recycling program. Watching the movie, you were supposed to be revolted.

Well I'll tell you what: A lot of the processed foods we're eating right now make Soylent Green seem like cordon bleu.

When I asked Eric Asimov of *The New York Times* if he thought fast food was good food, he had a funny response.

"You have to question whether it's food or not. If you've got something that's created in an assembly line somewhere hundreds of miles away, comes in on a truck, is thawed out and heated, and is adulterated with chemicals from some processing science company in New Jersey, I don't know if that really is food."

Eric Schlosser explains how this nonfood food came to be. Clarence Birdseye—yes, *the* Birdseye—had patented a lot of techniques for flash-freezing food in the 1920s, but it wasn't until after World War II that frozen food began to take off. In the boom years of the 1950s, everybody was buying refrigerators with freezers, all the supermarkets were installing them too, and it was what one historian calls "the Golden Age of Food Processing." The American housewife was encouraged to simplify her chores and feed her family frozen OJ, frozen TV dinners, the Chicken-of-Tomorrow, "Potato salad from a package!", Cheese Whiz, Jell-O salads, Jet Puffed Marshmallows and all that other crap. Whole restaurants sprang up boasting that they only served frozen foods.

And then there were all those fast-food joints popping up all across the country. Processed frozen foods were perfect for them. Instead of having a bunch of trucks drive up to a location, each one hauling a different, bulky product, now a single freezer truck could deliver loads of preprocessed patties, fries and whatever, slide them right into the back of the joint and drive off in no time. Fast-food chains could eliminate most of the cooking at each outlet, reduce time and staff and costs by a lot and make a killing simply reheating processed crap for their customers. The profit margins were, and remain, dazzling. Fast-food companies purchase frozen fries for about 30 cents a pound, reheat them in oil and sell them for about $6 a pound. That's one hell of a markup.

A big problem was that the canning, freezing and dehydrating kinda killed the taste. They also kill the smell and the color. So a billion-dollar industry sprang up to make processed food not taste like cardboard. Mostly they do that by injecting chemicals. A simple example is methyl anthranilate, which is used as a metal corrosion inhibitor in jet engine lubricants and also to make grape Kool-Aid taste like grape. Amyl acetate (also used as a paint and laquer solvent) tastes like banana. But the formulas are usually much, much more complicated than that. To simulate an old-fashioned strawberry milkshake, the "artificial strawberry flavor" in a Burger King shake contains forty-six chemicals. None of which is strawberry.

When they finally perfected a frozen french fry, customers didn't notice any difference in taste between the old-fashioned made-on-premises fries and the newfangled, E-Z-2-Serve McFries. Adding that beef flavoring didn't hurt. As the number of fast-food joints exploded in the 1970s and '80s, potato farming got corporatized and centralized. Over the last twenty-five years, Idaho has lost about half of its potato farmers. Now it's vast corporate farms that stretch for thousands of acres. To maximize output and minimize costs, they use all sorts of high-tech methods, including chemical fertilizers, pesticides, fungicides, and herbicides, all of which have a highly questionable impact on the environment—not to mention the impact on our bodies.

"The fertilizers they use are synthetic," John Robbins explained to me. "They're primarily nitrogen, phosphorous and potassium. But all the other micronutrients are not replaced in the soil, and so the food is deficient in or void of them. Also, they're grown in these large monocrops that attract pests, which are dealt with by poisons: herbicides, insecticides, fungicides, a whole gamut of poisons. Isn't there something bizarre about growing our food with poisons? Chemicals that have been designed and produced specifically to kill life?

"Now, residues from those pesticides invariably are higher in conventionally grown food than in organically grown food. You can wash the produce, which might get most of the pesticides off the surface, but because they're grown in the milieu of pesticides, they take it up into the plant. You can't wash off what's within the cells of the plant. In the long run—in fact, in the not so long run—these residues build up in your body, and they start to cause toxic overloads. It causes problems in your liver at first, and then eventually throughout the organs."

For a while, McDonald's was even working with the giant chemical company Monsanto, former producer of the herbicide Agent Orange, to produce genetically modified spuds that had the pesticides programmed right into them. (You can read more about it in Michael Pollan's book *The Botany of Desire*. They were called NewLeaf potatoes, genetically engineered to produce their own insecticide, called Bt (short for bacterial toxin). Supposedly, any Colorado potato beetle—the scourge of potatoes—that took a bite from a NewLeaf leaf was doomed. NewLeafs were actually registered as a pesticide with the EPA.

Let me repeat that:

NewLeaf potatoes were actually registered as a pesticide with the EPA. Potatoes! And we were eating them! Lots of them! (Mmmm, pesticide.)

NewLeafs were introduced in 1996, and McDonald's started using them immediately. Although they were also used in Pringles, Frito-Lay potato chips and Hardee's fries, according to *The Wall Street Journal*, McDonald's was by far the biggest buyer, and a Monsanto executive told Pollan that, without McDonalds' early support, the NewLeaf might never have gotten off the ground. In 2000, growing public unease about genetically modified (GM) food convinced McDonald's and others to drop the NewLeaf and go back to plain old Russet Burbank spuds. Without McDonald's as a customer, the NewLeaf was discontinued.

I don't think we'll ever be told how many millions of pounds of these toxic spuds we ate as McDonald's fries or Frito-Lay chips in the late 1990s. Nor will we ever know if they made any of us sick. Pollan says that organic farmers had been using bacterial toxins for decades—of course, they hadn't been gene-splicing it with their vegetables, but still, that's a bit discomforting. Speaking to Pollan for a 1998 *New York Times Magazine* article, Monsanto claimed "that it has thoroughly examined all the potential environmental and health risks of its biotech plants, and points out that three regulatory agencies, the U.S.D.A., the E.P.A. and the F.D.A., have signed off on its products. Speaking of the NewLeaf [a Monsanto biologist told Pollan], 'This is the most intensively studied potato in history.' " Which I don't find any more comforting than Pollan did.

Pollan visited a potato farmer in Idaho who grows Russet Burbanks—the taters most used in french fries—for McDonald's. Along with various insecticides, pesticides, herbicides, chemical fertilizers and fungicides, this farmer dusts his crop with some of the most toxic chemicals now in use, including Monitor, a deadly chemical that damages the central nervous system. He tells Pollan he won't go into a field for four or five days after it's been sprayed. Monitor kills aphids, which are harmless but transmit a virus that causes a problem called "net necrosis"—sounds spooky, but all it means is brown spots on the potato's flesh. But McDonald's doesn't want brown spots on its fries. This farmer could plant other kinds of potatoes that aren't susceptible to net necrosis, but then he'd lose McDonald's as a buyer.

And then there's dioxin, "a hideous poison," as John Robbins described it to me, and a by-product of pesticide manufacturing. "It's in a lot of the food we eat, in very small amounts. But it's so concentrated a poison, so damaging and devastating, that even very small amounts raise cancer rates, raise the level of birth defects in newborns, cause a lot of autoimmune problems, a lot of inflammatory problems. It's been linked in some studies to chronic fatigue syndrome. There are some questions about those studies, but cancer is incontrovertibly linked to dioxin exposure. Most of the dioxin exposure in the United States comes from animal products: meats, dairy products, eggs." This is the same poison that gave formerly handsome Ukraine president Viktor Yuschenko his new bulbous spudlike complexion.

These are just hints of the frightening things that happen to beef, chicken and dairy on the way to becoming that Egg McMuffin you had for breakfast yesterday, that Whopper you devoured for lunch today and that tub of KFC you're picking up for dinner tonight. Kinda makes you wonder what's in the Colonel's secret recipe! Hmmm.

Speaking of secret recipes: As if bacteria and pesticides involved in the main ingredients weren't delicious enough, McDonald's adds even more stuff to the food when they prepare it: lots more chemicals.

For instance, you think a standard Chicken McNugget is like this little piece of breast meat with a little flour and breadcrumbs sprinkled on it to make it crunchy, right? Sorry. There's no one place on the chicken that the McNugget comes from. A McNugget is pieced together from the mushed-up little bits of a dozen or more chickens. And then they throw in

> water, modified cornstarch, salt, chicken flavor (yeast extract, salt, wheat starch, natural flavoring (animal source), safflower oil, dextrose, citric acid, rosemary), sodium phosphates, seasoning (natural extractives of rosemary, canola and/or soybean oil, mono- and diglyc-

erides, and lecithin). Battered and breaded with: water, enriched bleached wheat flour (flour, niacin, reduced iron, thiamine mononitrate, riboflavin, folic acid), yellow corn flour, bleached wheat flour, modified corn starch, salt, leavening (baking soda, sodium acid pyrophosphate, sodium aluminum phosphate, monocalcium phosphate, calcium lactate), spices, wheat starch, whey, corn starch. Breading set in vegetable oil. Cooked in partially hydrogenated vegetable oils (may contain partially hydrogenated soybean oil and/or partially hydrogenated corn oil and/or partially hydrogenated canola oil and/or cottonseed oil and/or sunflower oil and/or corn oil).

Yummy! There's the partially hydrogenated oil again, as well as dextrose (sugar) and chicken flavor. Should they really have to *add* chicken flavor to Chicken McNuggets? What are these mad scientists creating?

By the way, when I combed the McDonald's locations in Manhattan, I found only about three out of four—or 75 percent—had *any* nutritional information available to customers. (Some only had the info in Spanish; that's *no bien.*) Translate that to a national level, and that means about 3,400 locations nationwide have *no nutritional info* whatsoever. When I asked McDonald's about this, they said, "All the ingredient and nutrition information is available on the website." Well, that's swell, considering only about 50 percent of American households have computers hooked up to the Internet. The rest of you just have to guess.

Not quite trusting the nutrition information on McDonalds' website, I purchased a sampling of McFood items and sent them to an independent laboratory. They tested the following items:

- a Quarter Pounder with cheese
- a Filet-O-Fish

- a Fiesta Salad with salsa dressing
- medium french fries
- a six-piece Chicken McNuggets
- a small Fruit 'n Yogurt Parfait

The first discrepancy the lab noted was that the portion sizes of the items I brought them were mostly larger than those listed on the McDonald's website. Granted, the website cautions that portion sizes may vary, but in our study, five out of seven varied on the high side. For instance, the website said an order of medium fries weighed 114 grams and contained 350 calories. But the medium fries we brought to the lab weighed 123 grams and contained 430 calories. So there were 80 more calories in our serving than the website said there would be.

But even when we compared the calories by equal, 100-gram servings, we still found discrepancies. One hundred grams of french fries should have contained 307 calories. But our independent lab found that 100 grams of the french fries it tested contained 352 calories. That's a 15 percent difference.

As you can see from the tables in Appendix 2 in this book, the differences were even greater in other categories. For example, the lab found a whopping 67 percent more saturated fat in the medium serving of fries we purchased than what was listed on the website . . . twice as much sugar in the Fiesta Salad . . . and 23 percent more saturated fat in the Quarter Pounder with Cheese—even though the Quarter Pounder we tested was actually a little *smaller* than the serving size listed on the website!

Obviously, if other independent lab tests supported our results, the nutrition information on McDonald's website is pretty useless. Refer to Appendix 2 of this book for all the test results—you won't believe it.

Anyway, after people got hip that your standard McNuggets were basically Assorted Leftover Chicken Parts Ground Up & Glued Back Together in Cute Little Shapes with Tons of Chemicals Added, McDonald's introduced the new, improved, premium version: Chicken McNuggets Made with White Meat. That's right, America, now there's actually chicken in these new McNuggets! Go to the website (if you can) and see what other scrumptious ingredients are in these new, improved, premium chicken breast McNuggets. What a surprise—they're still packed with all those chemicals. (*Mmmm*, chemicals.)

How about some fries to go along with those premium white-meat McNuggets? In the United States today, the most eaten vegetable is the french fry. No, not the potato, the french fry. People say, "Well, french fries are made from potatoes. How bad can they be for you?" In certain instances, I'd agree. The kind of place I like to go eat a burger and fries actually slices the potatoes in the kitchen and deep fries them right there. The ingredients: potato and oil. Some salt sprinkled on it. That's it. It's only one step away from being a potato.

But even those aren't good for you if you eat too many of them, because they're soaked with fat. You've got to remember that potatoes are four-fifths water. When you drop those fries into hot cooking oil, the water is blasted out of them as steam, and the fat from the oil rushes in to replace it. It's the fat that makes them taste so good—and makes them so bad for you. Your body can't burn off all the extra calories in that fat, so it stores it in your butt, your thighs and your belly.

And those are *real* fries. McDonald's fries are not much like real fries. By the time it gets to your mouth, a McDonald's fry is somewhat removed from that pesticide-coated field where it was once a Russet Burbank spud. Check out these ingredients:

> *Potatoes, partially hydrogenated soybean oil, natural flavor (beef source), dextrose, sodium acid pyrophosphate (to preserve natural color). Cooked in partially hydrogenated vegetable oils (may contain partially hydrogenated soybean oil and/or partially hydrogenated corn*

oil and/or partially hydrogenated canola oil and/or cottonseed oil and/or sunflower oil and/or corn oil).

Did you even know all that stuff was in a simple french fry? I know I sure didn't. I thought french fries were just deep-fried potatoes and no more. Simple. The way they should be. But to keep the shape and taste and look and smell of their fries uniform all over the world, McDonald's has turned this American classic into a chemical by-product. It's more like plastic than food. (To this day, their fries taste like smoked plastic to me. The most unnatural, unreal, chemical-ridden "food" I can imagine.)

Don't believe me? To test how long McFrankenfood lasts, I bought various McDonald's items—a Filet-O-Fish, le Big Mac, fries, the usual suspects—and also some real fries and a real burger from a non-fast-food sandwich place. I put them all in big, lidded glass jars in my office and watched nature take its course. Two weeks, a month, six weeks. Everything gradually decayed and decomposed, the way God intended it to. My office got awful stinky. Only those McDonald's fries refused to die. Those freaks of nature didn't decompose one bit in ten weeks. They didn't mold, they didn't break down, nothing happened. After ten weeks, they still looked brand new. That was the point at which my intern freaked out at the disgusting sights and smells and threw everything away, so I have no way of knowing how long those Frankenfries would have lasted. For all I know, they're still looking as new as the day I bought them, somewhere in the Fresh Kills landfill.

That experiment was inspired by something I did to a friend of mine at MTV a few years ago. A producer and I would play pranks on each other, like hiding food in each other's office where it wouldn't be found until the stink of rotting grub permeated the space. I had just found a ham sandwich that had turned green under my desk and smelled like Shaq's jockstrap after four full quarters. How to get back at him? I walked down to the neighborhood McDonald's, bought a McChicken sandwich and snuck into his office. I unwrapped it and placed it on top of his bookshelves, behind a bowling pin and a basketball he'd collected during his days at MTV Sports.

He'll never find it, I giggled to myself.

Boy was that right. Weeks went by. Nothing happened to alert my friend. No odor of rotting chicken to send him on the hunt. Two months went by, and still nothing. Once, when he was out, I snuck into his office and checked. The sandwich was still up there where I'd hidden it. The sauce had dried up and the lettuce had wilted away to nothing, but the bun and the chicken looked like new.

It's bound to start stinking soon, I thought.

Two more months went by. My show was canceled by MTV. I made the rounds to say my good-byes. My friend's office still did not stink of dead McChicken. He said nothing about it as we shook hands and parted.

Many more months passed. Then one day he called and asked me when I'd been in his office.

"What are you talking about?" I said. I was genuinely puzzled. So much time had passed, I'd forgotten all about the prank.

"I found the little present you left for me." He chuckled. "When were you here?"

"I left that thing there almost a year ago!" I cried.

"What? No way," he answered.

"Why? How does it look?"

"It looks," he said slowly, "like you bought it yesterday."

It turned out he'd only found the sandwich by accident. Nothing, no smell, had alerted him to its presence. Had he not seen it, how long would it have lasted, pristine and uncorrupted? Another year? Forever?

The answer may be "forever." After *Super Size Me* came out, I heard from a guy named Matt Malmgren, a thirty-eight-year-old software engineer in Burlington, Vermont. Back in 1991 he was out with some friends in Boston for New Year's Eve, and they stopped into a McDonald's on the way home. Matt bought a couple of cheeseburgers, ate one and put the other in his coat pocket for later.

"I didn't wear that coat again until the following fall," he told me, "and the burger was still in my pocket. It had dried out, but other than that it was well preserved. That was pretty cool."

He kept it as a kind of memento. And then he started collecting them, one a year. In the fall of 2004, Matt's museum of indestructible McFood had grown to include:

- the original '91 McDonald's Cheeseburger
- '92 McDonald's Cheeseburger and Big Mac
- '93 Burger King Hamburger
- '94 McDonald's Hamburger
- '95–'03 McDonald's Cheeseburgers

What can I say? He's a collector, and he sent me the photos to prove it.

"I keep them on the bookshelves in our living room. They still smell like burgers, but our dogs lose interest after the first couple days. You can see the special sauce, lettuce and pickle on the top bun, and cheese below the bottom patty. The buns tend to get fragile over time, but the rest of the stuff stays pretty much the same. The most amazing thing about this is the meat. It retains its shape and color—all years look exactly the same."

Matt says his wife "tolerates" the collection, though at one point she did try to convince him to sell it on eBay.

Matt told me that my experiment could have gone on much, much longer if I hadn't put the food in those glass jars with lids. They trapped the moisture and condensation that promote fungus and decay. I should have left it all out in the open air to age gracefully and glacially, like he did.

Asked how his experiment has affected his family's fast-food consumption habits, he said his two daughters, two and four, had eaten at McDonald's a couple of times, but otherwise "we haven't eaten red meat for about ten years, and rarely go to fast-food places, other than for the playgrounds. There's not a lot for toddlers to do around here during the winter."

Think about this: Food isn't supposed to be indestructible. Food is supposed to decay if just left sitting around. Food is supposed to be the most biodegradable of all products.

Now ask yourself this: What allows this food to defy nature? And what is this indestructible, nonbiodegradable McFood doing to your body?

You know the answer: nothing good.

EIGHT

PHYSICAL MISEDUCATION

Excuse me—I'm getting another call from the McCritics' Corner.

"This is a game of hysteria and sound bites."

Hey kids, it's our old pal Tricky Dick Berman, talking to the *Los Angeles Times*.

"Why are we heavier?" he asks. "Is it food or a sedentary lifestyle? We believe in freedom of choice and the concept of personal responsibility."

In one way he's right. It's true that Big Food is just one Big Piece of the obesity puzzle. Another huge problem, and one that really *is* our personal responsibility, is our lack of exercise and physical activity. Physical exercise is one place where we truly can make a difference in our lives.

Let me just say that I am a huge proponent of personal responsibility. My number-one form of transportation in New York City is riding my bike, and if you ride a bike in NYC, you'd better be fully prepared for personal responsibility. I've been hit by all kinds of things—buses, cabs, old ladies with their walking sticks—and I never jump up and say,

"That's it! Get me a lawyer! I'm suing you . . . you . . . old lady." No, I get back on my bike and ride away with my pride in tow: personal responsibility.

Like I said before, it really couldn't be simpler: overeating + under-exercising = obesity, and all the disastrous health consequences that come with it. If you take in more calories than you work off, your body is going to store those extra calories as fat. Those few million years of lean times programmed our bodies to do that. Until extremely recently in human history, food was usually pretty scarce. When you got it, you ate it. All of it. Your body used some of that energy to keep you going about your daily grind of hunting woolly mammoths and scrounging for roots and berries and then stored what it could as fat, to keep you alive during those long, cold winter months when you were huddled in the back of your cave with nothing to eat.

Now, for the first time in human history, we live in an all-you-can-eat world, where food is produced in overabundance and pushed on us everywhere we go. *Mangia! Mangia! Mangia!* There's more where that came from!

Marion Nestle, one of the country's leading nutritionists, whom I quoted earlier, edited the Surgeon General's Report on Nutrition and Health in 1988 and is currently the chair of the Department of Nutrition, Food Studies and Public Health at New York University. When I asked her why we all seem to be overeating, she put it really simply:

> We overeat because food's ubiquitous in our society. If you're a food company, your objective is to get people to eat more of your food, and you do that by making food closer to people, putting it in vending machines where they can easily get it. You do it by making larger portions. You do it by advertising. You do it by making it as easy as possible for people to eat as much food as they possibly can, twenty-four hours a day, seven days a week, 365 days a year.

And, of course, they're loading up all that food with delicious fats and scrumptious sugars, which only makes us want to eat more and more and more.

We're shoveling in all these extra calories, but we're not doing any extra work to burn them off. So we're getting fatter and fatter.

That ain't rocket science. It's not new math. Yet it's appalling how many of us don't even know these basic facts. I asked a bunch of people on the street if they knew what a calorie was. Not one of them could tell me. Not one! If I'd asked them who had won the last *American Idol*, or how many games it had taken the Red Sox to win the World Series, I bet they coulda told me. But ask Americans about basic issues of their own health, and all you get are blank stares.

I had to go back to Nestle to get the answer: "A calorie is a measure of the energy content of food," she explained. "One calorie, the kind that you usually see when you see the caloric content on food labels, is the amount of energy that's needed to raise the temperature of a liter of water by one degree centigrade."

Don't say I never taught you anything, America.

If you want to stay trim and healthy, every one of those calories you take in is a calorie you should burn. It's a simple equation. You eat 100 calories' worth of fries, you should get in 100 calories' worth of physical activity. You eat 100 calories' worth of fries and then only use up 50 of them, the other 50 calories are going straight to your waist, thighs and arteries.

As we all know, putting on pounds is a helluva lot easier than taking them off. And since nothing in this world is idiotproof, figuring out how much exercise you need to do to burn off X number of calories can be tricky. The number of calories you burn depends on your weight, the activity you're doing and the intensity of the activity. You can go to the gym five times a week, but if you're just going there to sit on a stationary bike and gab with your friends on your cell, then those pounds aren't going to melt away like magic. (Nothing makes me madder than people who talk on their cell phones in the gym. *Leave it in the locker, pal!* You'll get a better workout, and everyone around you will be happier.)

If you do go to a gym, try to get a trainer to work with you on setting up an exercise routine that matches your weight and diet. If you don't belong to a gym, get a book or go online, where there are comparison tables you can follow to design your own program.

The average man weighing 150 pounds can burn off 115 calories with every ten minutes of high-intensity aerobic exercise. Ten minutes of racquetball will burn around 90 calories. Running at a good clip for those ten minutes buys you a handsome 131 calories. Sitting on your behind for ten minutes only uses up 12. A woman weighing 123 pounds can burn 56 calories in ten minutes of bicycling at a decent speed, 77 calories playing basketball, 78 playing soccer, and 88 calories in ten minutes on the StairMaster.

Some things people like to consider "exercise" don't really burn many calories. Like bowling. If you're 160 pounds, a half hour of bowling only burns 48 calories. If you drink two beers and slurp a slice of pepperoni pizza while you're at it, you're kinda defeating the purpose. Riding around the links in a golf cart isn't much better: In a half hour of golf, that same 160-pound guy will use up only 84 calories.

Now compare that to how many calories are in the crappy food we eat. A single Whopper with Cheese contains 800 calories. It's gonna take that guy eight full hours of bowling—and no beers or pizza—to work off that one Whopper. A Big Mac has 560 calories. That's about seven straight hours of golf! Just for one Big Mac. Throw in the large fries, the 32-ounce Coke and a yummy shake, and you gotta be on the links 24/7 not to gain weight.

I know a lot of people complain that they don't have time to set aside for regular exercise, or they can't afford membership at a gym. Believe me, I hear ya. I really don't understand why gyms have to be so damned expensive. I belong to a little gym downstairs from my office that costs me $89 a month. With tax, that's $1,200 a year! What the hell am I paying for? I'll tell you: I'm paying to be able to walk downstairs to the gym. Period. If I had to go across town, I'd never make it.

When I go home to West Virginia, I always work out at the YMCA. They have everything that the fancy Reebok Sports Club in New York does, for a fraction of the price. Basketball, swimming, racquetball, cardio equipment, you name it. You should look into the Y in your own neighborhood. They are usually very affordable and will often offer breaks as well as payment plans that will enable you to get a membership. Think about joining as a family. Like I always say, "The family that sweats together rides home in a smelly car together."

We live in the fattest nation in the world—shouldn't gyms be one of the *cheapest* places you can go? Shouldn't they be tax-deductible? You know what gyms should do? Give free memberships to women. Write off all those free memberships as tax-deductible donations to the health of our nation. Then every guy in town would have reason to (a) come to the gym and (b) get his fat butt into shape.

But there are also some everyday things you can do to use up some calories. Just working around the house, instead of hiring some local neighborhood teen to do it for you, will get you some exercise. And walking's good. Jogging is even better, naturally, but if you don't feel you're up to that, walking is better than nothing. I mean, you have to walk at a good speed for almost an hour to burn up the calories in one Sausage McMuffin, and almost an hour and a half to offset one Taco Bell Gordita Supreme. But you won't burn those calories couch-sitting—believe me, I've tried.

Unfortunately, walking is another thing Americans don't do. I spoke with Mark Fenton, former editor of *Walking* magazine. Fenton is also a former Olympic race walker—you know, those folks who walk funny really quickly? You may think they're funny, but I challenge you to do that full-speed for even one mile. I did it when I met him, and I've got new-found respect for those guys. The next day, my ass hurt in places I didn't even know I had muscles.

Fenton told me that fewer than half of all Americans get any form of exercise at all. Not even walking. We walk about half as much as we did twenty years ago. The average American walks 1.5 miles a day. For all you pedometer junkies out there, that's only 3,000 steps. Think about that: 3,000 steps a day is nothing.

Part of the reason for the decline of walking, obviously, is the spread of suburbs. There's nowhere to walk in the suburbs. Everything is a drive away: work, school, shopping, entertainment. It's because so many suburbs are zoned for "single-use" houses only. That's a brand new development in human civilization. It came along with the automobile. Before, you never saw miles and miles of only houses, because it was totally impractical. From little villages to big cities, everything was "mixed use"—houses, shops, schools, churches, workplaces were all jumbled together. You could walk almost everywhere. Or rather, you had to. Now you can't.

Walking out in the 'burbs can be dangerous, too, if you do want to walk (or ride a bike) to the grocery store and back. In a lot of communities, there aren't sidewalks. You walk on the shoulder of a busy road or, God forbid, a highway. And don't even think about crossing that highway—it'd be like a game of human Frogger. Becoming roadkill does not promote a healthy lifestyle (although you might end up in our "circle of life" food chain).

Ah, you say, but so what? We live in the modern era. We don't walk because we don't have to. That's why God—or Henry Ford, the God of mass production—made cars. That's why there are golf carts, so we don't tucker ourselves out when we're getting our weekly exercise. And those little electric scooter things they advertise on cable TV that are great for the handicapped and old folks. And those chairlifts you can put on your stairs. It's why God—or Dean Kamen, the God of not walking—invented the Segway Human Transporter. We don't have to walk anywhere, or climb stairs, our use our lower bodies at all. It's evolution! Humans are evolving past the point where we need our lower limbs for locomotion. Soon we'll roll out of bed into a little electric cart, which we'll ride to the chairlift at the top of the stairs. At the bottom of the stairs, another little cart will be waiting for us. When we're ready to leave the house, we'll Segway from the front door to the door of the SUV. Our legs will become vestigial organs, as useless as wisdom teeth or wings on an ostrich.

Not even the mailman will walk anymore. He'll ride a Segway. Oh yeah, he'll be fast. Until the diabetes or the clogged arteries or the cancer knocks him off the transport for good. I was at the airport recently and was passed by a cop riding on a Segway. He met up with another cop on a Segway and then they sped off together, like a remake of *CHiPs*. (Maybe it should be called Chocolate CHiPs.)

It's bad enough that all us adults are sitting around on our behinds all the time, only getting exercise when lifting a beer and a slice to our faces while watching our favorite ball team on TV. But what's worse, what's downright criminal, is the example we're setting for our kids. A nation of couch potatoes, raising a nation of pudgy little couch spudlings, whose only exercise anymore comes from using the remote or the joystick.

The decline in physical activity among American kids over the last twenty years is scary. You want to hear something that'll really make you feel guilty? *Today's grandparents are more active than their grandchildren.* I don't mean that grandparents were more active than today's kids back when they were kids themselves. They're more active *now!* That's just pathetic! While American seniors are walking, hiking, gardening, doing Tai Chi and yoga, their grandkids are home, staring slack-jawed at *Spongebob Squarepants* or *Halo 2.* Or they're in a Mac Shack, loading up on Happy Meals.

In parents' defense, a big part of this stems from the rise of single-parent and two-earner households. Adults spend so much time at work, trying to stay afloat in this economy, that they've got far less time to monitor their kids' activities the way parents used to. So many American kids at all economic levels come home from school to an empty house, plunk themselves down in front of the TV or computer or maybe even homework, and no one's there to shoo them outside. Or they hang out with other kids at the mall food court, making sure they get home just before their exhausted folks do. In poor city neighborhoods, conscientious parents don't even want their kids outside where the violence and drugs are; they'd much rather they stay inside, plopped in front of the afternoon cartoons.

Kids used to at least get some exercise, lousy as it often was, at school. Remember phys ed? Did you hate it? Lots of kids did. Well, you can breathe a sigh of relief, because the presence of PE has sharply declined in American schools in the last fifteen years. Partly it's through lack of funding for gyms, teachers and equipment, but it's also because of legislation like the "No Child Left Behind Act"—state education boards are pressuring schools to cram as much teaching into the day as possible, to replace "downtime" like phys ed and recess with more academics.

Phil Lawler, who runs a model phys ed program at Madison Junior High School in Illinois (we'll meet him again later), says, "I've often referred to art, music and physical education as the sacrificial lambs of education. We're now in a society of high-stakes testing. Everything that we're trying is to improve science, reading and math scores." Out of Madison's nine-period schoolday, which includes one period for lunch, Lawler has had to fight to maintain one period of gym.

The sad irony, he says, is that there are studies showing that gym is actually good for the brain as well as the body. The increased flow of oxygen to the brain that comes with physical exercise can make kids better, more focused students when they return to the classroom.

The CDC reports that in 1991, about 43 percent of America's high school students took phys ed daily. By 2003, that was down to around 28 percent. In 2003, only a little more than half of high school students were taking any sort of PE at all. And when they did, most of them just stood around, anyway—only a bit more than a third of them were physically active during PE class.

> Kelly Brownell, a professor of psychology at Yale, and director of the Yale Center for Eating and Weight Disorders, said, "There's only one state in the country that mandates daily physical education in schools, and that happens to be Illinois. In the rest of the country it's district by district and highly variable. In some places children get almost no physical education in high school. In other places they might get one or two days a week. But even then, studies have shown that out of a typical gym period, only six minutes are spent being physically active! The rest of the time it's standing in line, visiting with your friends, standing around waiting for the ball to come to you, things like that. So the amount of physical education students get is actually very small—it can be measured in minutes per week. It's hard to imagine that we're going to have a fit nation if that's what we're teaching kids in school."

What difference can a little PE make? In August 2004, the RAND Corporation announced a study suggesting, "Increasing physical education instruction in kindergarten and first grade by as little as one hour per week could reduce the number of overweight 5 and 6 year old girls nationally by as much as 10%. . . ." And one hour a day of PE "could cut the number of overweight girls in those grades by 43%, and the number of girls in those grades at risk for being overweight by 60%." Boys would not be much affected, presumably because they're more active than girls at that age.

. . .

It's not like Americans don't know they *should* be doing something. According to a 2004 survey, 97 percent of Americans are aware that the United States is the world's fattest nation. More than 64 percent said it's embarrassing. But then, when it comes time to doing something about it, only one in four who said they were overweight were trying to diet, and only one in five belonged to a gym. (Too bad just belonging doesn't help you lose weight. If only somehow through osmosis that gym membership card could suck away the pounds. They should make gym cards that weigh 50 pounds, so that even when you just carry it around in your wallet you'd be exercising. Bally's, Crunch, take that one and run with it.)

So, we're overeating and embarrassed, but too lazy to do anything about it. Ain't that America, babe? That's as American as baseball—well, not playing baseball but watching it, while eating hot dogs and apple pie and driving a Chevrolet. And not a little Chevy either, but one big enough for our big ol' overfed and undermoved bodies. You think it's coincidence that great big SUVs have become so popular?

That's why for the thirty days of my McDiet I tried to become as sedentary as the average American. I tried not to exercise at all, and to walk no more than 5,000 steps a day, a bit less than twice the daily American average.

Let me tell you, it was *tough* trying to get as little exercise as the average American does. I live in New York City, where limiting how much you walk turned out to be like limiting how often you can flip someone the bird or scream obscenities at a cab driver. I walk and ride my bike nearly everywhere, and I quickly discovered that I walk an average of 10,000 to 12,000 steps per day.

The thought of suddenly having to cut that in half was daunting, especially when you take my apartment into account as well. I live on the sixth floor in one of those old-school East Village tenement buildings.

There's no elevator. It's a building where you know just a few decades ago there was only one toilet for the whole floor. So the fact that you have to walk up six flights every time you come home is somewhat off-set by the plus that at least you have your own toilet—so what if it's in the closet, and the shower is between the front door and the apartment's only sink? I can shower, sign for a package from Fed Ex and do the dishes all at once! I'm multitasking! And it's mine, my little piece of heaven, six magical floors into the sky.

But it's 100 steps from the front door of the building to the front door of my apartment. One-tenth of a mile roundtrip, every time I come and go. And I come and go a lot.

NINE

SEX, FRIES AND VIDEOTAPE

Looking back, that month of February 2003 is kind of like a surreal dream, an endless procession of McMuffins and Big Macs, shakes and sodas, cookies and Chicken McNuggets and Salad Shakers, marching in a line that stretched all the way from the horizon to my mouth. What circle of Hell did I say it was where the gluttons were stuck in Dante's *Inferno*? That's what that month looks like to me now. Day after day, staring down into the bottomless pit of buckets of fries . . . And the fries never stop coming; it's like there's a hole in the bottom and someone keeps poking more fries up through it.

Then there was the headachy torture of sucking an entire Super Size Shake through a straw. Before making this film, I didn't even know they had Super Size Shakes! Who on earth wanted to suck down a shake that could fill a wastepaper basket? It was 42 ounces of shake, 1,400 calories of sugary chemical goodness! You'd have to run eight or nine miles just to work off that one "dessert." I felt so sick and bloated afterward. Once I knew these things existed, I started listening to people order in the stores, and you would be blown away by how many people actually order them. I did it one time in the whole month and that was one time too many, trust me.

> You ever notice they don't call them "milkshakes" anymore? Someone once told me they had to stop that long ago, when they stopped making them like real milkshakes and started mass-producing them from chemicals. I guess calling them simply "shakes" sounded better than "chemshakes." That may just be an urban myth, but it's still a great story.

And then there's the "ambience": the weird lighting and plastic chairs and painful colors. The constant smells of hot oil and griddle grease. The kids behind the counter staring at you like zombies, like dead-eyed lost souls stuck in *Inferno* with all the gluttons. Only instead of Cerberus, the demon that torments us is a giant Hamburglar, and our eternal punishment is to eat one more burger, one more filet, one more fry. . . .

Aaaaiiiieeeee!!

As the days and weeks progressed, or maybe I should say digressed, other weird shit happened to my body. The first zits sprouted on my face before the first week was out. Pretty soon I felt like I was thirteen again—pimply, pale, greasy and funny-looking. Thank goodness I already had a girlfriend. (For the time being, at least.)

In my chest, I started to have . . . not chest pains, exactly . . . and not man-breasts, at least not early on. It just felt like there was a weight on my chest, a strange pressure pushing on my chest. It's hard to describe. It felt like someone had stacked weights on my chest. I didn't know what it was, but I knew it was probably not a good thing.

Worse, I started getting this really weird feeling in my penis. Those buzzing pulsations I'd felt in my arms were now in my penis. It was like I could feel the blood pumping in and out of it with every pulse. It was a freaky feeling. You know what it feels like when you put your finger on a cat's throat when it's purring? That's what this felt like inside my penis. At first I thought the wireless mike I was wearing for the filming was sending some sort of small energy charge into my body, so I went into the bathroom and took it off. But it didn't stop, and it totally freaked me out. I mean, I like it when my penis is happy, but I don't want to feel it purring like a cat. This was beyond worrisome.

Pretty soon it was difficult for me to go back to work after lunch. By the time I'd get back to the office, I'd feel really lethargic and scatter-brained, and I just couldn't focus. As the month progressed, I got more and more forgetful. Feeling fuzzy most of the time. My friend Scott Ambrozy, the director of photography, kept saying the diet was making me dumber. I wished I'd taken some sort of cognitive test at the beginning to see if we could measure how it affected my ability to process information. It made me think of kids going back to class after a lunch of Mc-Crap. It's hard enough to stay awake in school. No wonder kids' test scores are going down. All I wanted to do was curl up under my desk and nap.

You think I'm exaggerating? Check out this UPI report from October 26, 2004:

> South Carolina researchers say eating trans fats, the kind in many fast foods, impairs memory and learning.
>
> Lotta Granholm, a neuroscientist at the Medical University of South Carolina, whose work was discussed at a San Diego conference this week, fed one group of rats a diet that contained 10 percent hydrogenated coconut oil, a common trans fat.
>
> She gave another group the same diet, but replaced the coconut oil with soybean oil, which is not a trans fat.
>
> After six weeks, the animals were tested in a series of mazes. The coconut oil group made far more errors, especially on the tests that required more mental energy.

"The trans fats made memory significantly worse," Granholm said.

She said trans fat seems to produce its effect on the brain by destroying proteins that help neurons send and receive signals. In animals that ate coconut oil, these molecules, known as microtubule-associated proteins, were much less common.

Granholm suspects trans fat increases inflammation in the brain, which damages the proteins.

That's us. Dumber and dumber lab rats for the fast-food industry.

In New Zealand, thirteen-year-old Justin Fletcher—a boy after my own heart—used himself as a guinea pig to test whether fast food can really make you dumber. He went on a two-day diet of nothing but junk food, then took a series of reading, math and typing tests. Then he ate two days of real food, and tested himself again.

The results? After two days of junk food, his reading speed dropped by more than 50 percent, his typing speed was down by half, and he solved math problems up to 35 percent slower.

He also reported experiencing mood swings and being irritable and sluggish.

I started getting prebreakfast, prelunch and predinner headaches, too. Massive, pounding thumpers that would rip through my skull. But the minute I started eating the food, the headaches would go away. Way too strange.

By the middle of the month, I swear the food was also beginning to affect my emotional state. Throughout the second and third weeks, I was prone to pretty radical mood swings. I would eat a McMeal and feel fantastic for an hour or so, pumped up by all the sugar and caffeine, really cruising. And then I'd crash and become a whiny, grumpy, moody bitch.

Snapping at Alex, at Scott, at the taxi driver, whoever. Depressed and lethargic and unmotivated. All I could think about was how long it was till dinner, when I'd get my next upswing. Does that sound like an addict or what?

Did you ever look at the actual burger in a McDonald's sandwich? I mean, really look at it? Ever eat it by itself? Try it sometime. Buy a burger at McDonald's or your favorite chain burger joint, and when it comes, scrape everything off it. Get rid of the bread, the cheese, the special sauce, those terrible dehydrated onions, the pickles, the ketchup, the mustard—everything. What you'll be left with does not look much like an actual hamburger. It's gray. Like the color of paint primer. And kind of flappy and rubbery. Like a lab experiment where someone was trying to create a burger and didn't come close to getting it right.

Now take a bite of that naked, flaccid Frankenburger, without the aid of all the fixings and distractions. It tastes *kinda* like meat, but more like an industrial meat-flavored substitute. If Mentos made a burger flavor, you know it would taste just like this. The consistency is disturbing, too. It chews like beef-flavored confetti.

Here's something else—I challenge you to eat the whole thing without reaching for something to drink. This food just dries your mouth out immediately. I'm sure it's all that sodium they pack into it. Sucks all the saliva right out of your tongue. When you bite into a real burger, one actually made from fresh ground beef, it's *juicy.* You don't need to wash it down immediately with a gulp of soda.

I'd try to have one of McDonald's "healthy" meals just to counteract all the bad effects. So I'd eat a Chicken McGrill dinner, which still packs over 1,000 calories with the fries and soda. Or I'd have a Chicken Caesar Salad Shaker, just to have something that approximated greens. The iceberg lettuce was tasteless. Half the thing was cheese. And the packet of dressing was loaded with fats and sugars. It was ridiculous. I nicknamed it the McTosser. I could have bought my own chicken breast, my own salad greens and my own cheese to grate for less, and it would have been better for me.

Once, I also had the pleasure of seeing where Ronald's orange juice comes from. It's delivered in a giant plastic sack of Day-Glo goo. On one side of it is a little tube they attach to the juice machine, then they roll the sack inside and close it up. The goo is mixed with water to deliver to you, the happy customer, a beverage that tastes a bit like orange juice and a bit like the inside of a garbage bag. (*Mmmm*, garbage bag.)

Speaking of delicious, nutritious beverages, when the movie came out, another criticism I got from the food lobby was, "Nobody drinks as much Coke as Spurlock does in this movie!"

Bullshit. Remember that statistic from earlier: The average American teen now drinks two or more sodas a day. And you know from personal experience it's not just kids. People all over America go around chugging down Big, Bigger, Giant, Swimming-Pool-Sized sodas every day, all day long. Drink four 32-ounce Cokes in a day—and don't tell me people don't do that—and that's 1,200 calories, all from sugar. I mean, there's nothing else in soda. It's water, sugar and a little flavoring and coloring.

But what about diet soda? Well, diet soda's not such a great idea, either. Diet sodas usually contain that synthetic sweetener, aspartame, that the Department of Health and Human Services has said may be linked to some uncommon but troubling side effects, including headaches, hallucinations, panic attacks, dizziness and mood swings. The Center for Science in the Public Interest's recommendation on diet soda is that "if you consume more than a couple of servings per day, consider cutting back. And, to be on the safe side, don't give aspartame to infants."

There was a hilarious moment during that McLibel trial when a McDonald's spokesman was on the stand and was asked about the nutritional value of the food. He said that all of McDonald's products contained nutritional value.

Oh really? said Dave Morris, the activist who was conducting his own defense. "So, for example, a Coke could not be described as nutritious, could it?"

The McDonald's flack sat on the stand, thinking, and then muttered, "Well, providing water, and I think that is part of a balanced diet. . . ."

Ri-ight. There's water in Coke, that's for sure.

Recently, the McLibel Two won their appeal against the British government in the European court of human rights. The court stated that, by not providing legal aid to its defendants, the government breached their right to a fair trial and freedom of expression. The two were awarded £24,000 in damages plus legal costs. More important, this decision paves the way for more people like Dave Morris and Helen Steel to confidently challenge the business practices of large corporations.

And don't get me started on the Filet-O-Fish. That has got to be one of the worst sandwiches I've ever eaten. When I was in elementary school in West Virginia, they served us fish for lunch every Friday, their nod to religious observance, and boy was that fish lousy—so breaded and processed it wasn't even real fish anymore. That's exactly what their McDonald's filet is like. I think they're breeding some new species of square fish that doesn't look or taste like real fish but is much more handy and efficient. It's like McNuggets of the Sea.

One morning during the McMonth, I got up really early to grab a flight from New York to Los Angeles. I didn't stop for breakfast on the way out of the city, because there's always an open McDonald's at the airport, right?

Wrong. The terminal we were flying out of didn't even have a

McDonald's in it. It has to be the only one in North America! The only one in the free world! How could there not be a McDonald's there?

"Isn't this America?" I cried. "Land of the freezer, home of the fries?"

"There's a Burger King right down there," the smiling sky cap said.

"What good is that going to do me? I can only eat McDonald's!"

"I'm sorry to hear that," he said thoughtfully, and slowly pushed his cart down the walk.

You and me both, pal. It was a good six hours before we landed in L.A., and those beckoning Golden Arches never looked better.

From L.A., I drove to Downey, California, in the San Bernardino Valley. Downey is the home of the oldest remaining McDonald's in the world. It was the fourth one built by Richard and Maurice McDonald, in 1953. It's still in operation and is actually registered with the National Trust as a historic site.

The McDonald brothers had moved from snowy New England to sunny Southern California in 1920. In 1937 they sold hot dogs; in 1940 they opened a diner where they pioneered their fast-food ideas. By the time they opened the Downey location in '53, many of the recognizable McDonald's basics were in place, but kind of in miniature. The Arches are there, but they weren't yet joined into the familiar M— there's one Arch on each side of the building. Speedy, the original mascot, is on the sign high above the highway. He stood for the "Speedy Service System," the way the McDonald brothers had innovated the burger production assembly line. The sign says, "More Than 500 Million Served." They stopped updating it a long time ago.

Standing in the parking lot at Downey, eating an old-fashioned—or should I say historically reenacted—sixty-cent cheeseburger, I really got a feeling for what a warped success story McDonald's is. From this little burger shack to world domination in half a century.

But it wasn't the McDonald brothers who made it happen. They'd have been happy spending the rest of their lives flipping burgers in San

Berdoo. The real Dark Overlord of the McDonald's evil empire was Ray Kroc, a salesman of milkshake machines who was their first licensed franchisee in 1954. By 1961 he'd bought the whole megillah from them. By '65 he had the corporation listed on the New York Stock Exchange. By '67 he'd opened the first McDonald's outside of the United States, in Canada. In '68 he introduced the Big Mac. The Egg McMuffin debuted in '73, the Happy Meal in '79, and blah blah blah. When Kroc died in 1984, McDonald's was well established as the biggest, baddest fast-food chain in the known universe. It had its competitors and its shameless imitators like Burger King, but its supreme world hegemony was unchallenged.

A string of corporate CEO types have struggled to live up to Kroc's legacy since then. It hasn't been easy. In fact, when they don't get fired, it seems to make them sick, as I mentioned earlier.

Not one of these guys has had Kroc's greasy-fingered magic touch on the pulse of America. Time was, when McDonald's dictated how Americans ate fast food. Customers gobbled up any new menu item McD's debuted. Now, the last really successful new meal they introduced was the McNugget, in 1983. Since then, all sorts of new brainstorms have come and flopped. Remember when McDonald's decided to offer McPizza? The McVeggie burger? The McFried Chicken? The McFajitas? The McLean Deluxe? The McLobster sandwich?

For over three decades, Mickey D's did nothing but grow in double digits, expand in all directions and make tons of money for its shareholders. Although it's still the Big Mac of food pimps, it has stumbled and struggled some in the 1990s and 2000s. Like all empires, it has shown itself vulnerable to attack on several of its borders.

In the United States, growth slowed and profits stagnated. It was only rapid expansion in the international market that propped up the Falling Arches. Burger-flipping competitors like Burger King and Wendy's chipped away some at McDonalds' domestic customer base, but the real problem was that more and more competitors were offering alternatives to the basic American burger, and people responded— especially if whatever crap the competition was offering looked more "healthy" than a Big Mac and Large Fries. Chains like Baja Fresh and Chipotle Mexican Grill were now the ones seeing double-digit growth. (McDonald's eventually bought Chipotle in self-defense. Did you know it also owns Aroma Café, Boston Market and Pret A Manger?)

And then there was Subway. No competitor's been more of a pain in Ronald's butt over the last few years than Subway, both at home and abroad. Fred DeLuca, Subway's Ray Kroc, was just your average Brooklyn mook when he and a partner started their first sub shop in 1965. But, like Kroc, he had visions of world domination.

In a period when McDonald's has been scaling back on how quickly it opens new outlets in the United States, Subway has been in an extremely aggressive new-franchise mode, expanding faster than the average American's waistline. By 2001, Subway had passed McDonald's as the fast-food chain with the most U.S. outlets—at the time of this writing, it has almost 18,000, compared to McDonald's roughly 13,000, and it's catching up internationally, too, with around 22,000 to McDonald's roughly 31,000. In the UK, where it has also passed McDonald's in the number of shops operating, Subway has been doubling its outlets every year. At this rate, Jared may even beat Ronald to the South Pole.

In 2004, Subway even beat Ronald to the Iraqi front. That September, while McDonald's was still negotiating to plant the Golden Arches in Iraqi soil, the first Subway opened in Tikrit.

Subway first leaped on to the our-food-is-healthier-than-McDonalds' bandwagon in 1997, when it launched a flotilla of low-fat sandwiches. Never mind that a lot of its other offerings are just as fat-laden as anything at McDonald's or Burger King. According to Subway's own website, the six-inch tuna sandwich packs a mighty 530 calories, 280 of them from fat. That's equivalent to a Quarter Pounder with Cheese. The six-inch meatball sub hits you with 560 calories. There are a whopping 960 calories in the six-inch Double Meat Meatball Marinara sandwich, 380 of them from fat. That's worse than a Burger King Bacon Double Cheeseburger.

And those are the "small" Subway sandwiches. Don't forget its famous foot-long behemoths. The twelve-inch Double Meat Meatball Marinara Sub whacks you with a mighty 1,480 calories, 46 percent of them from fat. That's like wolfing down two BK Bacon Double Cheeseburgers!

Subway also boasts about how its sandwiches are "made on the premises from rows of 'fresh' ingredients and meats" that are laid out for the customer to salivate over—they want to seem closer to an old-fashioned sub shop than the fast-food production-line assembly process. The franchise is now, for instance, the largest single purchaser of tomatoes in the world.

In 2000, Subway introduced the world to Jared Fogel, the college student who said he'd dropped from 425 pounds to 192 on a yearlong Subway diet. (One British paper dubbed him "Mini-Size Me.") I was really interested in what it's like to be a living human being who's been turned into a Ronald McDonald–style corporate mascot, so I set up an interview with him. We had lunch—at a Subway, of course (long after my McMonth was over).

When you meet him, Jared doesn't strike you as the corporate shill, to put it bluntly, he has become. He's just kind of a nerdy, geeky guy who somehow became a media star. Mr. Deeds Goes to Subway. And you have to admire how much weight he lost—over 230 pounds. That's more than one of me, even at my McFattest.

But you don't have to talk to him for more than ten minutes to realize that Subway's "healthy" food had nothing to do with it. Jared Fogel lost weight the old-fashioned way. After a lifetime of serious overeating, he put himself on a strict diet. He went on a program of draconian calorie reduction and exerted a tremendous amount of willpower to stick to it. He significantly increased his level of physical activity. He changed a lifetime of bad habits, bad attitudes and unhealthy behaviors. He owes his success to self-discipline, not to a six-inch sub and a Diet Coke. He told me:

> I started to eat a lot of fast food at an early age on my own. I would get on my bike to get a burger, or I'd ride my bike to get tacos, or I'd ride my bike to get pizza, whatever it may be. That [was] coupled with my starting to play less and less sports as I got older. But also, I was a bit of a socially awkward kid as I was growing up. And not fitting in so well with some of the other kids, I had time on my hands. I didn't have a lot of friends, so I started eating. To top it off, I started liking video games . . . so it was just a combination of factors. . . . It was that domino effect. The more weight I put on, the less I wanted to move. The less I wanted to move, the more I wanted to eat. It just was that vicious cycle.

Asked what his favorite kinds of fast food were, he replied,

> It didn't matter to me. It could be anything. No matter what it was, I was always super-sizing it. There was never a question of am I just going to have a small burger and small fries. It was always, "I'm going to have the largest sandwich they have, and I'm going to have the largest french fry they offer, which is now a popcorn-size bucket, and I'm going to have the largest soft drink they offer, and I'm going to have dessert, because no meal is complete without dessert. . . ."
>
> Say I was going to a burger place. It would be the half-pound,

which is usually the biggest burger, sometimes three-quarter-pound at some restaurants, and extra cheese. Not just cheese, but extra cheese. I would have to add bacon to it. I would make them put mayonnaise on it if it didn't already have mayonnaise. Then, of course, I would get the extra-large onion rings or french fries, and an extra-large soft drink. Usually an apple pie, or two apple pies. Three, four, five cookies. That would be lunch. At a pizza joint, I could easily eat an entire ten-piece pizza for dinner. . . . I didn't feel satisfied unless I was completely stuffed.

By the time he was in college, Jared had tried numerous diets—the SlimFast-style liquid diet drinks, the Weight Watchers–style frozen diet meals—and none of them worked. He'd have one of those diet shakes for breakfast, one for lunch and then was allowed a "sensible meal" for dinner. But for him, "a sensible dinner" was an entire pizza. Or an entire Chinese buffet, or whatever it may have been. But it definitely was *not* very sensible.

I remember cooking at home and measuring out cups of this and ounces of this and teaspoons of this. I was so heavy back then, it doesn't sound like a lot, but to me that was a lot of effort back then. I was so worn out by the end of cooking a meal, it wasn't even funny. And then to have to portion it out at the end of a meal, and have to not eat the rest of it, was impossible. Inevitabily, after leaving half the pot or three-quarters of the pot, I'd come back a few minutes later and eat some more, and come back a few minutes later, and before I knew it, the whole thing was gone, whatever I had made. And so that didn't work either. I just didn't have control over it.

After a lifetime of eating like that, bingeing every single day, Jared finally bit the bullet instead of the cheese-filled pizza crust. He massively reduced his food intake to a daily regimen of two Subway six-inch "low-fat" sandwiches and a couple of diet sodas. And he started getting a lot more exercise.

Of course he lost weight. The fact that it was two of Subway's sandwiches is immaterial. He chose Subway because there was an outlet very nearby. He could have reduced his intake from his daily supersizing to any two comparably small meals and he would have dropped a lot of weight.

Still, you have to hand it to him for sticking to his diet, even though any nutritionist would warn you against such a drastic crash diet, and even Subway doesn't endorse it. But that doesn't stop people from thinking they, and Jared, have discovered the Magic Bullet. Jared admits that it was an extreme first step, but, more important, "it really was a lifestyle change. Losing the weight was only half the battle. The rest of it is keeping it off for the rest of your life and living a healthier life. . . . I'm just learning to eat moderately. I had to retrain myself how to eat, because, you know, I could easily slip back to a whole pizza. But I can't do that. Diets are the short term, lifestyle change is the long term."

Partly because of competitors like Subway attacking its flanks, the period from the mid-nineties through 2003 was the worst in the history of McDonaldland. There was also all the terrible press from the McLibel, from the pockets of resistance to its imperial power in places like France and from the backlash from the lies it told about the beef and the partially hydrogenated oils in the fries. Then there was all the news and the government warnings about the obesity epidemic, all citing the American fast-food diet as a major cause. Then came the E. coli 0157:H7 and mad-cow scares, which didn't do much to drive new business into burger joints. Throw in the best-selling *Fast Food Nation*, and Ronald was rocked. *The Economist* reports that "McDonald's ended 2002 with its first quarterly loss since 1954," the year Kroc took over. The stock price plummeted. Earnings slumped. Shareholders grumbled. Franchisees rebelled. Heads rolled in the Oak Brook corporate offices.

On one level, McDonald's reacted the way it always has, denying the problems while hurling blame and insults at everyone else. Concerned franchisees were shrugged off as a minority of malcontents. When journalists wrote about the company's troubles, a McDonald's spokesman called their reporting "bullshit" (*The Wall Street Journal*) or called the whole publication "corrupt" and "a scandal sheet" (*Crain's Chicago Business*). Nutritionists, physicians, pediatricians, lawyers, child psychologists and pretty much anyone else who dared to speak negatively about fast food in public were vilified as extremists, alarmists, ambulance-chasers, tree-hugging loonies or "the food police of the nanny state."

But Ray Kroc's brainchild did not grow up into McGoliath by being stupid, and as I write this in fall 2004, the company has been showing signs of bouncing back. As then-CEO Charlie Bell (the one fighting the Big C) admitted in a startlingly frank *London Times* interview in September 2004, it was more like McDonald's had just let itself become "fat, dumb and happy."

Maybe McGoliath had been eating too much of his own McFood.

I know I was.

TEN

RONALD & ME

I got very excited the day my toys arrived.

When I was a kid, I had a Ronald McDonald train set that I loved. I played with it all the time. I was around six or seven. This was a little circular track that went around a foldout McDonaldland, with a cardboard forest behind it where the talking tree and Fry Guys hung out. The train set complemented a full line of McAction figures: Ronald, Grimace, Big Mac, Mayor McCheese, Hamburglar, Captain Crook and the Professor. Most people forget that McDonald's actually had a character named Crook, who I always thought to be the funniest thing ever.

The train had three cars, an engine, a passenger car and a prison car for the Hamburglar. I loved the Hamburglar when I was a kid. He and Big Mac were by far my favorites, so when I was playing with that train, you could pretty much bet that Ronald would be in the prison car.

I hadn't seen these dolls in years. When I opened up the box that arrived at my office, all those memories came rushing back. None of the characters' arms or legs could bend, but their heads could turn with the help of a little knob in the middle of their backs. Except for Grimace.

He has no moving parts. (What a coincidence, considering he's the obese one of the bunch.) They were definitely pre–Star Wars toys.

It's interesting to note that in his earliest incarnations, Grimace had four arms, so he could grab as many shakes as possible. Apparently people were freaked out by that, and I suspect that McDonald's didn't want to seem to be promoting the idea of drinking four shakes at once. Not that they would discourage it.

The Ronald doll has stiff arms; they move at the shoulder but don't bend, and his hands are turned palms-up. It's a curiously uncomfortable-looking gesture. But as I sat at my desk and played with it, I could see why it was done: If you raise his arm over his head, had the hand been palm-down he would've looked like he was giving the Nazi salute. I'm sure there was a flurry of memos in Oak Brook about that before these toys hit the market back in the mid-seventies.

During my McMonth, I couldn't get over how many kids there were almost any time I walked into a McDonald's. Kids with their parents. Gaggles of kids stopping in for breakfast or for a predinner snack in their cute little Catholic school uniforms. Kids in all the Playlands, the cheap alternative to a trip to Six Flags. Kids as little as three and four having Happy Meal McBirthday parties.

By far the saddest and most disturbing example I saw was in a McDonald's in Houston. At the time, Houston had the dubious honor of being rated the fattest city in America. (In 2004, Detroit rolled ahead of Houston to take the fat crown, but Texas managed to put five cities in the top ten: Houston, Dallas, San Antonio, Arlington and Fort Worth. And Chicago, Philly and Cleveland are also way up there.)

So here I am in a McDonald's at 9 a.m., ordering breakfast at the counter, when I turn around and see a mother with her two very overweight kids, who had just finished their fat-filled breakfasts and were now eating hot fudge sundaes.

It's nine in the morning, Mom! *Hot fudge sundaes?!?*

This is a huge problem in America (no pun intended). I couldn't help thinking of Ashley and Jazlen in the Bronx, who'd gotten me started on this whole project, not to mention their parents. Parents are their children's primary role models. Kids learn their life habits, good and bad, from their parents. If you're a mom or dad who eats crap all the time and you don't exercise, what are your kids going to do? If you let your already-overweight kids eat hot fudge sundaes for breakfast, they stand an extremely good chance of developing diabetes by the time they're thirty, if they haven't already. "And afterward, kids, we're gonna go play in traffic!" Sounds good, right?

There's no question in my mind that adults in America bear an enormous responsibility for the obesity epidemic among America's kids. And yet there's also no question that even conscientious parents and guardians, who really do try to do well by kids and teach them healthy life choices, are not playing on anything like a level field. They're going up against billions and billions of dollars spent every year in corporate marketing—what Kelly Brownell calls a "toxic environment" of advertising and promotion that is all aimed at teaching kids to make exactly the opposite sorts of choices.

McDonald's and the other fast-food chains make no secret of the fact that kids are their primary targets. "We have living proof of the long-lasting quality of early brand loyalties in the cradle-to-grave marketing at McDonald's, and how well it works," James McNeal, a well-known kids' marketing guru and the author of *Kids As Customers*, has said. "We start taking children in for their first and second birthdays, and on and on, and eventually they have a great deal of preference for that brand. Children can carry that with them through a lifetime."

I mean, Ronald McDonald and his goofy fry pals weren't created to attract you and me. Burger King doesn't cross-promote with Little Tikes toys to get my girlfriend into their joint. The Playskool Weebles that Wendy's is pushing as I write this aren't luring anyone over five into their joints. Not to mention the insidious promotional tie-ins with Disney and Pixar movies, with Pokémon and Yu-Gi-Oh! with *Sesame Street* and Teletubbies.

> In the summer of 2004 alone, Burger King cross-promoted with *Shrek 2*, *Spider-Man 2* and *Yu-Gi-Oh!* Wendy's sucked up to *Garfield*. Ironically, McDonald's, stuck in an exclusive ten-year promotional deal with Disney, was having a lousy summer—the studio was producing nothing but crap. The summer before, McDonald's had had a field day with *Finding Nemo* and *Pirates of the Caribbean*, but Disney's big movies of 2004 were flops like *The Alamo* and *Home on the Range*—a film McDonald's couldn't exactly promote, since the lead characters were all cows. Couldn't you just see the ads? "You've seen them on the screen, now come eat them in person!"
>
> Mickey D's must have been pining for the good old days, like 1993, when it launched the whole Super Size deal with a cross-promotion of the mega-box-office smash *Jurassic Park*. Do you remember that? They called Super Sizing "Dino Sizing." A meal fit for Fred Flintstone. (Cue Edith Bunker, "Those Were the Days . . .")

According to Marion Nestle, by the end of the twentieth century, American children were getting half of their calories from added fat (35 percent) and sugar (15 percent). "Only 1 percent of them regularly ate diets that resemble the proportions of the Food Pyramid." The diets of nearly half of them failed to meet *any* of the serving numbers recommended in the Pyramid.

In her book *Consuming Kids: The Hostile Takeover of Childhood*, psychologist Susan Linn, associate director of the Media Center at Harvard University's Judge Baker Children's Center, explains how marketing to kids—which before the 1970s was practiced only by a few toy makers, cereal companies and entertainment companies—has ballooned. Today, corporations spend over *$15 billion every year* on marketing, advertising and promotions meant to program kids to consume, consume and consume some more.

Why? Because they realized that children not only have more expendable income of their own, but they influence how their parents spend *their* hard-earned bucks, too—to the tune of over $600 billion in annual spending. What do children choose to buy with all that expendable income? What do you think? When buying their own food and drink, half of kids ages seven to twelve choose candy, more than one-third will also buy soda and ice cream and about one-fourth might go for fast food as well. That doesn't leave too many who are buying stuff that's not bad for them.

And they wheedle their parents into buying crap, too: 25 percent of the salty snacks, 30 percent of soft drinks, 40 percent of frozen pizza, 50 percent of cold cereals and 60 percent of canned pasta are all sales "influenced" by kids pestering their parents. Advertisers have learned that if they can brainwash kids into believing they have to have that toy, that Happy Meal, that new game, that Disneyworld family vacation, then those kids will pester their parents until they give in and buy it for them.

It's called the "nag factor." I mean, there was actually a marketing study put out in 1998 called *The Nag Factor*. Was it published to help parents learn how to say no to their kids? *Tzzzzzt*. Sorry. Nope, it was done to help advertisers and marketers learn how to target kids better, to *get* them to nag. I couldn't make this up. The press release that went out to advertisers to announce the publication of this study was called— I'm not kidding—"The Fine Art of Whining: Why Nagging Is a Kid's Best Friend." Another industry nickname for it is "pester power."

So what did these evil geniuses find out? Things like: Divorced parents, and those with teenagers or very young children, are most likely to give in to nagging. The different tactics kids use to nag: the whine, the threat, the guilt trip, the suck-up. How marketing and ads can be designed to trigger these different tactics.

The big cereal companies were among the first to figure out how to get kids to nag their parents to buy specific brands. Before the Civil War, Americans didn't eat cereal for breakfast. They got up and chowed down on pork, beef or even chicken. The first breakfast cereal was Granula, introduced in 1863. It was made of bran nuggets that had to be soaked overnight to be soft enough not to break your teeth. C. W. Post introduced Grape Nuts in 1897. The Quaker Oats man became the first registered breakfast-cereal trademark in 1877. John Harvey Kellogg, a doctor, Seventh-Day Adventist and vegetarian, invented Toasted Corn Flakes, and with the help of his brother, W. K. Kellogg, came out with them in 1906. General Mills scored big with Wheaties in 1924 and Cheerios in 1941. GM also invented "puffed" cereals like Kix and "shredded" ones like Shredded Wheat.

As televisions spread to every American home in the fifties and sixties, Kellogg and Post and General Mills and the rest discovered the kids' market, and that's when all the sugar got shoveled onto (or "toasted into") cereal. They blanketed the Saturday morning kiddie shows with ads for these cereals, breakfast drinks and assorted other sugary junk. (You can see some egregious examples at TVparty.com.)

Back in those pre-health-conscious days, they could be a lot more upfront with their messages. So a kid might see the Trix Rabbit complain, "I have a problem. I'm a rabbit, and I'm supposed to like things like carrots. Yuck!" He'd much prefer some Trix, but of course, "Everyone knows Trix are for kids." My researcher, Karen Pelland, says, "I remember being in a supermarket and telling my mom that I had to have Trix because I *was a kid!* I actually believed that, and was pissed off when she refused to buy them for me."

Bugs Bunny and Daffy Duck shilled for "New Natural Orange Flavored Tang," with "Vitamins C and A"—about the same amount of calories and sugar as Coke. Tang, you may remember, was also the healthy drink of our NASA astronauts. Come on, they drink it in space, it must be good for you!

Cap'N Crunch's jingle went, "Oh sing a song of Cap'N Crunch, the sugary sweet cereal that's fun to munch!" Quisp, my brother's favorite cereal, which featured the space-age cereal shaped like sugar-coated flying saucers, told kids, "Nothing's impossible with sugary sweet Quisp! It's vitamin charged for Quazy energy!" General Mills innovated the inclusion of marshmallow bits in cereal when it introduced Lucky Charms in 1963, and from then on you couldn't turn on the TV during kiddie prime-time without seeing that damn leprechaun. And no one seemed to question the dubious proposition of feeding their children marshmallows for breakfast.

Need I mention Kellogg's Sugar Frosted Flakes? Back then, cereal brands were *proud* of their sugary content, and a bunch of them had the word in their name. Remember Super Sugar Crisp? And don't forget Sugar Jets, which Rocky and Bullwinkle promoted: "They make you feel jet-propelled!" Yes, I'm sure they did. It's called ADD. Later, they dropped the word "sugar" or replaced it with euphemisms like "golden."

Naturally, once they decided that kids were their target, they instantly started to cross-promote with the toy companies. To this day, you can hardly open a box of kids' cereal without some kind of friggin' toy falling out of it. In 1999, to pick one of the more disturbing examples, Kellogg stuffed something like 25 million Muppet Beanie Babies—Muppets! as in *Sesame Street!*—into specially marked packages of Rice Krispies, Corn Pops, Apple Jacks and Marshmallow Blasted Froot Loops. The accompanying ad campaign was handled by Leo Burnett Company, McDonald's and Marlboro's agency. (If you're gonna manipulate kids, Burnett is the go-to guy.)

In 2002, General Mills went so far as to create a whole new brand of cereal based on a movie: *Star Wars Episode II* cereal! With little marshmallow bits shaped like light sabers and R2-D2! Talk about the Dark Side.

Meanwhile, when they're marketing kiddie brands to the kiddies' parents, they use a very different tactic: They tell parents their brands are good for kids. That they're "fortified" with essential vitamins and minerals. That they're low in cholesterol and fat (most recently, trans fat). That they're "enriched" with wholesome goodness.

It's a brilliant pincer attack on the food budget of the American family. Get the kids to whine at their parents for the cereal with the mini Muppets in it while you tell the parents it's okay, Marshmallow Blasted Froot Loops are good for them.

Even conscientious parents have to be really careful about buying their kids food that claims it's good for them. The whole business of "fortified" foods can be a scam. That cereal may be packed with vitamins— but it may also be packed with sugar and be really low in fiber.

Food manufacturers have been fortifying products for a long time. Vitamin D–fortified milk first appeared in 1931. In the 1950s, lots of cereals began to be "enriched" with thiamin, niacin, riboflavin and iron. By the mid-eighties, 92 percent of cereals were fortified in some way. Vitamins A, C and E got added to the mix.

Meanwhile, calcium got thrown into all sorts of candies, soda and snack foods as a way to make them seem good for kids. Yeah, those vitamin-enriched Gummi Bears, they're part of every kid's balanced diet.

Once they've guilted parents into "making the healthy choice," the manipulating food companies raise the price on their fortified products! A cereal that claims it's "fortified" with all the vitamins and minerals your kids need can cost as much as 40 percent more than a regular one. It would be much cheaper for parents simply to buy their kids once-a-day vitamins, but the guilt factor still has them reaching for that more expensive cereal.

The whole scam of labeling kids' food as healthy and good for them came to its most despicable low in 1988, when, as Marion Nestle explains, "the American Heart Association (AHA), long a distinguished champion of research and education promoting low-fat and other dietary approaches to prevention of coronary heart disease, decided to raise funds by labeling foods 'heart-healthy.' The AHA would identify foods that met certain standards for content of fat, saturated fat, cholesterol, and sodium with a logo consisting of a red heart with a white check mark and the words 'American Heart Association Tested & Approved.' The AHA planned to collect fees from food companies that made approved products and expected to benefit from company advertising and promotion of the partnership."

Get it? For a fee, we'll declare your product healthy! Pretty soon, you had manufacturers like Kellogg promoting all their "heart-smart," AHA-approved brands . . . like the notoriously sugar-laden Cocoa Frosted Flakes, Fruity Marshmallow Krispies and "Low-Fat (but by no means low-sugar) Pop-Tarts." Remember? And now, General Mills is making the same American Heart Association claims for most of its cereals, including Cocoa Puffs and Frosted Cheerios. Sure, none of these cereals and others like them are fat laden, which most people associate with heart trouble, but the AHA seal of approval sends an overall message that the product is healthy.

One irony is that Post cereals can't participate, because Post is owned by Philip Morris, and American Heart Association rules prohibit endorsements of any product owned by a tobacco company. So General Mills Cocoa Pebbles is AHA approved, but Post Cocoa Pebbles, virtually identical in nutritional content, is not. (See Appendix 3 of this book for a list of all the foods manufactured by cigarette companies!)

And it's not just the AHA looking to cash in; everybody's in on the game now. Brand logos for all sorts of crap now turn up on nursery blankets, crib toys and mobiles. In my office, I have a collection of baby bottles shaped like little bottles of 7-Up, Dr Pepper, Pepsi, Mountain Dew and Slice. I found them on eBay. When we contacted the California manufacturer, Munchkin Bottling, they told us they'd produced these things for a few years in the mid-nineties. They'd developed the concept themselves, then licensed the various soda companies' names and logos.

Think about the associations formed in infants' minds by these things. Think about the mentality that sees nothing wrong in marketing them. The parent who would fill a miniature Mountain Dew bottle with formula for her baby might not think twice about putting Mountain Dew in it—and that's all part of their unspoken master plan.

Not to be outdone, McDonald's marketing genius M. Lawrence Light, the guy who rolled out the "I'm lovin' it" campaign, wants to surround the youth of the world with McDonalds' brand images. "Now, Light wants to turn everything he can into an ad for McDonald's," *BusinessWeek* wrote in July 2004. "He's pushing the Oak Brook chain to open clothing shops so kids will walk around in T-shirts with the Golden Arches logo, just as they already do with Old Navy or Disney. He envisions a deal with the National Basketball Association to play the five-note tagline of the 'I'm lovin' it' ad in the stadium every time a player shoots a three-pointer. He's even toying with making the jingle available over the Internet so it could be downloaded as a mobile-phone ring tone." (If I ever have that ring tone on my phone, someone please kill me.)

Light chose China as the market in which to open the first McKids store. "There will be twenty-five McKids stores there," he told *BusinessWeek*. "It's got a line of toys, a line of clothes, a line of videos, all directed at young kids. The first one will hit the U.S. next year." Why China? Because after years of commie rule, these kids can't get enough American products. A company like McDonald's can easily swoop in and corrupt young consumers from the start.

Even the venerable National Geographic Society has sold out. Its magazine *National Geographic Kids* is packed with more junk-food ads than a Snickers has peanuts. *NGK* runs ads for wholesome, nutritious kids' foods and snacks like Twinkies, M&Ms, Frosted Flakes, Froot Loops, Hostess Cup Cakes, and X-TREME JELL-O Pudding Sticks. One issue came with a wrap-around fake-cover ad for an Arby's "Adventure Meal."

Why did National Geographic sell out? Well, they get anywhere from $31,825 to nearly $169,000 per ad—and that pays for a lot of photos of topless natives!

Television advertising accounts for $60 billion of the yearly brainwashing in America, up over three times what it was in 1980's. Why? Because the average American kid between the ages of two and eighteen spends two hours and forty-six minutes a day in front of the tube. Two-thirds of kids age eight and up have a TV in their bedroom. Even babies under two now watch an hour or two of TV a day. The average American kid now sees around *40,000 TV commercials* a year. Forty thousand! Up 100 percent from twenty years ago.

And kids, especially little kids, have a very hard time distinguishing advertisements from reality. You and me, when we see a commercial for the latest hair-restoring drug or miracle cleaning product, we know that, at least theoretically, we should take whatever they're saying with a grain of salt. But when Ronald McDonald and his weirdo friends come dancing and prancing across the screen, telling little kids that if they want to be happy they just gotta come eat a Happy Meal, they believe it. And start whining at Mom or Dad to take them to McDonald's now, *pleeeeeeeaaaaaase!*

As early as 1978, the Federal Trade Commission proposed a rule to ban or severely restrict children's advertising on television. Predictably, the broadcasting, advertising, food and toy industries howled. Congress caved. It actually passed legislation in 1980 stripping the FTC of its authority to restrict advertising. Since then, parents have found themselves hopelessly outfoxed by the evil advertising geniuses who target their kids.

Since 1995, when the rules for corporate underwriting of programs were revised, not even PBS is safe for your kid to watch. Now even shows like *Teletubbies* and *Clifford the Big Red Dog* are involved in promotional tie-ins with joints like Burger King, McDonald's, Wendy's and UpChuck E. Cheese.

Teletubbies is a really interesting case. It began on the BBC in England and hit PBS in 1998. And from their first day in the United States, those furry, potbellied little creeps were making pots of money for all sorts of folks, including the chronically cash-strapped PBS. PBS Kids, along with Ragdoll Productions, itsy bitsy Entertainment and Warner Home Video, celebrated the release of a series of Teletubbies videos by making Teletubby Gift Packs—including the videos and a mini-Teletubby toy made by Hasbro—available to newborn babies. Hospitals handed them out . . . *to newborn babies.* Yes, we start our little brand-conscious consumers early in this country. A PBS exec told *The Christian Science Monitor*, "Merchandising was never, ever a consideration in choosing that show. Educational content was always first and foremost in our minds."

Uh-huh.

When the ethics of promoting fast food to infants and toddlers was questioned, itsy bitsy Entertainment (don't you already want to kill them just for that name?) put out a Teletubbies exercise video for infants and toddlers. Let me repeat that: *an exercise video for infants and toddlers* . . . who need to exercise because they got fat eating . . . what? The itsy bitsy press release announcing the video proudly declared, "Teletubbies Stand Up to Obesity in Kids." Really? By whoring for Burger King and McDonald's?

And the Teletubbies aren't the only PBS kids' characters on the take. *Sesame Street* characters shill for Apple & Eve fruit juices. Characters from *Dragon Tales* sell for Mott. Not to be outdone, Nickelodeon's *Rugrats* sell bubblegum, fruit rolls, Kraft Macaroni & Cheese and Good Humor peanut-butter-flavored ice cream sandwiches. Yeah, I'm sure those are wholesome and nutritious. And Spongebob seems to be everywhere, on just about every kind of kid food you can imagine. (I bet the creators never intended for these characters to be so heavily merchandised, either.)

> Dr. Susan Linn analyzed a bunch of studies and found an alarming but not really jaw-dropping pattern:
>
> • Kids who watch four hours or more of TV a day are most likely to be obese. Kids who watch the least TV are least likely to be fat. (Hey, now I know why they're called Tele*tubbies*!)
> • Preschoolers with TVs in their bedrooms are more likely to be fat.
> • In teens, "the incidence of obesity increases by 2 percent for every additional hour of television watched."
>
> It's not just the boob tube anymore. It's the teenage man-boob tube.

Marketers know that for many kids, when they aren't in front of the TV, they're at the computer or fiddling with their Game Boys. That's why McDonald's and others have reached out to embed their images and messages into Cyberworld.

Neopets.com is the most popular children's site on the Web, with more than 70 million pet owners worldwide (according to the site). As of 2004, it got 7 million page views a month and had 22 million members, with 27,000 new ones joining every day. It's free to play and supports itself through "immersive advertising," a really insidious, interactive form of product placement that turns commercial items into part of the Neopet environment. Kids create their own cyberpets, then spend time playing games, solving puzzles or going on quests through various imaginary worlds. They earn Neopoints, which can be used to buy food, toys and other luxuries in the Neopet world. They are even invited to take consumer surveys and are rewarded with hundreds of Neopoints for answering questions about their shopping habits.

In a Neopet food store, a player can buy virtual snacks, Uh Oh Oreo Cookies, Nestle SweeTARTS and Laffy Taffy. Or they can just go to the virtual McDonald's, whose Golden Arches are prominently displayed on the screen. Kids can also earn points by watching cereal ads or movie trailers in the Disney theater.

Neopets skirts TV practices intended to alert children to upcoming commercials, such as bumper announcements like "Hey, kids, we'll be right back after these messages!" With immersive advertising, there's no way for the kid to separate the fantasy world of Neopets from the reality of McDonald's. A recent study by the American Psychological Association says kids under eight have a hard time distinguishing ads from entertainment anyway. When asked about McDonalds' association with Neopets, Kathy Pyle, director of kids marketing, said, "McDonald's wants to be integrated into the online experience. We have been doing it for entertainment purposes, not directly selling."

Yeah, I'm sure that's why in the summer of 2004 McDonald's offered Neopets toys in Happy Meals as part of their "25 years of Happiness Happy Birthday Happy Meal Celebration," which just happened to be cross-promoted on the Neopets website—for the "experience." This was the largest Happy Meal collection of all time—109 different designs! Still think they're not trying to lure in your kids?

McDonald's also teamed up with the electronic game manufacturer Electronic Arts to embed the Golden Arches into The Sims Online. Players can now build their own McDonald's burger kiosks and make "virtual profits" on sales in their Sims world. In a 2004 co-promotion with Shockwave.com, McDonald's gave away 2 million thirty-day subscriptions to Shockwave.com's GameBlast. In fact, McDonald's has shifted a substantial amount of its TV budget to interactive formats, quadrupling its spending on web advertising.

Personally, I find all this virtually disgusting.

Of course, your friends in government do try to counteract all that advertising and marketing. In 2000, government agencies spent about $48 million to promote nutrition and health for kids. But McDonald's alone spent fourteen times that amount—$665 million—to advertise its McGrub in U.S. media alone (TV, radio, print and outdoor signs) that year. In all, the food industry spent $2.7 billion advertising fast food, junk food, soda, candy, snacks and sugar-coated cereal in 2000—56 *times* what the government spent on its nutrition promotions.

You get the sense that the good guys are a bit outgunned? How do you think parents feel?

One thing that really pisses me off is the way sports figures and other celebrity "heroes" are used to sell crap to the kids who look up to them and want to grow up to be just like them someday. Like the ridiculous spectacle of McDonald's at the Olympics. McDonald's has been an Olympic sponsor since 1976, and the "Official Restaurant" since 1996, a role it will play again in 2006, 2008, 2010 and 2012. It's a brilliant promotional coup: a global stage, where people the world over watch their greatest athletes compete, courtesy of Chicken McNuggets, and Coke, Swatch and other consumer crapola.

At the 2004 Summer Olympics in Athens, McDonald's employees from thirty-five countries staffed three restaurants at the stadium, the press center and Olympic Village. It was, in fact, the only brand-named food-and-beverage concession in the Village. McDonald's boasted that it would serve 230,000 Big Macs and 400,000 orders of french fries during the Games.

In the months leading up to Athens, you couldn't open a magazine in the States without turning to a page with an American Olympic athlete posing with McDonalds' new premium salads. How many

McSalads do these athletes actually eat? Not many. If you're a professional athlete, one of the last things you'll be shoving in your body is food like this.

The deal backfired in a funny way during the spring before the '04 Games, when some clever reporter asked the tiny American gymnast Carly Patterson, whose picture was about to be pasted across 70 million McDonalds' bags that summer, when was the last time she actually ate at McDonald's.

"Gosh," the poor innocent kid admitted, "I couldn't even tell you. It was when I was real young. I can't really have McDonald's right now, you know?"

The media loved it, but I bet there were some heart attacks in McDonald's public relations offices. (Apart from their regular health-related ones, I mean.) After all, McDonald's had contracted Patterson as a spokesperson well before the Games began. I half-expected Carly to mysteriously disappear from the U.S. Olympic team. Instead, after what were probably some grueling behavior modification sessions with the publicists, she changed her tune. By the time of the Games, she was dutifully dipping the tip of a plastic spoon into some yummy sugar-loaded yogurt parfait and telling reporters, "It's fruit and yogurt. It's good for you."

But of course the goal of all this isn't really to get a few athletes to try the McSalads. While at the Games, the real market is the tens of thousands of sports fans who attend, and the tens of millions of others watching on TV. McDonald's and other sponsors also use the Olympics as a way to expand their markets in the host countries, the way McDonald's is hurriedly increasing its number of outlets in China before the 2008 Games.

No, the whole point of sponsoring athletes is to tell the general public, and especially the impressionable kids who look up to sports heroes, exactly what Carly Patterson learned to say: *It's good for you.* Just like Cocoa Puffs. I call it "health by association."

You know what I'd like to see someday? A whole team of athletes whose jerseys are "branded" with an anti-McDonald's logo. Like the Golden Arches inside of the ∅ symbol, for NO MCDONALD'S. Now that would be a good message for athletes to send their millions and millions of young fans.

By the way, you want to know what sort of control the big food sponsors have over what gets consumed at the Olympics? Total, that's what. Complete food fascism. At the Athens Games, according to the *London Times,* spectators—not the athletes, but the paying spectators—were told that "they could be barred for taking a surreptitious sip of Pepsi or an illicit bite from a Burger King Whopper. Strict regulations published by Athens 2004 dictate that spectators may be refused admission to events if they are carrying food or drinks made by companies that did not see fit to sponsor the games."

Since Coke was the official soft drink, Pepsi was of course confiscated at the gate. But you couldn't even walk in carrying any brand of bottled water except for a Greek one called Avra, a subsidiary of Coca-Cola. Even T-shirts with a competitor's logo on them could get you into trouble, and if they thought you might be on TV when the cameras panned the stands, they'd tell you to wear it inside-out. If you were on staff or a volunteer at the Games, the only sneakers you could wear were Adidas. "It is not even possible to buy a ticket to the Olympics using a credit card other than Visa," the *Times* reported.

How insane is that? I thought the Olympics were supposed to be all about international brotherhood and fair and open competition. Guess not.

That same summer, McDonald's was also a sponsor of the Euro 2004 Football Championships, shucking their grub to avid soccer fans all over the continent. You couldn't turn on a TV in Europe without seeing some sort of logo placement or advertisement. McDonald's even sponsored almost 1,500 kids to act as "player escorts," accompanying the players on to the field. This is marketing at its twisted best. Cute, right?

The kids get to kick a few balls around with their heroes—and billions of the rest of us watch and smile and absorb the unspoken message that McDonald's can make your dreams come true. McDonald's has similar relationships with a lot of youth sports organizations in the United States, like the American Youth Soccer Organization in Southern California and the University of Miami Hurricanes.

No sports hero has shown himself to be a more willing corporate pitchman and mascot than Michael Jordan. Arguably the greatest player in the history of basketball, he's also been one of the most aggressively self-merchandised. Mr. Basketball is Mr. Endorsement. The guy CNN once called "a golden marketing tool" (think about that for a second, Michael) has sold everything from Nikes to Hanes undies to Bugs Bunny movies and merchandising to Gatorade to perfume to WorldCom long-distance services to, of course, McDonald's fries.

How often was he actually wolfing down McDonald's fries? Not too often, I'd bet (and Michael's a betting man). The message was clear: If you dress like Michael Jordan, smell like Michael Jordan and eat lots of fries like Michael Jordan, you can grow up to be like Michael Jordan.

Beautiful job, Michael. You're a role model to millions and millions. Did you really ever stop to think about what you were selling? I mean honestly, how many more gazillions of dollars did you need to make?

But he's not the only one, of course. The Williams sisters have shilled for McDonald's. Tiger Woods, Lance Armstrong, Dale Earnhart Jr., Shaq, Kobe Bryant (oops!), A-Rod, George Foreman, Anna Kournikova (woo hoo!)—the list of sports celebs who've sold us crap is pretty much endless. Sports celebrity endorsements are a huge, huge business. Not everything these "heroes" endorse is bad for kids, but a lot of it is. In 2003, the British medical journal *The Lancet* called the practice "especially bizarre since sports celebrities need a properly balanced diet to achieve fitness. Such celebrities should be ashamed, as should others who get caught in the web of junk-food promotion."

Pop stars do it all the time, too, of course. Somehow that's slightly less shocking. I mean, everybody already knew that Madonna and Britney were easy before they ever sold out to Pepsi, right? Every year, tons of Hollywood celebrities slip quietly over to Japan, where they appear in TV commercials for all sorts of stuff they'd probably never be caught dead endorsing in America, and hope their American fans never catch them doing it. Arnold, Sly, Harrison, Mel, Leonardo, Cameron, Meg and Madonna have all snuck over there to sell things like beer, deodorants and gift-wrapped hams (*mmmm*, ham) to their adoring Japanese fans.

In 2003, when McDonald's rolled out its new "I'm lovin' it" campaign, Justin Timberlake was its icon. How much more money do you need, Justin? Is selling out your zillions of young fans to the Fat Farm worth it to you? Beyonce Knowles and Destiny's Child have signed up to do the same in 2005. (At least they hired a singer who knows what will come from eating this diet—remember, Destiny's Child does have a hit song called "Bootylicious."

"McDonald's shares our passion for music," Beyonce was quoted saying in the press release, "so we can't wait to start connecting to our fans, McDonalds' customers, all over the world."

When some media critics and Beyonce fans did not take this news well, Beyonce came out with a statement defending herself and McDonald's. The *Los Angeles Times* noted:

> *Knowles is sure to horrify* Super Size Me *documentary director Morgan Spurlock, who became ill after living on McDonald's food for 30 days, by admitting she feasts on McDonald's food on a daily basis.*
>
> *She explains: "I ate McDonald's every day when we were recording. We get the chance to visit children at Ronald McDonald houses,*

where some are sick and some have different things going on with them.
So hopefully we get a chance to help put smiles on their faces. To be
part of that is beautiful."

I'm not horrified. I'm disgusted.

But it's not just me. Even other pop stars don't like it.

"I love her voice," Bjork told an interviewer. "I'm really pissed off
she's doing all of those commercials." She said it's "like selling your soul
to the devil."

One of the funniest pop-star endorsements ever was announced in
September 2004, when McDonald's signed Mary-Kate and Ashley
Olsen to promote Happy Meals in France. "Sales of Happy Meals are
down in France," *Newsweek* snickered, "and marketers evidently believe the eighteen-year-old twins send just the message needed to re-
verse the trend." So Mary-Kate came straight out of a rehabilitation
clinic for her eating disorder to be a spokesperson for Happy Meals.
(Hey, look, McDonald's just wants people to buy the Happy Meals. No
one said anything about eating them.)

Look, I'm not a commie. I'm not against people making money, even
money they obviously don't need. But they're role models to hundreds
of millions of young people, and they need to act like it. They're imi-
tated and emulated, and they have a responsibility to live up to.

The evil geniuses at one fast-food company even tried to turn *me* into
an endorser. No lie. When *Super Size Me* opened in Germany in the
summer of 2004, the German distributor of the film partnered with
Subway to promote it. Since Subway is McDonalds' major competitor,
it was a clever move. I knew nothing about it. I only heard about it when
conservative media back here in the States, responding to a "grassroots"
protest generated by the right-wing Center for Individual Freedom,
ranted that it was "un-American" of Subway to be sponsoring a film like
mine overseas. That's because the ad the Germans designed featured an

obese Statue of Liberty, and asked the question, "Why are Americans so fat?" The CFIF sent out a bombastic press release saying that it "demands that Subway apologize to American consumers immediately. If it fails to make amends for this transgression, it risks once again feeling the wrath of angry consumers across our nation!" I was on the phone immediately to the distributor to kill the campaign, since I had never approved it and I personally don't support Subway or their food.

Like I said, it was both evil and genius of Subway to hijack my film as a way both to slam its competitor and to position itself as the "healthy" alternative. But I believe Subway's mass-marketed and mass-produced food to be, at best, not much better than that of its burger-pushing colleagues. The ad was soon pulled.

A representative from Subway also contacted the U.S. distributor of our DVD prior to its release in the States. Subway wanted to buy 5 million copies and give them away in its stores to customers who purchased $15 or more of food. "It'll be a great way to get the movie into the hands of the people who are actually buying fast food," went the pitch-man on the phone. Although we would have made an instant $2.5 million on the deal, it took about two seconds for me to turn it down. Sorry, Jared, that's not what the movie's about.

Ray Kroc understood that kids were his target market from Day McOne. He'd no sooner bought the company from the McDonald brothers than Ronald McDonald was brought in to attract the kiddies to the burgers and shakes. The first Ronald was the TV weatherman Willard Scott, in his younger, but apparently not leaner, days. Scott had been doing Bozo the Clown on local TV. When the show got canceled, an enterprising McDonald's franchisee asked him to come up with a clown figure that would lure the kids into the restaurant. Kroc saw it, liked it and took the idea national. But first he canned Scott. Kroc understood the negative publicity implications of an icon who looks like he's been eating too much of the company's food.

And, in fact, to this day you'll never see Ronald McDonald eating the food. Not in any commercial. He dances and sings, grins and giggles and smiles at the kids while they stuff their faces, but he never touches the grub. Why? Because like the late Eazy-E said in the song "The Dopeman": "Don't get high off your own supply."

Kroc also understood the value of promoting McDonald's as a caring, family-friendly sort of place, a place with a heart, not heart disease. Early on, he began linking McDonald's with various children's charities. One exec told John F. Love, author of *McDonald's: Behind the Arches*: "It was an inexpensive, imaginative way of getting your name before the public and building a reputation to offset the image of selling fifteen-cent hamburgers. It was probably ninety-nine percent commercial."

Thus the Ronald McDonald House Charities were born, which have now provided housing (and McMeals) for the families of more than 2 million seriously ill children. (Never mind the fact that today an increasing number of kids are going into the hospital because of eating-related illnesses.)

> Pay no attention to that man behind the clown:
>
> It is ridiculous to call this an industry. This is not. This is rat eat rat, dog eat dog. I'll kill 'em, and I'm going to kill 'em before they kill me. You're talking about the American way—of survival of the fittest.
> —Ray Kroc, business visionary and humanitarian

But it's not enough to get kids to come to your joints—you gotta keep them coming back. McDonald's currently operates something like 8,000 "Playlands" around the country; they're especially attractive to kids in neighborhoods where things like playgrounds are mighty scarce. Burger King has about 3,200 of its own. (Of course, it's UpChuck E. Cheese that took this concept all the way, an entire chain of kids'-themed restaurants, 500 at last counting, where you can book your kid's birthday party, and your kid and all his/her little pals can spend hours gorging on pizza, mozzarella sticks, buffalo wings and cotton candy.)

And then there's the Happy Meal, launched nationally in 1979. It cost a buck in those days. Inside a cardboard box with a circus theme, kids found a McDoodler stencil, a puzzle book, a McWrist wallet, an ID bracelet and McDonaldland character erasers. The meal-plus-toys packaging proved to be an instant hit with the first *Star Trek* Happy Meals that very year. Soon, toy versions of all your favorite McDonald's mascots were included: Ronald, Grimace, Hamburglar, Mayor McCheese, Big Mac, Birdie and Captain Crook. Later toys would be themed for tie-ins with Barbie, Hot Wheels, The Little Mermaid, Finding Nemo and so on. By 2003, Happy Meals accounted for about 20 percent of all meals sold (about $3.5 billion in annual revenue).

And let's not forget the Mighty Kids Meal, introduced in 2001. McDonald's realized that by the time kids were eight or nine years old they felt they'd outgrown the Happy Meal. Happy Meals were for little kids, not them. So the Mighty Kids Meal comes in a slightly more "grown-up" package, offers them bigger meals—a Double Cheeseburger, Double Hamburger or a six-piece Chicken McNuggets—but still comes with a toy. We may be older, but we still like toys.

In 2004, McDonald's celebrated the twenty-fifth anniversary of the Happy Meal with a year-long barrage of promotions and ads. The company also launched a Happy Meal for adults, the Go Active! Adult Happy Meal. It included a salad, a 16-ounce bottle of water, a book that told you how to exercise, and an adult "toy": a Stepometer, so you could measure how few steps it was from the counter to your car.

Yeah, good old Ronald. Under his smiling, caring guidance, an entire generation of overweight American adults who grew up following him into their local McDonald's are now raising their own overweight children to follow in their heavy footsteps.

Recently, *Advertising Age* cited Ronald McDonald as number two on its list of top-ten advertising icons of the twentieth century.

Who was number one? The Marlboro Man.

ELEVEN

A LUNCHROOM NAMED *DESIRE*

It's lunchtime in the cafeteria at Madison Junior High in Naperville, Illinois. Cute adolescents milling around, lining up at the counter, carrying trays to the long tables, where I'm sure there are complicated social rules for who gets to sit with which crowd. Giggling, laughing, talking over one another. Generating that bubbly hubbub of energy that kids throw off.

Several kids are crowded around the near end of the counter, where pizzas are stacked one above the other, slowly spinning to display all their cheesy, doughy goodness. A Tower of Pizza. Kids reach in, grab a slice or two, and push their trays down the line.

Let's see what else they're being tempted with. *Mmmm*, a big aluminum tub of mac and cheese, glowing an artificial neon orange under the fluorescents. A tub of spaghetti and meatballs you just know was reheated out of an industrial-size can. A tub of succotash that's more gray than green and yellow.

Down at the end of the line is where all the fun stuff is. Tubs of french fries and ketchup packets. Piles of plastic-wrapped cinnamon buns and snack cakes. Rows of candy bars. To drink, your choice of milk, water, "fruit" beverages, canned lemonade, or bottles of Gatorade.

Most kids cluster at the two ends of the line. A few kids lean over the succotash, sniff at it and move on. Yeah, the staff is gonna haul a lot o' succotash to the dumpster this afternoon. Unless they just reheat it and try again tomorrow?

Now, it's no surprise that adolescents choose pizza, fries and candy. If you were a kid, which would you choose? *That's why kids need adults to supervise how they eat.*

At home, it's the parents' job. It's your mom or dad who says, "No, you can't just have fries for dinner. Eat some string beans, then you can have some fries." Or, under extreme conditions, "Young lady, you will sit there until you eat your vegetables." How many nights when you were a kid did you sit at the table for hours, staring at a pile of Brussels sprouts as they got colder and colder? You may not have eaten them that night, but a message was imparted, and later, as you got older, you discovered that vegetables actually taste good.

The average kid spends one-third of the day at home, one-third asleep and one-third in school. During those school hours, teachers and administrators are the surrogate parents. But in too many of our schools, the surrogate parents abandon the kids in the cafeteria. No adult is there monitoring what they eat—certainly not the people behind the counter. The kids are left to make "wise" food choices on their own.

Is it any wonder that they don't? We don't expect adolescents to make other kinds of crucial health choices on their own. We don't hand a thirteen-year-old the car keys and let the kid go joyriding. We don't hand a thirteen-year-old a rifle to play with. We don't say to our kids, "It's okay if you want to raid the liquor cabinet. Just be smart about how much of my vodka you drink."

But that's pretty much what we say to kids in schools. That's certainly what the food lobbyists say. Whenever they hear criticism about the kinds of foods kids choose to eat in school, one of their stock an-swers is, "Proper nutrition should be taught in the home, then the chil-dren would make the right choices here," or they'll proclaim, "Teach the kids proper nutrition in class, and when they come to the cafeteria they'll choose a balanced meal." The buck is passed, and passed again. But the fact remains, given the choice between peas and pizza, we know what nine out of ten kids will eat. Hell, that's the way many adults will eat. I've stood in line behind you at McDonald's—I know!

The cafeteria staff and school nutritionists try to put the best face on it. They'll tell you that, yes, kids buy a lot of fries, but they eat them as a side dish with a sandwich. But what I observed were kids—not just a few kids but *lots* of kids—whose entire lunch consisted of fries, cookies and a lemonade, or fries and milk or even a tray loaded up with bags of chips and candy. When I followed them to their tables to see if they'd brown-bagged a sandwich to have with those goodies, they rarely had. Fries and ketchup was their lunch. (Well, ketchup is a vegetable. Rea-gan told us so.) Some schools won't serve sodas, but they'll sell so-called "fruit" drinks that are just water, a little artificial fruit flavoring and coloring and 36 grams of sugar per bottle. In other schools, Coke and Pepsi and the like are prevalent. One girl I saw bought two packs of Ruf-fles, a Twix bar, a soft pretzel and a Gatorade for lunch. When I followed her back to the table, I saw that she also had brought a Coke from home to drink with all that!

The sad fact is that in many, many of our schools, we're teaching kids terrible habits of diet and health. Often they get no gym class. They get no nutrition education. And they get few good choices in the lunchroom. Whether it's through the federal government's school lunch program or because the school district has farmed out the feed-ing of kids to a lowest-bidding commercial outfit, cafeteria food is dis-tinctly sub-par.

Worse, while schools should be the one place kids aren't inundated with junk food messages, fast food and lousy processed food, it's just the opposite. In fact, a lot of school lunchrooms look like mall food courts. Coke, Pepsi, Taco Bell, Burger King, McDonald's and the rest have taken over thousands of American schools.

And for that we have no one to blame but ourselves. As voters, as taxpayers and as parents, we've sold out our schools to the corporate takeover artists because we don't want to pay more local taxes. As federal and state officials continue to slash education budgets, these corporations step into the "funding gap." We're sacrificing our children's health so that they can turn a profit in our schools.

First, let's look at those cafeteria lines.

Since the mid-1990s, an increasing number of school districts have been licensing out the management of their cafeterias to commercial food-service outfits like Sodexho, Aramark and Daka. Sodexho manages the school district that is the home to the Madison Junior High cafeteria and a few hundred others across the United States. These are the same companies that provide food service to prisons, hospitals and many college campuses. And now they run the lunchrooms in thousands of school districts.

Why are public schools farming out their lunchrooms to these companies? For the same reason many of them don't have gym equipment, or instruments for a school band, or biology labs or any books in their libraries that aren't twenty years out of date: They're broke. Broke because we don't fund them.

Farming out lunchroom management is one way school districts cut costs. They may even make a little money out of the deal. These companies are supposed to follow those federal nutrition guidelines, ensuring that our kids are eating right, but it's all very loosey-goosey, and the kids' welfare is more observed in theory than in fact.

But even schools that aren't outsourcing their lunchrooms are failing our kids nutritionally—and they're doing it with the full support of our friends in the federal government. Through the National School Lunch Program (NSLP), the United States Department of Agriculture provides lunches for some 26 million children each schoolday. About 99 percent of all public elementary, junior high and senior high schools, along with a number of private schools and residential child-care institutions, participate in the program. Schools get a cash reimbursement and donated goods for serving the meals.

Any student can avail herself of these meals, but kids from households below certain income levels get them free or for a greatly reduced price (40 cents max); students who aren't from poor homes pay more for them. Of course, kids don't have to participate, and can bring their own lunches from home.

All NSLP lunches are supposed to meet federal nutrition requirements, based on the USDA's own Dietary Guidelines for Americans: no more than 35 percent of calories from fat, with less than 10 percent from saturated fat. Plus the meal should provide one-third of the Recommended Dietary Allowances for calories, protein, vitamins A and C, iron and calcium.

Sounds great, right? Good ol' USDA, feeding all those poor kids nutritious, wholesome meals every day!

Well . . . not exactly.

An encyclopedia (Wikipedia) definition of the USDA reads like this: "The United States Department of Agriculture, also called the Agriculture Department, or USDA, is a Cabinet department of the United States Federal Government. Its purpose is to develop and execute policy on farming, agriculture and food. It aims to meet the needs of farmers and ranchers, promote agricultural trade and production, work to assure food safety, protect natural resources, foster rural communities, and end hunger in America and abroad."

Notice the priorities. The interests of agriculture and ranching come first. In the twenty-first century, that means corporate agribusiness, the corporate beef industry, the corporate poultry and dairy industries—in short, Big Food. Notice how the interests of the consumer—things like food safety and hunger—come last.

That's a pretty apt description of the USDA's agenda. Some critics call it "USDA Inc.," and say it's basically agribusiness's department in Washington.

It hasn't always been that way. In Abe Lincoln's day, it was known as "the People's Department," because it represented the needs and interests of American farmers and farm workers, which meant most of the people in America. In the early twentieth century, largely as a result of the uproar about unsanitary meatpacking plants described by Upton Sinclair in his muckraking book *The Jungle*, the USDA took on a more regulatory role—and took it seriously.

But as the century progressed and nearly all the family farms and ranches were swallowed up by giant corporations, the USDA became less and less about serving the needs of the People and more and more about protecting the profits of Big Business. Nowadays, the only time the USDA seems to take its regulatory role seriously is when it's forced to by a huge public scandal like the mad-cow scare.

In fact, a lot of the time the USDA seems to function like a Big Food lobby that conveniently just happens to be a wing of the federal government. That's partly because so many of its executive offices, from the Secretary of Agriculture on down, are occupied by people who came from the executive offices of the Big Food corporations and will go back there when their tour of duty in D.C. is completed. In 2004, something like forty-five of the top offices of the USDA were filled by people recruited from Big Food and its lobbies. "Incestuous" hardly seems like a strong enough word to describe the revolving-door relationship between the USDA and Big Food.

In 2004, according to their bios on the USDA's own website:

- Former Secretary Ann M. Veneman served on the board of the biotech company Calgene.
- Her chief of staff, Dale Moore, had been an executive of the National Cattlemen's Beef Association, the enormously powerful corporate meatpackers' lobby.
- So had her director of communications, Alisa Harrison.
- Her deputy chief of staff (who left in 2004) was a vice president of the International Dairy Foods Association, the also extremely powerful milk-and-cheese industry's lobby.
- Deputy Secretary of Agriculture James Moseley was a partner in Infinity Pork LLC, a corporate pig farm in Indiana.
- Under Secretary J. B. Penn was an agribusiness consultant.
- Under Secretary Joseph Jen came from Campbell Soup.

"Conflict of interests" is hardly apt. These people have no conflict of interests. They know exactly whose interests they serve.

These are the people you're trusting to inspect the National Cattlemen's Beef Association members' meatpacking plants. To keep an eye on what the International Dairy Foods Association's members are feeding their milk cows. To make sure the pork chops you get from Infinity Pork don't give you trichinosis. Last time I checked, banks weren't guarded by bank robbers. How can this be happening in the highest branches of our government?

But wait—they're also the ones responsible for disseminating the one bit of nutritional education every kid, and every adult, is supposed to know by heart: the Food Pyramid. Which boils down the USDA's Dietary Guidelines into an easy-to-follow, at-a-glance graphic. Eat more of the foods at the bottom, less of the ones at the top. Simple. Couldn't be clearer.

Yet nothing illustrates the USDA's conflicts of interest like the wheeling and dealing that have gone on over the last couple of years as the department has tried to figure out how to revise and update both the Guidelines and the Pyramid. The Guidelines are updated every five years by a panel of experts jointly appointed by the USDA and the Department of Health and Human Services. The Pyramid, however, had not been changed since it was introduced in 1992.

The friggin' Great Pyramid in Egypt wasn't as hard to build as this revised Food Pyramid. All the Big Food lobbies—meat, sugar, dairy, even salt (who even knew salt had its own lobbyists?)—have been jockeying to get the best positions on the new Pyramid and to soften anything said about them in the new Guidelines. Even the Fatkins Diet lobby got into the act, demanding that the Guidelines reflect the late, great and overweight Dr. Atkins' anti-carbs campaign. It's also worth mentioning that the panel appointed to update the Guidelines was packed with more Big Food industry types than a fruitcake has cherries.

Everybody got to throw their two cents in. The Peanut Institute, the California Walnut Commission and the National Barley Food Council all fought for their fair share. The lobby for the vitamin-supplements industry tried to convince the panel that the Pyramid should have a little flag waving from the top of it—the flag would represent vitamin supplements.

Private citizens were allowed to write to the panel to express their views, too. Hey, it's the democratic way, even if it does open up the process to the lunatic fringe. Between the lobbies and the loonies, there were numerous arguments that the Pyramid shouldn't be a pyramid at all, but a clock, a wheel, a plate, a pie, balloons, a mountain range, an hour glass, a cross-section of a diamond, a menu, an upside-down pyramid superhero or a "nourishment tree."

One guy, who claimed to be a "foodician," wrote in to argue stren-
uously that the Pyramid should be a Food Merkabah. (For those of you
who haven't been shopping for incense and New Age reading materials lately, a merkabah is a kind of multidimensional mandala.) He also
complained that "the cleansing properties of urine are not even ad-
dressed in the food pyramid. This must be corrected. We cannot allow
small minds and prejudice to bury this useful health information from
our brothers and sisters in light." He went on: "Write back IMMEDI-
ATELY and tell me where to report with my diagrams. I am including
corn muffins prominently in my calculations. That alone should tell you
that I know what I am doing!"

Thank you, Gandalf. We'll get back to you.

The Food Pyramid got the USDA into trouble the very first time it
was unveiled, in 1991. The department's friends in the beef industry
were outraged at what a small space they got on it, and it took a year of
haggling to come up with a version that pleased them. So, right from
the start, the USDA was compromising your health to appease one of
its true constituents.

When the USDA released its preliminary and unofficial 2005 Dietary Guidelines report in the summer of 2004, it appeared that sugar
would come out as the big winner. Previous editions of the Guidelines
used to say choose a diet "moderate in sugar" or "avoid too much sugar."
Big Sugar has lobbied long and hard to get that wording softened over
the years, and the New York Times reported in August 2004 that the new
guidelines wouldn't even list sugar among the foods that are bad for you.
But thankfully, that part of the preliminary report didn't quite make the
final cut. The official Guidelines released in January 2005 make clear
statements about limiting added sugars, much to the chagrin of those
at Big Sugar who defended their lobbying efforts, saying they stood firm
in their assertion "that there is not a direct link between added sugars
intake and any lifestyle disease, including obesity." That was Andy
Briscoe, president and CEO of the Sugar Association, who went on:

"For the guidelines to infer any type of limit on added sugars is not science-based." Better luck next time, guys.

I presume the government's recent focus on combating obesity had a lot to do with this small but important victory for our health. The Guidelines also include more and more advice on preventing obesity, including a recommendation to exercise for sixty to ninety minutes daily, up from thirty minutes in previous guidelines.

The sugar lobby also tried to throw its weight around with the UN's World Health Organization. As draft versions of the WHO's new dietary guidelines, which were released in November 2004, became public in 2003, it became clear that the final report would recommend stiff restrictions in sugar consumption. The Sugar Association went ballistic, firing off letters to the WHO's director general grumbling that the "report reflects poorly on WHO and, if allowed to stand, will mislead and confuse the public," calling it a "shabby affair" and saying, "It is difficult to believe the standards of the World Health Organization have slipped to such a low point. . . ."

The Sugar Association CEO wrote to the WHO, promising, "We will exercise every avenue available to expose the dubious nature of the 'Diet, Nutrition and the Prevention of Chronic Diseases' Report, including asking Congressional appropriators to challenge future funding of the U.S.'s $406 million contributions (including both regular and voluntary funding) to the WHO." And the association got its people in the Senate—Louisiana Democrat John Breaux and Idaho Republican Larry Craig, cochairs of the Senate Sweetener Caucus (who knew?)—to complain to cabinet members as well. The WHO didn't cave.

It's also worth noting that advice on carbohydrates warranted its own section in the new Guidelines, whereas past reports barely mentioned carbs. Thanks to relentless lobbying on the part of the Atkins folks, the USDA now tells us to "choose carbohydrates wisely."

The dairy lobby is also celebrating. Reporting in August 2004 on the USDA's preliminary Guidelines, *The Wall Street Journal* said, "In a shift that has major implications for the U.S. dairy industry, the Dietary Guidelines Advisory Committee on Friday endorsed what amounts to a 50% boost in milk consumption, up from the two servings long suggested for many adults. . . . The new advice is a major victory for the $50 billion U.S. dairy industry, which has long lobbied for increased consumption guidelines. Currently, Americans eat or drink about 1.5 servings of dairy products per day, according to the Agriculture Department. Despite the dairy industry's iconic 'Got Milk?' ad campaign, per-capita fluid milk sales have fallen nearly 3% over the past five years. The suggested boost in dairy intake could spell big profits for the industry, as federal nutrition programs such as school lunch menus are adjusted to conform." When the final version of the 2005 Dietary Guidelines were unveiled six months later, the 50 percent recommended boost in milk intake held steady. (Actually, the article was misleading: That ubiquitous "Got Milk?" ad campaign was produced by none other than the USDA, yet another example of the department doing Big Food's work for it.)

Actually, the "Got Milk?" ad campaign was a product of what are called checkoff programs, which are designed by the USDA and made mandatory by acts of Congress to help promote various agricultural commodities. The USDA oversees and must approve all checkoff activities. In this case, milk producers forked over a percentage of their revenues to the Dairy Board, which in turn paid for the "Got Milk?" and other promotions. Have you seen the new McDonald's Milk Jugs? If you think that was a McDonald's idea, think again.

And don't forget pork—the National Pork Board paid McDonald's thousands of dollars to help create and promote the McRib Sandwich. It's not just dairy and pork, either. The USDA uses checkoff programs to gouge farmers from almost any area—beef, eggs, cotton, mushrooms, honey, watermelon, popcorn, soybeans, potatoes, lamb, etc. Farmers from across the spectrum hate these programs, and in 2001 they cheered when the U.S. Supreme Court declared the mushroom checkoff program unconstitutional because "it compels producers to finance and/or to be associated with political or ideological speech to which they are opposed." At the time of this writing, beef producers are awaiting what they hope to be a similar Supreme Court decision, and the pork checkoff has been flopping around the courts for years.

Never mind the fact that, as the article notes, "Walter Willett, a physician and chairman of the department of nutrition at Harvard University's School of Public Health, calls the committee report 'egregious,' saying it excludes at least six major studies linking dairy consumption to prostate cancer. 'There is no nutritional requirement for dairy at all,' he insists. 'Huge parts of the world do not even consume dairy.' "

One reason the Get More Milk lobby may have won out over concerned nutritionists like Dr. Willett, according to *The Wall Street Journal:* "At least three of the 13 committee members, Connie Weaver, head of the department of foods and nutrition at Purdue University; Theresa A. Nicklas, a professor of pediatrics at Baylor College of Medicine; and Penny Kris-Etherton, professor at Pennsylvania State University, have received National Dairy Council funding within the past five years." Milk, it does the lobby good. Pass it on.

All I know is, that's gonna be one lopsided friggin' Pyramid.

And these are the same people who are feeding 26 million kids a day in 99 percent of America's public schools.

How did the USDA get in the business of running school cafeterias, you ask? It started during the Depression. The total collapse of consumer markets left the farm industry with tons of surplus product. Meanwhile, millions of American kids were going hungry. The USDA killed two birds with one biscuit: It bought up all those farm surpluses to save the agriculture industry and dumped all that food into the schools and prisons.

The NSLP operates basically the same way to this day, still using schools and prisons as dumping grounds for surplus agri-product, propping up sagging sectors of the food industry like beef and dairy as needed. As of July 2004, 200 of the 26,000 school districts in the country were even serving kids that irradiated beef I talked about earlier. "The meat industry has used the NSLP as a gravy train, and our kids are paying the price," says Jennifer Keller of the Physicians Committee for Responsible Medicine.

It's not hard to tell which of the USDA's constituents, Big Food or impoverished schoolchildren, gets first priority. The USDA's main job is promoting and supporting agribusiness; feeding kids is just a convenient sideline. When dairy prices fall, for instance, the USDA buys up lots of milk and cheese, then ships it off to school cafeterias, prisons and hospitals. Never mind that although a lot of kids are lactose-intolerant, the USDA won't reimburse schools for serving alternatives to cow's milk, because the powerful dairy lobby won't allow it. Got milk? Boy, do our schools got milk! Similarly, the USDA buys hundreds of millions of pounds of surplus beef, chicken, cheese and pork every year, and then dumps them on your kids. Like it or not.

TWELVE

LORD
OF THE
RING DINGS

Food corporations have waltzed through the schoolroom doors in even more insidious ways than through their influence over the USDA.

The soda, snack and fast-food industries are everywhere in our schools, pushing junk on kids through vending machines and snack bars, and in the cafeteria line, where chicken nuggets are offered right next to all that government cheese and beef. By the mid-nineties, Pizza Hut, Taco Bell, Burger King, Domino's, Subway and of course Mickey D's were operating virtual franchises inside many schools. Some 23,000 of our public schools now have fast-food franchises in them. In the 1990s, several high school cafeterias actually became licensed fast-food franchises themselves.

Attorney John Banzhaf put it bluntly: Schools that let the fast-food and soda companies into their lunchrooms "get a bribe for every fat burger or sugary soft drink which is sold," he says. "Even those who defend it seem to say, 'Well, it's bad, we know it's not good for the kids, but we do it for the money.' We have a simple word in the English language for people who do something they know is wrong for money. We call it 'prostituting' yourself."

Vending machines are strategically placed at other points around many schools. Soda and snack vending machines began appearing in schools in the 1960s. The Secretary of Agriculture banned them from school cafeterias in 1970, but that didn't last for long after the food lobbyists got to work. Now something like nine out of ten high schools, and seven out of ten middle schools, have soda and snack vending machines in them. Some schools have only one, others as many as twenty-two. As nutrition advocate Kelly Brownell put it, American schools have become "7-Elevens with books."

And what kinds of nutritious goodness are they vending from those machines? A study conducted in some 250 schools around the country in 2003 found that 7 percent of the beverage choices and 85 percent of the snacks were high in sugar and fat and low in nutritional quality. Seventy percent of the drinks were sugary sodas, iced tea, so-called sports drinks and so-called juice drinks (usually less than 50 percent juice). Only 7 percent were really juice, and 12 percent were water. Eighty percent of the snacks were junk food, candy, chips, cookies and cakes. Of the almost 10,000 vending machine slots surveyed, only *twenty-six* offered a fruit or vegetable. Twenty-six!

Way to promote healthy eating habits, Mr. or Ms. Principal! Have a Snickers.

"These schools were really strapped for money," Eric Schlosser said when I interviewed him, "and made a bargain with the devil, letting in the soda companies and the fast-food companies, who get them more money for school bands and school uniforms and text books."

In 2003, New York City, still in the grip of a wicked post–9/11 local recession, got a cool $166 million for awarding Snapple exclusive rights to sell from vending machines in all of the city's schools. The idea was that the city was replacing those bad, sugary sodas with a "healthy fruit drink." The problem is, as *The New York Times* pointed out, "An 11.5-ounce container of the new Snapple has 160 or 170 calories and the equivalent of about 10 teaspoons of sugar, 40 or 41 grams. A 12-ounce Coca-Cola has 140 calories and 39 grams of sugar."

In 2004, Illinois Governor Rod Blagojevich took that a step further when he floated the idea of letting the big soft-drink companies compete for the exclusive sales rights from vending machines in state office buildings, parks and rest stops across the state. The winner would simply be whichever company ponied up the most cash. As an added benefit, their brand would be named the official Illinois state beverage!

"As a nation we owe it to parents to create an environment that makes it easy for them to raise healthy children," Kelly Brownell said. "And we are doing almost everything the opposite of that. No parent can compete with the amount of food advertising aimed at children. Parents may focus on healthy eating at home, but then they send their children to schools where they're given ice cream, can buy bags of potato chips, buy soft drinks out of the machines. It's extremely hard today for a parent to raise a healthy child."

College campuses have been invaded, too. Here's an e-mail we got on the *Super Size Me* website:

Hey, I am a student at the University of South Carolina. I was watching your movie and when I heard that Sodexho does children's lunches, I cringed. That kind of stuff did not go on when I was a kid. Candy, chips, and soda weren't allowed in schools, but now it's an everyday thing. And it never stops. Not even when you get to college. Sodexho is our food supplier, and *now we have a Burger King, Chick-Fil-A, Marble Slab Ice Creamery, AND a Taco Bell on campus. . . . I think that everyone should adopt the "penny per calorie" rule. If a calorie cost a penny, then would you really want to spend $3.60 on a candy bar? Or $11–12 on a fast-food sandwich? Maybe that would be a way to get the obesity level in America down without spending money on surgeries, or listening to your doctor lecturing you on obesity. Then maybe we could have a more healthy America.*

For Big Food, it's not enough just to sell crap to kids in school every day. They want to train those kids to be good, brand-loyal consumers for the rest of their lives. In schools, they have a captive audience, 180 days of the year, from the ages of five to eighteen.

"Not all families own television sets or computers," Marion Nestle explained, "but most American children attend school. Given their purchasing power, numbers, potential as future customers and captive status, it is no wonder that food companies view schoolchildren as an unparalleled marketing opportunity."

Over the last twenty years, cash-strapped school districts have allowed kids marketers to indoctrinate kids with advertisements, promotional messages, brand logos and mascots. The companies pay the schools for the privilege. They fund textbooks and gymnasiums and football teams and, well, just about anything the schools will let them slap their logos on. Fast food, candy and soda companies now "sponsor" all sorts of study materials, classroom videos and educational software—even nutrition guides! They get their names, message, logos and mascots all over them, of course. For instance, in the mid-1990s, Mars Incorporated sponsored math materials that had a Snickers logo on every page, and included such educational info as, "Eating SNICKERS is a good way to get quick energy that will keep you kicking all day long."

Some corporate-sponsored education materials for really young students (from the Dairy Council, for example) come disguised as fun toys or coloring books or what have you. Coca-Cola and McDonald's cosponsored the Little Known Black History Facts Education Kit, and McDonald's has produced materials on subjects ranging from fire safety to suicide prevention. For grades K–5, teachers could even call their local McDonald's and arrange for "inspirational lessons, hosted by Ronald McDonald."

"Several companies license counting books for young children that require the purchase and use of brand-name candies, cookies, and sugar-sweetened cereals," Nestle writes. She cites an Oreo book that instructs kids to count down from ten Oreos to none—obviously suggesting they gobble up the cookies as they counted them—and included discount coupons.

One parent wrote this to the *Super Size Me* website:

> My daughter just started kindergarten. October 1 she came home with
> a paper describing a reading incentive program. We have to make a list
> of books read every month according to the goal set by the teacher. . . .
> [W]hen the students turn in their list of 12 books read, they will re-
> ceive a coupon for a free meal at McDonald's. And this will happen
> EVERY MONTH of the school year. . . . These children are five
> years old!

And did you hear the one about Krispy Kreme Doughnuts' offer to schoolkids in Florida? In 2004, the Associated Press reported that "Krispy Kreme stores will give Palm Beach County students in kindergarten through sixth grade a free doughnut for every A on their report card. Another program has students decorate posters of doughnuts with 'success sprinkles' when children meet goals. The posters can be turned in for a class set of doughnuts."

No wonder McDonald's has been rumored to be interested in buying Krispy Kreme—they must have fallen in love with their marketing techniques immediately. I remember when I was in high school, and each year the dance squad would sell Krispy Kreme doughnuts to raise money for their season. This was at the time when there were few franchises around, so anytime you could sink your teeth into a KK doughnut was a good time! The team would sell thousands of them and raise tons of money, while the rest of us—the ones who weren't dancing and practicing every day—gained thousands and thousands of pounds.

Even outside these specific incentive programs, teachers often use candy and snacks as rewards. In Arkansas, a new law "requires schools to calculate the body mass index for each student and bars access to vending machines for elementary school students," AP reported in 2004. This led the Pulaski county school district, where our first Fast-Food President went to school, to tell teachers they "could no longer hand out candy or ice cream as rewards." I love that they had to be told not to do this.

What were they thinking? If teachers are rewarding kids with ice cream, how are parents supposed to instill healthy rules at home?

As if selling crap to kids on the TVs in their bedrooms wasn't enough, in 1990 Channel One debuted TV in classrooms throughout the nation. Created by the now-defunct Whittle Communications and now run by Primedia, Channel One makes schools an offer many feel they can't refuse: It installs free TVs and video equipment in classrooms, in return for which the school promises that 8 percent of its students will watch Channel One's twelve-minute morning news program on 90 percent of schooldays.

That twelve-minute program, not surprisingly, includes two minutes of commercials. It is now beamed into 12,000 schools across the United States, where 8.3 million students see it. That's 40 percent of the nation's high school students—more than watch MTV. That's why advertising on Channel One costs over $200,000 for a thirty-second spot, same as network TV.

And who advertises? Who do you think? Pepsi, Doritos, candy companies, zit-cream makers, sneaker companies—pretty much anyone who'd like to reach a literally captive market of 8.3 million kids.

And what do the evil-genius marketers have to say for themselves?

"There's only one way to increase customers," kids marketing guru James McNeal told the *National Review*. "Either you switch them or you grow them from birth. Parents who are concerned about in-school marketing are complaining about something they created. They begin taking babies to the mall at a median age of two months."

There is a bright side. Things have gotten so out of control in our schools that dozens of states have begun to consider changes in their cafeterias, their vending-machine contracts, their nutrition classes and their phys ed programs. Texas, one of the fattest states in the land, banned the sale of soda, candy and "foods of minimal nutritional value" from hallways, lunchrooms and common areas during mealtimes in 2002. In California, a number of school districts have banned junk food, and in 2004 Governer Schwarzenegger expressed his support for a bill introduced in the state legislature proposing sweeping statewide changes.

As I write this, politicians, educators and food lobbyists in Massachusetts are discussing a bill that proposes sweeping changes throughout the state's public school system. *The Boston Globe explains:*

The bill would require that:

• All food available in schools, whether in the cafeteria or in vending machines, will comply with nutritional standards set by the state Department of Education.

• All drinks available in schools be water, fruit juices that are 50 percent or more natural juice, or low- or nonfat milk. Soft drinks would be out.

• All food from vending machines have no more than 35 percent of calories from fat, 10 percent of calories from saturated fat and 35 percent of calories from sugar. Many chips and candies would be out.

• Students have access to nutritional information on all food available.

• Students get 120 hours of physical activity, in a class or recess, each school year.

• Students get 50 hours of nutrition or wellness education annually.

At least it's a start.

Bills like one proposed in Massachusetts in 2004 would take responsibility for school lunches and vending machines away from the state's local school districts—which have, after all, dropped the ball—and put it at the statewide level. The bill's one glaring weakness is that it says nothing about where the funding would come from to replace revenues schools get from the soda companies for the vending-machine contracts. If they don't pay for gym teachers and equipment, who will?

I have an idea: Why not a statewide tax on candy and sodas? Just a few pennies per? It worked with cigarettes. In New York they taxed the hell out of smoking—a pack of smokes in the city now costs more than $7! And it has generated a financial windfall for the city and state.

Naturally, the food lobby opposes the bill and in fact killed previous versions. The American Beverage Association, which lobbies for companies like Coca-Cola and Pepsi, says it's inappropriate for state and federal governments to dictate what's available to kids.

In 2004, the Seattle school board unanimously agreed to ban foods containing high levels of sugar and fat from sale in elementary and middle schools, including the end of soft-drink vending machines. A number of other big cities—Los Angeles, Philadelphia, San Francisco, Oakland and more—have made similar moves. Fayette County public schools in Kentucky changed its vending contract to up the healthy beverages offered—water, sports drinks and real fruit juices—from 21 to 72 percent. (But beware sports drinks—they can be as full of sugar as those so-called "fruit drinks.") Healthy snacks, which were only 1 percent of what was stocked in the machines, were upped to 40 percent.

On the national level, one guy who's shown he truly gets it is Senator Tom Harkin of Iowa. The ranking Democrat on the Senate Committee on Agriculture, Nutrition and Forestry, he introduced a bill in 2004 called the HeLP America (Healthy Lifestyle and Prevention) Act, a really sweeping piece of legislation that would include tight regulations on all aspects of what the junk-food industry is doing in our schools, a ban on food marketing and advertising in schools and funding for schools to give kids alternatives to junk food. And this part I love: The bill would be funded by fining tobacco companies if sales of cigarettes to minors don't decline.

Naturally, Harkin's swimming upstream in Congress, where Big Tobacco and the junk-food industry have so many politicians in their pockets. But you gotta love the guy for trying. And who knows? It could actually happen. (And you can help—send your Senators and Congressmen e-mails telling them you support HeLP, and if they want your vote, they better support it, too. (Go to www.DontEatThisBook.com for more information.)

Harkin did get something called the Local Wellness Policy passed, which means that every school in the country has to have a wellness policy by the start of the school year in 2006. That means setting goals for nutrition education and physical activity. And as part of the 2002 Farm Bill, he launched the really cool Food and Vegetable Pilot Program (FVPP), an attempt to improve fruit and vegetable consumption among kids at elementary and secondary schools in eight states and on three Indian reservations. All around these schools, in free vending machines and boxes, in the hallways and in the classrooms, there's fresh fruit and veggies kids can snack on during the day, instead of corn chips and Twinkies. Schools report the response from kids has been overwhelming; they're even eating more fruit and vegetables in the lunchroom now.

Senator Hillary Clinton has long proposed a ban on advertising in schools and an end to all advertising aimed at preschoolers. It could happen. Someday. Sweden, Norway and Finland banned marketing to children under age twelve. In Canada, the province of Quebec bans marketing to children under age thirteen. Greece prohibits TV commercials for toys between 7 a.m. and 10 p.m., New Zealand bans junk-food marketing to kids and the UK has announced plans to do the same.

You don't have to wait for the feds, the state or even your local school board to wake up. Individual schools have come up with some amazing programs of their own.

At Madison Junior High, where I saw all those kids eating fries and ketchup for lunch, at least one thing is going right: Phil Lawler's phys ed department. Lawler has created a model program, with daily classes where the kids get to run, climb and work out on equipment that's better than in many health clubs. Where'd the money come from? Lawler gets $1 per year for each student from the board of education, and the parents and students raise additional funds from local businesses. It's a win/win situation: It's a tax write-off for the businesses, and there are *no ads* for their companies anywhere in the school.

He's been getting some fantastic results. His kids take the same fitness tests as kids in California, and while 48 percent of California freshmen were in the healthy zone, "We were at 80 percent."

The 120 students at Appleton Central Alternative Charter School in Wisconsin are so-called "problem kids," grades eight through twelve. Their "problems" range from ADD, drug addiction and obsessive-compulsive disorders to physical handicaps, asthma, allergies and "behavioral" things ranging from teen pregnancy to truancy and "anti-social behaviors."

Over a single weekend in 1997, the Appleton staff completely transformed the kinds of food available to the kids. In a five-year test project proposed and funded by Paul and Barbara Stitt of the Natural Ovens Bakery, the staff got rid of the vending machines, sodas and junk food and replaced them with water coolers, 100 percent fruit juices, skim milk, whole-grain breads and bagels, a salad bar with dark greens (instead of just iceberg lettuce), homemade applesauce and other good, healthy stuff. Cooks employed by the bakery prepared vegetable stir-fries and ground-turkey tacos. Food was always prepared fresh, never frozen and reheated. Nothing was deep-fried, they never used dairy in any of the cooking and they served very little red meat.

The entire five-year pilot program cost only $125,000. When it was completed, the school brought in ARAMARK, one of the commercial outfits, to run the cafeteria, still trying to stick to the high standards set by the Natural Ovens program.

Teachers and administrators were blown away by the improvements in the kids' behavior, their attentiveness in class and their general attitudes. English teacher Mary Bruyette says she no longer sees "disruptions in class or the difficulty with student behavior. . . . I've been able to demand more academically" from the kids. Deb Larson, the school's social worker, says, "It's made my job easier because I don't have the angry outbursts. Instead we get to deal with some of the real issues that are underlying and causing some of the problems. . . . I think it's easier to talk to kids today than it was a few years ago before we started the program."

Larson also says there's a full-time "police liasion" officer at the school, who used to deal with outbreaks, fights and misbehaving students almost daily. When the food changed, so did most of the students' attitudes, and the officer now spends far less time handling outbreaks and much more time developing positive relationships with the kids.

In 2003, school officials voted to phase in a similar plan for all 15,000 students in the Appleton school district. The board also voted unanimously to ban the sale of soda and candy in vending machines.

The Stitts' nonprofit Nutritional Resource Foundation, which is supported by their bakery, is now working with the Perspectives Charter
School in Chicago, a new high school for underprivileged kids. The NRF
put up the money for the kitchen/cafeteria area, and found a culinary-
arts expert specializing in whole natural foods to run the program.

The Olympia school district in the state of Washington began an
Organic Choices salad bar at Lincoln Elementary in 2002. The idea
came from Vanessa Ruddy, a concerned parent, who organized other
parents and community members to work with Lincoln staff. The salad
bar features organic fruit and vegetable choices, whole-grain breads,
vegetarian meat alternatives, free-range eggs and organic soymilk. Al-
ternate protein choices include cottage cheese, sunflower seeds, salmon,
tuna, garbanzo beans, organic soy beans and kidney beans. The school
still participates in the NSLP but has eliminated all junk food and
sweets, including chocolate milk (which is loaded with high-fructose
corn syrup). The cafeteria recycles everything that can be recycled, it
replaced the paper plates and plastic utensils with real china and sil-
verware and the kids help load the dishwasher after lunch!

In class, the kids learn the "Three out of Five" federal food guidelines, which recommend that kids' lunch choices include three of the
five food groups: fruit, vegetable, protein, bread (grain) and dairy. Lincoln also has an organic garden and greenhouse, where students from
kindergarten up grow greens, herbs, gourds, beans, potatoes, strawberries, raspberries, pumpkins and more. In-school snacks come from the
garden and greenhouse, and leftovers from lunch are composted.

Ruddy says the kids, the school and almost all parents have been ec-
static about the whole thing. She has a few critics who think the program's "too radical. I tell them it's just the opposite of radical," Ruddy
says. "It's going back to the way things used to be."

Browne Junior High School in Washington, D.C., has a strict "no
junk food in school" policy—no candy or soda sold—and if a kid is
caught with any during school hours, it's confiscated and chucked.

In Montana, Whitefish Middle School switched from selling sodas and candy to 100 percent fruit juice, water and healthy snacks. Before, kids would often act out right after lunch, working off all that sugar and caffeine energy. Disciplinary problems have been greatly reduced since the switch, and making the switch hasn't cost the school a dime.

Oh, and remember that Krispy Kreme "reward" gimmick? Schools in Massachusetts are doing the opposite: They teamed up with a local fruit-and-produce wholesaler to reward students who choose items like salad, hummus and stir-fry veggies in the cafeteria. By eating right, kids earn points that can be redeemed for prizes like sports watches and skateboards. And no sit-on-your-butt prizes like Gameboys, either.

But watch out. Big Food sees which way the wind is blowing, and it's making all kinds of promises to improve school foods and nutrition info—promises that you should be very wary of. ConAgra Foods has introduced seven new "low-fat, high-fiber" pizza varieties in schools. Sodexho has debuted the Cyclone Salad, a funnel-shaped tortilla shell filled with salad and low-fat dressing that kids can eat on-the-go without utensils. Both Sodexho and ARAMARK also want you to think of them as expert advisors in nutrition and exercise now. They're rolling out nutrition education pamphlets and lesson plans to be distributed in classrooms and PTA meetings (sounds just like what the fast-food companies are doing now, right?).

Beware. Never forget that at the same time the food industry is making these small, good-for-publicity gestures toward improvement, lobbyists are busily opposing and undermining every real policy change or piece of legislation that comes up. There's no substitute for kicking all this crap out of your kids' schools altogether.

And here's my own humble proposal. Faced with an epidemic of obesity, I think we should make food education a priority in schools, the same way we've taught sex education and AIDS education. (Not that I got any sex ed in school back in West Virginia—when it came to sex education, we were homeschooled.)

Call it Survival 101. Prepare our kids for life in the real world when they grow up. Students could learn how to cook something different and good for themselves every day in cooking classes. Schools with available grounds, or even just windowboxes, could teach them how to garden vegetables or at least herbs and spices, like at Lincoln Elementary. For homework, kids would cook dinner for their parents, then the whole family would actually sit and eat it together. Take them on field trips to supermarkets and show them how to read the labeling for fat, sugar and sodium content. Take them to greenmarkets and farmers' markets, if there are any nearby, and teach them about seasonal fruits and vegetables. Continue it in college with Survival 202, where each and every freshman will be required to continue these "life lessons." Set up communal kitchens in the dorms, and let the students cook for themselves on a rotating schedule.

Instead of teaching our kids bad habits, feeding them crappy food and making them unwitting subjects of the evil marketing geniuses' experiments in brainwashing, we could be teaching them useful survival strategies for long, healthy lives.

In Appendix 1 of this book, I've listed the names and contact information for all the schools we discussed in this chapter, so that you can follow up with them to find out what you can do to get the ball rolling in your school district.

THIRTEEN

HEALTH CARE
OR
SICK CARE?

I knew I was going to gain weight during my McDonald's month, but I and my team of health advisors were startled at how much I gained, and how fast. When I had my first weigh-in at Haelth on Day 5, I had ballooned from 185.5 to 195 pounds. Almost 10 pounds in five days of a McDonald's diet!

At my second weigh-in on Day 12, I was up to 203 pounds. I was adding roughly nine pounds every six days! I'd turned myself into the Anti-Jared! If we'd met during my diet, we both might have exploded, like matter and antimatter. At the rate I was going I'd gain 45 pounds by the end of the month. That didn't seem possible, but 18 pounds in two weeks wouldn't have been conceivable either if I hadn't just done it.

I have heard from a few doubters who refused to believe I put on that much weight. Believe me, I understand your skepticism. All I can say is, watch the movie again—it's all on the tape. Most of the experts I talked to afterward tend to think that a lot of the weight gain was water weight due to the massive amounts of sodium in the food. I'm sure I was packing on real fat, but the water retention probably played a significant role.

Bridget, my nutritionist, was already concerned by Day 5. She said gaining weight that fast is not healthy and suggested I stop eating McBreakfast, or only have a banana and a coffee. Sorry Bridget, I said, but McD's doesn't sell bananas. Okay, she said, then have a yogurt instead of a sundae for dessert. I could tell she didn't eat at McDonald's often. It was true that a small yogurt had fewer calories than one of their sundaes, but the regular size, especially if you added the crunchy granola topping, had more calories than even the hot fudge sundae. So at least take a multivitamin, Bridget said. They don't sell multivitamins, either, I replied.

I could feel the weight piling on. By the second week I had a gut where I'd never had a gut before. It became a welcome mat for food stains as I sat and ate. I was starting to get man-boobs, too. And I could feel my muscles shrinking and weakening. Bridget even said the loss of muscle mass was probably offsetting a little the weight gained in fat.

All I knew was, when these thirty days were over, I was going to have to go on a diet, big time.

Dieting is, after all, one of America's favorite pastimes. Americans spend more than $40 billion a year on dieting and diet-related products. That's roughly what the federal government spends on education in a year. It's more than twice what we spend on fitness and health products.

- An estimated 40 to 50 percent of American women are trying to lose weight at any point in time.
- One recent study showed that 91 percent of women on a college campus had dieted; 22 percent dieted "often" or "always."
- Four to six out of ten high school girls are on diets; almost half of nine- to eleven-year-olds are sometimes or very often on diets.
- Roughly four out of ten girls in the first, second and third grades report that they wish they were thinner. First-graders!

How often do fad diets work? Not often. Some 95 percent of all dieters regain their lost weight, or even add more weight, within one to five years.

Bonnie Liebman, director of nutrition at the Center for Science in the Public Interest, says that "miracle diets come and go like hemlines, hair-dos, and celebrity romances."

"They all have a brief flurry in the market," Kelly Brownell said. "They're all condemned by health professionals either because they're dangerous or because there's no data to support them. And then another comes along, and people say 'Oh, maybe this is the real one.' When I get calls about the latest diet fad, I imagine a trick birthday cake candle that keeps lighting up and we have to keep blowing it out."

We think of dieting as a particularly American craze. It's probably true that nobody's tried out as many wacky diet plans as Americans have. And no society has ever been as fat as we are (which tells you something about how well most diets work).

Apparently, though, weird diet plans have been around for at least a thousand years. They say that by 1087, England's William the Conqueror had gotten so fat he couldn't ride his horse—guess his conquering didn't include his appetite. So he went on the first recorded liquid diet in history: He stayed in bed and drank liquor instead of eating, thinking he'd lose weight that way (or maybe he just wanted an excuse for being a lazy drunk). At any rate, liquid diets have come and gone over the millennium, right up to SlimFast.

People have come up with thousands of other diet plans since the days of William the (Cake) Conquerer, even though no one really understood how food and fat are related until very recently. They could tell that if you didn't eat you wasted away, but no one understood that certain foods are required for survival, while others aren't. Food was just food, you ate what you could get, what you could afford, what you liked or what you could grow, raise or catch. And unless you were well-to-do, you ate pretty much the same thing all the time.

Another liquid diet, the vinegar diet, was a fad in Europe in the 1700s and 1800s. Men used to weigh themselves on public scales at the time. Don't ask me why. Entertainment was harder to come by, I guess. On the vinegar diet, Lord Byron went from "13 stone 12" (194 pounds) in 1806 to 9 stone (just under 128) in 1881.

In the 1830s, Sylvester Graham, an American Presbyterian minister and vegetarian, who invented one of the world's tastiest crackers, dreamed up one of the most boring diets in history, the Bland Diet. He believed that rich and spicy foods not only made you gain weight but influenced your behavior, making you act all, you know, "spicy." He was also against alcohol, coffee and tea. People on his diet, which no doubt included lots of Graham crackers, were too boring to sin.

I don't know why anyone would follow an undertaker's advice on eating well, but in the 1860s many people did. William Banting, a London undertaker, started a fad for cutting sugar, starch and root vegetables from your diet. In effect, he invented a low-carb, high-protein diet a century before Dr. Fatkins came up with his in 1972. Banting's book, *Letter on Corpulence*, was widely read on both sides of the Atlantic and may be the first best-selling diet fad book in history.

In 1913, an art importer and ink manufacturer named Horace Fletcher ("The Great Masticator") wrote his own best-selling diet book advocating chewing slowly to lose weight. The idea behind "Fletcherizing" was to chew a mouthful of food thirty-two times to wring all the nutrients out of it, then spit it out. (J. H. Kellogg, the cereal guy, was a big fan of Fletcherizing.)

The grapefruit diet, huge for a while in the 1920s, advocated massive consumption of grapefruit and an extremely strict 800 calories a day. There was also a molasses diet (perhaps promoted by the citrus and sugar cane industries?). One of the weirder and more disgusting diets, also from the 1920s, was the tapeworm diet. Apparently no one actually swallowed live tapeworms, but there were diet pills on the market that claimed to contain tapeworm segments.

Since 1970, as Americans' weight has ballooned, the diet fads have been coming hot and heavy:

• Dr. Robert Atkins came out with his low-carb diet in 1972. It faded, then made a big comeback in the late 1990s.

• Herman Tarnower's low-cal, high-protein Scarsdale diet swept the land in 1978.

• The low-fat Pritikin diet was all the rage in 1979.

• Judy Mazel's Beverly Hills diet, which was basically an update of the grapefruit fad, hit the best-seller list in 1981.

• Dean Ornish's low-fat, vegetarian Life Choice diet was big in the early nineties.

• The Zone plan had people loading up on lean meat, egg whites, fish and chicken in the late 1990s.

• And more recently, of course, there's the South Beach diet.

Not to mention the cabbage soup diet, the boiled egg diet, the Abs diet . . .

It's no big surprise that the Fatkins diet is popular again. It's the one that best fits our yuppie, consumerist, gluttonous age—the Rolls Royce of diet programs that promise you can eat what you want and still lose weight.

The key to all fad diets is that people think they're seeing immediate, magical results. And the reason people have to keep switching from one fad to the next is that that's all they see: short-term results. Because "most of the weight a person loses is water weight and lean muscle mass, not fat," according to the National Women's Health Information Center. That's why more than nine times out of ten, people gain back the weight they lose, or even more.

One way you can spot quack fad diets is that they always spin elaborate theories for why you should eat a ridiculously unbalanced diet. They're always telling you to cut out all the carbs, or all the fat, or all the protein or everything but fruit juice. That's how you know they're bunk. There's not a nutrition expert on the planet who'll tell you that a wildly unbalanced diet is a healthy diet.

Behind all the fancy-sounding theories, the ones that do seem to work, in the short term, work for the same reason: reduced calories. The Zone diet tells you to restrict yourself to about 850 calories a day. Anyone who eats only 850 calories a day is going to lose weight, whether they "enter the zone" or not. Recent studies suggest that the Atkins all-protein-all-the-time diet inhibits hunger. Foods high in fat seem to lead quickly to a feeling of satiation. So Atkins dieters may simply be losing weight the old-fashioned way: by reducing their caloric intake.

Sorry, there's no magic bullet. You gotta eat healthy and live healthy to be healthy and look healthy. End of story.

And don't get me started on diet pills. Thousands of brands of diet pills have littered the market over the last century, and not one of them, not one, produced real, healthy weight loss. At best they produced misleading short-term results. At their worst, they've been deadly.

In the 1890s, "thyroid extract" pills were big. Unfortunately, the weight you lost on them was all lean tissue, and they were bad for your heart. Laxatives were popular in the 1920s. In the 1930s it was dinitrophenol, an ingredient found in insecticides and explosives. Amphetamines also hit the market in the thirties and were widely prescribed, even for overweight kids, through the 1970s. Unfortunately, as we all know now, speed kills.

And remember Fen-Phen, the weight-loss magic bullet of the nineties? It was yanked off the market in 1997 after it'd been shown to lead to deadly pulmonary hypertension (PPH), valvular heart disease and endocardial fibrosis, as well as sleep disturbances, diarrhea and depression. Thousands of lawsuits were filed, leading to record-setting product liability payouts.

Meridia weight-loss pills, which flooded the U.S. market after Fen-Phen was pulled, have been linked to high blood pressure, rapid heart rate, heart arrhythmia, heart attacks, dilated cardiomyopathy, mental impairments, heart disease, stroke and seizure. Death is a high price to pay for the minimal, temporary weight loss the pill produces.

In 2000, the FDA issued a warning about the use of phenyl-propanolamine (PPA) in over-the-counter appetite suppressants like AcuTrim and Dexatrim, and urged manufacturers to pull all products that contained it. PPA causes something called hemorrhagic stroke: *It makes your brain bleed.* In 2004, the FDA banned ephedra, associated with high blood pressure, heart problems, stroke, seizures and death. It was the first time an over-the-counter herbal supplement was banned. Ephedra-based products had been popular with athletes, but the NFL, NCAA and International Olympic Committee had quickly outlawed their use. Major League Baseball had not, however, and when Baltimore Orioles pitcher Steve Bechler died of heatstroke that year, his use of ephedra was blamed.

But don't worry, there are plenty of diet pills still on the market. You can even buy them online. Phentermine, Xenical, Tenuate, Didrex, Adipex, Xenadrine and my fave, MetaboSpeed XXX (at least that one has an honest name).

Folks, I hate to be the bearer of bad news, but *there's no magic cure for obesity.* Sorry. The only way to lose weight and keep it off is to eat sensibly and to exercise.

If you want to hear some stories about how fad diets don't work, attend an Overeaters Anonymous meeting. You'll meet smart, breathtakingly honest people who've had the courage to face themselves and their problems head-on. They'll tell you how overeating is a product of a lifestyle formed when we're very young, in environments, both at home and outside, that encourage unhealthy habits, attitudes and appetites.

They'll describe how by eating they're trying to fill a void, an emptiness, that's got nothing to do with food. They'll tell you that the struggle to change those lifestyles is a physical, emotional and spiritual one. And they'll explain how no thirty-day miracle-cure diet fad can possibly bring a real change, because correcting a lifetime of bad habits is a 24/7/365 process.

"My history with food goes back to about five years old," Allen (not his real name) recalled. "Through therapy, I remembered my first food-related event. I was five, and I can recall an incident where my father was physically abusive to my mother. I went to the kitchen and made a sandwich and went to the boiler room and stuffed the sandwich down my throat, while I could hear the commotion of my father being abusive to my mother and my mother crying. So ever since I was five, I've been stuffing my feelings with food. . . . By age thirteen I was over three hundred pounds.

"When I got to college. . . . I went on a crazy diet and lost over one hundred and fifty pounds. When I put the food down, I started to pick up excessive alcohol and drugs. By the time I was in my late twenties, I had been in two or three rehabs for alcohol and drug abuse. My life didn't really change and get better until I came to the rooms of OA, simply because [food] was my primary addiction."

Allen had tried various diets. "I gained and lost over a hundred pounds since I was twenty years old, about seven times. The only success of any length was when I was with OA. Diets only took care of the symptom, they didn't take care of the problem. My problem was that I needed help, I needed people. I needed a program for living, I needed a spiritual life. I needed a lot more than just a diet plan."

Jane's overeating also started when she was a kid. "I came to OA about four years ago. Food has been a problem for most of my life. I grew up in a very controlling home. Both my parents are very heavy. Food was the only thing that the kids in my family had control over, we could eat whatever we wanted. . . . Feelings were not discussed in our home. When I left home . . . food was a major function in my life. I did not have a social life.

"When I was forty, I decided that I needed a shift, so I started looking at things to help me out. I decided to come to OA. At the time, I thought that I handled everything in my life and the only thing that I needed to change was how I handled my weight. I came and I lost the weight over time, but I put it back on.

"My problem is mostly my attitude. I tend to isolate more than anything else. Since I don't have much in my life, I tend to turn to food. I'm at a point now where I recognize that I have a choice to deal with my life in a different way. . . ."

"I was anesthetizing myself," Lena admits. "I can't deal with sadness, I can't deal with loneliness, I can't deal with feelings. . . . My dad died from obesity at age fifty-two. I'm forty-seven, and that scares me. February of last year I had an emotional breakthrough, I put pain down and joined Weight Watchers. I lost seventy pounds from then until now, but a month ago, the feelings showed up. The sugars call and the carbs call, and it's like this is an addiction. . . . But the minute that stuff is in my body, it might has well have been a needle or a bottle. Because it has the same effect."

Gaining weight wasn't the only bad physical reaction my body was having to my McDiet. The headaches persisted and got worse. They settled right behind my eyes. It felt like teams of little demon workers were hauling on my optic nerves, trying to drag my eyeballs into my skull.

And the tightness in my chest would not go away. Sometimes it was hard to catch a breath. Getting up those six flights of stairs to my apartment became a real chore, especially after the trip to California, where I spent the whole time in the car. By the third or fourth landing I'd be gasping and leaning on the railing like an old man.

It got to where the only time I felt good anymore was right after a meal. The fat, the sugar, the caffeine would be coursing through my body, and I'd experience a weird crackhead high, all jitterbuggy and goofy. But it was always fleeting, and way before the next meal I'd be back to what had become my normal self: lethargic, groggy, depressed and cranky. A total junk-food junkie.

There were times when I'd be so spaced-out and foggy in the head that I'd shuffle up to the McDonald's counter like a zombie and just stare at the menu overhead without being able to order. The whole ordering process was confusing. You ever notice how people walk into fast-food restaurants and stare at the board like the menu has changed since the last time they were there? These places have had the same menu for *decades!* What are you waiting for? There's no filet mignon today. Or lobster bisque. Just the same old McCrap they've been serving for years.

But now I understand. They're junk-food zombies, just like I'd become.

By Day 18, I was really feeling terrible. My whole body felt like it was in the midst of a complete breakdown. Have you ever had food poisoning? Your whole body kind of aches, your head pounds and you feel sick to your stomach? That's kind of how I was feeling in the hours between my feedings. And on top of everything else, my sex drive was down to nil. Nothing. I couldn't even think about sex. Which was probably just as well, cuz I don't think that Alex was real attracted to the lethargic, wheezy, McMusk-exuding slob I was becoming.

It was time for a check-up. I wanted to know how much worse this was going to get over the last twelve days of the experiment, and so did Alex.

So the next day I went and gave blood at all three of my docs. When Dr. Ganjhu saw me, the first thing she said was, "You look horrible. Where's your energy? It's completely sapped out of you."

At Dr. Isaac's office I got a lecture as he reviewed the results of my blood work. It was not good. Very not good.

My cholesterol when I started was 165. Now it was 225. My triglycerides were at 40, and now they were at 220. Dr. Isaacs kept leaning over the print-outs, muttering, "Oh my God, oh my God . . . I can't believe it. . . . Look at this. You were the picture of health before. It's crazy. I can't believe your cholesterol has changed so much. What you've done to yourself, it's not good."

He was especially shocked by the deterioration of my liver. Overeating can be as bad for your liver as alcoholism. It's called NASH syndrome, or nonalcoholic steatohepatitis, a liver disease that closely resembles alcoholic liver disease but occurs in individuals consuming little or no alcohol. The first step is excess fat deposited in the liver, which can cause inflammation and scarring, which can lead to cirrhosis. And cirrhosis is irreversible and potentially fatal. A lot of people don't know about this until it's too late and they're showing the symptoms. Biopsies on the livers of overweight and obese children reveal that some of them are already showing the scarring that suggests they're on the road to cirrhosis unless they change their diets.

On both of the scales they use in blood tests to monitor your liver function, SGOT (serum glutamic oxaloacetic transaminase) and SGPT (serum glutamic pyruvic transaminase), I was showing damage. My SGOT count, which is supposed to be under 37, had gone up from 21 to 130. My SGPT count had been 20 and was now 290—it is supposed to be under 40!

Basically, Dr. Isaacs said, my liver was turning into pâté.

Oh, and my blood pressure was up, another bonus.

Dr. Isaacs was not pleased. "I recommend you go on a low-salt, low-fat, low-cholesterol diet, which I know you're not going to do because of your project," he sighed. "But as soon as this is done, you need to get off this food. You need to stop."

But that's the whole problem, isn't it? People can't stop. Or they don't know how. Maybe some don't know they should. So they keep eating until it's time for drastic measures.

One of the most amazing experiences I had during the project was to be in a surgery room in Houston, Texas, and watch Drs. Adam Naaman and Carl Giesler punch a few small holes in a man's belly, sew his stomach into a little pouch about the size of a small apple, attach it to his small intestine underneath it and close him up again. It's the scene I bet most people fast-forward through on the DVD (that, or me puking).

It's called bariatric surgery, gastric bypass surgery, or a Roux-en-Y Gastric Bypass. Once a radical procedure with a lot of frightening possible complications, it's now become the weight-loss method of last resort to the stars. Carnie Wilson, Al Roker and Sharon Osbourne's successes with the operation have all helped to popularize it.

In 1998, around 25,000 bariatric surgery operations were performed in the United States. In 2004, 144,000 were performed.

It was first performed in the 1950s. Back then, they'd cut through the chest to do the surgery, attaching the stomach to the lower intestines and bypassing a big part of the intestines, which reduced how much food the body absorbed. It was complex, involved several weeks in the hospital and complications weren't unusual.

It's been refined a lot since then. An alternative to the intestinal bypass is to reduce the size of the stomach, either by stapling it or actually putting a kind of rubber band around it. And now they do it laparoscopically, which is much less invasive, and you're out of the hospital much quicker. The patient I saw operated on, Bruce Howlett, was up and walking by the end of the day; he checked out the next morning. He would go on to lose more than 100 pounds over the next several months.

I met Bruce and his wife, Tammy, before the surgery. She'd had the surgery three months before and had lost 50 pounds, gotten off all her diabetes meds and her blood pressure had gone down. Her lifestyle had changed as well. She walked more and ate less. For the first time in years she said she felt sexy and attractive.

Tammy also said a funny thing to us. Everyone in her family is big, and when they went to those family-style restaurants, they'd pile giant plates with huge portions and eat every bit of it (just as those university studies indicated people will do). After her surgery, she said, "If I go to a place like that now, that's like six or seven meals to me."

But wasn't surgery an extreme step? Couldn't she have changed her ways without it?

"Look, I got no willpower," she confessed. She had been yo-yo dieting for years.

Bruce said the same thing. He was also diabetic. He was drinking almost two gallons—I'll say that again for those of you who may have missed it the first time—he was drinking almost *two gallons* of soda every day. He had this giant mug that held 64 ounces—a half gallon of soda. He said he would go through three or four of those *a day*. It was nothing for him and Tammy to go through 100 two-liter bottles of Dr Pepper every month. And don't think that he's the only person in America doing this.

One day at work, Bruce went blind. Completely blind. He had to call Tammy and have her pick him up. He remained blind for a week. That's how he learned he had diabetes. His blood sugar count was so high that his doctor's machine couldn't register it. But even then, he said, he couldn't stick to any of the diets he tried. Surgery seemed the only option.

Drs. Naaman and Giesler have revolutionized the procedure. Tag-teaming the work like a pair of skilled dancers, they've cut the actual operating time down to thirty or forty minutes. They claim a 100 percent post-op cure rate with diabetes, and that the operation relieves hypertension in almost all their patients.

But does it work for significant weight loss? Bariatric surgeons seem reluctant to publish detailed results, but one who did reported that 9 percent of patients lost a fourth of their excess poundage. Pretty impressive. However, only 8 percent "attained normal weight." Also, some regained weight is almost inevitable, because what remains of the stomach stretches, and people often compensate for smaller stomachs by eating more frequently.

"I saw my doctor and he suggested gastric bypass surgery," Allen of Overeaters Anonymous told me. "I have two children, and they mean the world to me. I want to see them grow up and start lives. I knew if I continued on the same road, I might not be around until I was fifty or sixty. So I had the surgery. I'm very grateful for it, but that didn't take away the problem." He still has a hard time controlling his appetite.

The procedure is not cheap, either. It generally costs about $30,000, but if there are complications, that can soar as high as $100,000. And given that "more than a quarter of the phenomenal growth in health care spending over the past fifteen years is attributable to obesity" (as *The Washington Post* has reported), insurance coverage for the operation has become a matter of hot controversy.

Fewer than one out of four American employers covered gastric bypass surgery in their primary medical plans in 2003 and usually would only cover it if a patient could document that all other weight-loss methods had failed.

And that number may be dropping as the number of claims rises. For instance, Blue Cross and Blue Shield of Florida, which had been covering the surgery, announced in 2004 that it would stop doing so in 2005. Claims had been doubling annually for a few years. Cigna HealthCare also dropped coverage.

"Gastric bypass surgery is an extremely risky procedure that is of questionable benefit to the patient," Blue Cross Florida's chief medical officer, Robert Forster, told the Associated Press. "We are concerned at the growing numbers of these procedures while significant questions remain regarding quality of care, safety, efficacy and long-term consequences."

The appropriately named Dr. Harvey Sugarman, president of the American Society for Bariatric Surgery, told the *Houston Chronicle*, "Given the increasing number of procedures, insurance companies feel threatened by the rising costs. It's unfortunate, because it's shortsighted. In the long run, the surgery will be cost-effective."

Then again, Blue Cross and Blue Shield of North Carolina does cover the surgery, and it has also begun to cover obesity-prevention services, including the cost of doctor's appointments and some prescription diet pills. The company is trying to cover its own ass as well as its members' needs. "The company estimates that about 55% of its 3.1 million members are either overweight or obese," the Raleigh *News & Observer* reports. "Treatments associated with the extra pounds, such as care for high blood pressure, heart disease and diabetes, cost Blue Cross about $83.1 million in medical expenses in 2003."

The federal government added to the confusion in 2004, when Secretary of Health and Human Services Tommy Thompson declared obesity a "health crisis," and announced that Medicare was going to consider whether the surgery should be covered. As many as 7.4 million Medicare beneficiaries are obese and have one or more risk factors for heart disease that would make them eligible for the procedure.

Previous Medicare guidelines specifically stating that obesity of and on its own was not considered an illness were erased, but Thompson stopped short of the next step, actually declaring obesity a disease. That would pave the way for coverage of things like weight-loss therapy and behavioral and psychiatric counseling, not to mention diet programs like Weight Watchers and Jenny Craig. (Curiously, the Internal Revenue Service has considered obesity a disease since 2002. Expenses for gastric surgery, certain weight-loss drugs and nutritional counseling are now tax-deductible.)

Although it was designed as a desperate kind of last-ditch intervention, bariatric surgery is now being performed more often on obese children as well as adults. No doubt it has something to do with the fact that obesity-related annual hospital costs for children and youth more than tripled over two decades. "At least half a dozen major hospitals in the New York City area are now offering surgical options for obese teenagers," *The New York Times* reported in November 2004. "All said they had long waiting lists, and some hospitals said that in the past year dozens of teenagers have undergone surgery." Nationwide, about 1,000 of the operations performed in 2004 were performed on children, and as more of our kids become obese, that number will likely keep going up.

In Houston, I met Dr. William Klish, director of the Texas Children's Hospital. He talked about the especially severe impact of diabetes on the large Hispanic community in Texas. Hispanic kids in Texas are developing type 2 diabetes at a really alarming rate. These are ten-year-olds who will be having heart attacks in their thirties if they don't start to change their lifestyle.

Dr. Klish said that "five years ago, most pediatricians would have been appalled at the thought of this surgery in children." Texas Children's Hospital opposed the procedure until 2004, when it performed its first two operations on teenage girls.

Then there was sixteen-year-old Brandon Bennett, who weighed 420 pounds, enough to be denied access to the rides at the local Six Flags and was often sent home from school with high blood pressure. Texas Children's was scheduled to do a bypass on him, but his insurance company turned it down. The story made the local papers, and the enterprising folks at a place called Obesity Surgery Specialists offered to do him for free.

I'm not sure how I feel personally about all this. On the one hand, it sure seems to have worked for Bruce and Tammy Howlett, and if it saves some kids' lives, how can you not be for it? On the other hand, it's another magic bullet—the Associated Press called it "the Holy Grail of weight loss programs."

It's so typical of how American medicine deals with health problems: Instead of prevention, you wait until it's really serious, then develop a high-tech, high-cost surgical procedure. But the jury is still out on the long-term effects of this procedure on a child whose body is still developing. It just seems to me we'd all be better off if we'd focus as much on prevention as on treatment.

In Houston, I met a doctor who does. Dr. Lance Gould is like the Clint Eastwood of cardiologists. He stands about six-foot-six, and he's got this permanent tough-guy sneer. He doesn't put up with a losing attitude in his patients, either. "I make 'em shape up," he said to me, and I believe him.

Which is how all doctors should be. Tell people the truth. Give 'em some tough love. Get 'em in line and tell it like it is. "If you don't take better care of yourself, you're going to be dead at thirty-five." Your doctor should be your health coach. If he sees you screwing up your health, he should blow the whistle on you, before you need those pills or that bypass.

Dr. Clint told me he does not believe in surgery. He'd rather change the way you look and feel through your diet and exercise, change your lifestyle and prevent your ever needing that surgery. Pretty amazing for a cardiologist.

Or for any American physician. Because the sad truth is, when it comes to obesity and related illnesses, physicians have been part of the problem for years. Most doctors have no idea how to talk to, help or treat their overweight and obese patients. They watch their patients get fat, and then when it's abundantly clear that it's become a problem, because the patient has finally developed some "serious" complication like gout or diabetes or clogged arteries, they respond with a pill or surgery.

For one thing, the American medical establishment has never focused on nutrition. Dr. W. Allan Walker, who directs the Division of Nutrition at Harvard Medical School, said, "Nutrition is essential to medical education [but] American-trained doctors . . . do not get the nutrition training they need from medical schools."

As of 2003, a nutrition course was required at only 40 percent of med schools and osteopathic programs; it was an elective in 13 percent, and 24 percent of the schools integrated the subject into other courses. That leaves about 23 percent that seem to offer no nutrition training at all.

Six out of ten medical schools do not require a nutritional education course at all. And of those that do offer it, rarely is more than a single three-credit course offered. Dr. Andrew Weil, the mega-bestselling health guru, puts it simply: "Physicians are nutritionally illiterate."

Why? Because physicians in Western medicine aren't taught wellness and preventive medicine; they're set up only to react to illness. As Phil Lawler, that model phys ed teacher at Madison Junior High, puts it, "We don't have health care in this country. We only have sick care."

Did you know that in Chinese culture, you don't pay the doctor when you're sick? It's his job to keep you well. If you're sick, he ain't doing his job, and he don't get paid. If he comes around and makes you well again, then you start paying him.

Nutrition isn't glamorous or lucrative, but surgery is the highest-prestige, highest-paying career med students can strive for. And the giant pharmaceutical industry works hard to ensure that prescribing pills for whatever ails us is also top in every physician's mind.

Not surprisingly, then, studies have shown that childhood obesity is underdiagnosed at the doctor's office; physicians shy away from it because they know they don't have the proper training to deal with it. In response, Brown University has developed a couple of quick tools doctors can use to assess patients' weight problems: WAVE gauges—Weight, Activity, Variety (of diet), and Excess (of diet); and REAP, the Rapid Eating and Activity Assessment, a brief survey patients fill out in the waiting room and hand to the doctor.

Also, the Department of Health and Human Services has produced a free DVD to teach pediatricians, family physicians and other health-care providers methods for assessing and treating childhood weight issues. (HHS also produced one for parents and kids. You can order it free from www.ahrq.gov/child or by calling 1-800-358-9295, though the one I ordered took more than three months to arrive).

One of the worst consequences of doctors' lack of nutrition expertise is that it leads to overprescription of medication. While I was on my monthlong McDiet, my body wasn't feeling good, and I wasn't feeling good. I don't think there's anything mystical about that. I experienced three symptoms that happen to be among the most heavily medicated for in America. For that massive depression, that emotional roller coaster I rode every day, we take Prozac or Zoloft. I also experienced sexual dysfunction—I couldn't salute the general, as they say—for which we prescribe Viagra. And I couldn't focus, I couldn't pay attention, those tell-tale signs of Attention Deficit Disorder, for which we prescribe Ritalin to little kids as young as five years old.

What are we doing to ourselves? What would happen if, instead of resorting to drugs, we just ate less of the typical American junk diet? What if we focused on the cause instead of the symptoms? Got more exercise? Made our bodies feel better. Wouldn't our minds and our emotions follow along? Wouldn't we need fewer drugs?

There's no question that antidepressants and other medications help an enormous number of people and save lives. But there is also a large number of people who would benefit as much or more with preventive and lifestyle care—diet, nutriton, exercise—to address depression, sexual dysfunction and attention deficit disorder.

When people used to feel sad or "get the blues," now about 19 million Americans a year are diagnosed with clinical depression, dysthymia and seasonal affective disorder. Their symptoms are treated with drugs such as MAOIs (Nardil, Parnate), SSRIs (Prozac, Paxil, Zoloft) and tricyclics (Elavil, Asendin, Anafranil), as well as Zyban, Wellbutrin and Effexor. All these drugs can alleviate depression, but they can also cause side effects ranging from severe headaches to sexual dysfunction and even suicide in children and teens.

What used to be considered just fidgety and bored behavior in class is now considered a condition requiring the prescription of all sorts of drugs for attention deficit problems, with all sorts of troubling side effects. And now there's even a new "disease" caused by eating a diet too low in carbs: LCTS, or low-carb tunnel syndrome. I'm not making that up! Pretty soon your friends at the pharmaceutical companies will be cranking out all sorts of anti-LCTS drugs. Maybe your doctor should just remind you to eat a potato now and then.

The FDA is supposed to be looking out for you, monitoring and regulating all these new drugs. But just as at the USDA, the FDA is rife with conflicts of interest. A big *USA Today* exposé in 2000 found that more than half of the experts hired by the agency to advise on the safety and effectiveness of new drugs had financial relationships—"stock ownership, consulting fees or research grants"—with the very pharmaceutical companies whose drugs they were reviewing! Whose interests do you think they were looking out for?

In the wake of the Vioxx recall in late 2004, various changes and "reforms" to the FDA's drug approval process were being proposed. We'll see if real change happens.

Speaking of the medical establishment's nearly total disregard for the importance of good nutrition to our health, when we visited Texas Children's Hospital, I saw something that blew my mind.

A McDonald's.

In the hospital.

A children's hospital.

A fucking McDonald's in a children's hospital that is now stapling obese children's stomachs!

To me, that is utterly irresponsible, a flagrant violation of the doctor's pledge of *primum non nocere:* first, do no harm.

There's been a McDonald's at Texas Children's for seventeen years. You know what the doctors there told me? They said they had kids dying of cancer, and it was hard to get them to eat anything. At least they'd eat some fries, take a bite of a burger. Food they were familiar with. Junk they'd been eating all their lives.

Fabulous. So how about a smoke shop for all the patients dying of lung cancer? You know, stock it with brands they're familiar with—the ones they've been smoking since they were kids. To help calm their nerves as they fight off *death*.

It's a line McDonald's was quick to pick up on. In 2004, I was reading a *New York Times* article and found Ken Barun, one of Mickey D's senior vice presidents, saying the exact thing to the reporter:

> *"The doctors liked McDonald's because they could get something fast, and they said, 'Our sick kids will eat this food,'"* Mr. Barun said. *"Happy Meals provide kids with the nutrients they need,"* he said. *"From the emotional side, it really does help them get better."*

The nutrients they need? Which Happy Meals was this guy talking about? The one with the plain burger that gives the kid 7 percent of his daily fiber, 23 percent of his sodium, 19 percent of his saturated fat and 280 calories? The small fries that provide no vitamins A and C and 2 percent of his iron, but 210 calories, including 90 calories from fat? The small Coke with absolutely zero vitamins or minerals in it, but five teaspoons of sugar?

I'm only singling out Texas Children's because I was there. In fact, hospitals all across this great, overweight nation have fast-food franchises in them.

A 2002 University of Michigan survey found that six of the sixteen hospitals ranked the best in the country by *U.S. News & World Report* had fast-food franchises in them—McDonald's, Subway, Wendy's, Hardee's, Burger King, Pizza Hut and so on. Those hospitals were Johns Hopkins, Cleveland Clinic, the UCLA Medical Center, Duke University Medical Center, Barnes-Jewish Hospital in St. Louis and the University of Michigan Health System. The top-ranked pediatric hospital in the country, Children's Hospital of Philadelphia, had a McDonald's outlet in it. Why shouldn't there be one in Houston, right?

Food Service Directors magazine conducts a survey every year of 100 hospitals around the country. In 2003, they found that forty-three of them had some kind of "quick-service restaurant" on site, and though many of those were coffee shops, they also included total junk-food joints like Dunkin' Doughnuts. In my city, Elmhurst Hospital Center in Queens and Jacobi Medical Center in the Bronx have McDonald's outlets. There are Subway outlets at Coler-Goldwater Specialty Hospital and Coney Island Hospital, which also boasts a Burger King. New York–Presbyterian Hospital has its own Burger King.

One hospital I visited, Harlem Hospital Center, booted its McDonald's franchise when my movie came out in 2004.

Actually, it looks as though the combination of good information and bad publicity is goosing many more hospitals to reconsider their food-service contracts. But Ronald's not always leaving the premises without a fight. This is from the Cleveland *Plain Dealer* of November 22, 2004:

> *Cleveland Clinic CEO Dr. Toby Cosgrove wants to rid the nation's premier heart hospital of its McDonald's franchise, purveyor of artery clogging burgers and fries.*
>
> *But McDonald's, which contends it now offers lots of healthy choices and will work with the Clinic to tweak its menu, isn't "lovin' it."*
>
> *McDonald's corporate veep Marty Ranft defended the franchise, and vowed in a letter to Cosgrove that "McDonald's has no intention of terminating" the remaining 10 years on its lease. . . .*
>
> *The Clinic still insists McDonald's must go.*

Kids who've become overweight can be taught how to trim down before they get so fat and sick that they need gastric bypass surgery. The

Academy of the Sierras in Reedly, California, is a boarding school for obese kids from thirteen to eighteen years old. Some of the kids have been as much as 350 pounds overweight. The school combines weight-loss programs, behavior and lifestyle changes and field trips to restaurants and grocery stores, where kids get a real-world education in how to choose and consume the right foods. The kids lose an average of four pounds a week over a four- to eight-week course. It's a small school—and not cheap at around $5,500 per month—but it's a model that could be replicated around the country.

Still, the key to fighting obesity is prevention. The federal government has woken up to the problem. Having declared obesity a national crisis, HHS Secretary Thompson put close to $36 million of federal funding into a twenty-two-community test program in 2004 to build "a healthier nation by motivating Americans to eat nutritious foods and be physically active."

BusinessWeek focused on one of those communities:

In March, 2004, Dan Marino's, a casual dining steak and pasta house in St. Petersburg, Fla., owned by the legendary Miami Dolphins quarterback, retooled its menu. In addition to the regular fare of burgers, hot dogs, and fries, Corporate Chef Thomas Costello decided to offer kids an expanded choice of lunch and dinner options like grilled salmon or chicken with steamed corn and green beans, a side salad, and a dessert choice of fruit skewers with orange slices, pineapple chunks, and strawberries.

Costello was shocked at diners' positive response, as were most of the restaurant employees. "Now, 40% of our customers' orders are for the healthier kids' fare," he says.

That experiment was part of a $2.8 million federal grant to Pinellas County. Along with some ninety restaurants changing their menus, the grant helped the county fund free yoga and pilates classes, get more nutrition education into schools and enlist area physicians to consult with overweight patients.

Kelly Brownell has one idea that would dramatically increase the federal money available for obesity prevention: a $1.5 billion "Nutrition Superfund" that would be created by charging one penny of federal taxes on every soft drink we buy. One penny. You wouldn't even notice. A billion and a half bucks would buy a lot of advertising, promotions and educational materials that could be aimed at kids to offset the billions thrown at them by the junk-food marketers.

We have to start seriously looking at ways to change things in our daily lives and in our communities if we want to shift this trend. As former Surgeon General David Satcher said to me, "If you don't make time to take care of yourself now, then you better make time to be in hospitals later."

Truer words were never spoken.

FOURTEEN

McFREE
AT LAST

This is from my diary entry for Day 22:

Oh man, this food just makes me feel sick. It's beyond not wanting to eat it now. It hits my mouth and I'm completely disgusted. It's so greasy. Anything on the menu that's fried—the chicken sandwich or the fries, anything—I feel like I'm going to explode when I eat it. It's just so rank. I've had enough. I've had enough of this whole fucking movie.

The truly weird thing is that no matter how bad I feel . . . no matter how sick my stomach gets . . . no matter how gross I feel after eating it, I still crave it. I crave it all the time. I can feel absolutely horrible and still want more. Just now I couldn't finish the chicken sandwich, but then I thought, "Oh, I gotta have a hot fudge sundae now, ooohhhh." I'm at the point now where I'm dreaming about eating this food, no lie. I go to sleep and dream about going to McDonald's and eating the same food I eat all day. The monotony of my life is bleeding over into the monotony of my dreams. . . .

I tried the Veggie Burger, hoping for the best. It was the worst. The patty was covered with this goopy brown sauce that I guess was supposed to give it its "smoked" flavor, a "meaty" taste, a "mesquite" flair. I found it revolting. The patty tasted like ground-up sweat socks. (*Mmmm,* sweat socks. Smoked sweat socks.)

One day toward the end of my diet, completely spontaneously, I jumped into the jungle gym at a McDonald's Playland. My body was that ready for me to start exercising again. I played with the kids. It was fun. But I was not in that thing for more than two minutes when I had to climb out. I was so winded. Literally panting and wheezing. I thought I was going to pass out. It was so pathetic.

Around this time, I also started to lose my mind. I even made up my own pledge of allegiance while I was in Washington, D.C. It makes sense for our country, don't you think?

I pledge allegiance to all beef patties of the United States of America, and to the special sauce for which it stands, one lettuce, under cheese, indivisible, with pickles, and justice on a sesame seed bun, for all.

God, I was dying for a home-cooked meal. I'd even cook it myself! It's such a manly thing to do. Just give me the grub!

Hey, I mean that. It has been said that the main causes of obesity's spread in America were the rise and proliferation of fast food and the return of women to the workplace. Whether she's a single or divorced working parent, or it's a two-earner household, Mom's not staying at home and slaving over a hot stove the way she did a couple of generations ago.

"There is no cooking in America," Phil Lempert, the "Supermarket Guru," said to me. "What we have now, especially with the 76 million baby boomers, is a generation of adults who never saw their moms cook, never learned how to cook from their mom. We think that assembling is cooking. You take this and microwave it, take this and add water, take this and bake it. This is not cooking. If you look at the size of kitchens in new homes, people have bigger kitchens than ever before. But not to cook with—to fit two microwaves in.

"The average American today at four o'clock doesn't know what they're having for dinner. You come home tired from work, take whatever's in the freezer and heat it up. It has become so easy and affordable. When the TV dinner came out in the 1950s, it was something for the divorced dad who ate alone, or somebody working the midnight-to-eight shift. All of America eats this way now."

But, at least in two-parent households, the onus should not fall just on Mom. Dad should get into the kitchen, too. If parenting is a joint effort, then so is cooking. You both have a responsibility to your kids to teach them well, feed them well and prepare them for the world at large.

Split the kitchen chores with your wife, Dad. And don't tell me you can't cook. It ain't astrophysics or NASCAR engine maintenance. We're not talking Beef Wellington every night, here. You can cook rice or pasta. You can steam or stir-fry broccoli. You can shove a chicken in the oven. You can bake a potato. You can even bake potatoes in the frickin' microwave! Try it, it works. Experiment. You're a guy, you like gadgets. You programmed the satellite/cable remote, didn't you?

Maybe the biggest myth about cooking is that it takes hours to make a meal. Cooking dinner doesn't take that long at all if you learn how to cook. You can get meals together in fifteen minutes. A full, healthy meal that's a billion times better for you than a delivery pizza with that weird stringy cheese built into the crust, and at about half the cost. You just need a little practice. It's a skill like anything else, and the more you do it, the better you get. I started out a disaster in the kitchen, with the typical American male attitude, but with Alex teaching me and some practice, I'm going to be really good by the time we decide to have kids.

And if you do have kids, get them in the kitchen with you to help out. Studies have shown that getting kids, boys or girls, involved in the cooking—beyond teaching them kitchen skills they can use all their lives—is an excellent way to get them interested in food. Kids who help out in the kitchen are much more willing to try stuff they'd normally turn up their noses at.

Then sit down as a family as often as you can and share that meal. Enjoy the food you've prepared together, enjoy the time with one another. No TV. Talk to one another. After dinner, go out for a walk together. Play. Toss a ball around. Show your kids that physical activity is a good and fun thing. Get them into the habit of moving their bodies around.

Alex and I don't have any kids yet, but each day I go home and we eat dinner together. Every day. No matter how much work I have to do, no matter what's going on in my world, I leave the office and we eat together. You know where all that work will be when I'm done with dinner? Right where I left it. Make your health and your family's health a priority in your life now. Alex and I are building a positive routine for ourselves—that way, when we do have kids, it's already a daily habit that we have formed, a good habit on which we can build a healthy foundation for our kids.

I know that in today's world this all can be hard to organize, but if you focus on it as an important part of your family's life—and what bigger priority do you have, really, than your kids' health and well-being?—you can find the time. You find the time to pile into the car and go to KFC, don't you? You can find time to eat at home together. And you'll enjoy it more.

There's a sort of support group you can join now for encouragement in cooking at home: Slow Food USA. I think this is one of the greatest ideas ever conceived. This international anti–fast food movement has members in seventy chapters around the country and more chapters around the world! This is from their website, www.slowfoodusa.org:

Slow Food U.S.A. is a non-profit educational organization dedicated to supporting and celebrating the food traditions of North America. From the spice of Cajun cooking to the purity of the organic movement; from animal breeds and heirloom varieties of fruits and vegetables to handcrafted wine and beer, farmhouse cheeses and other artisanal products; these foods are a part of our cultural identity. They reflect generations of commitment to the land and devotion to the processes that yield the greatest achievements in taste. These foods, and the communities that produce and depend on them, are constantly at risk of succumbing to the effects of the fast life, which manifests itself through the industrialization and standardization of our food supply and degradation of our farmland. By reviving the pleasures of the table, and using our tastebuds as our guides, Slow Food U.S.A. believes that our food heritage can be saved.

Find a chapter near you at www.slowfoodusa.org.

It's not just the cooking that Americans don't feel they have time for. It's also shopping for the food.

Food shopping should be a pleasant, richly sensual experience, engaging all our senses—sight, touch, taste, smell. The way we used to "go to market" generations ago. The way many people in the world still do.

But for us, "going to market" means a drive to some giant supermarket, where we rush our squeaky cart down mile-long aisles past endless rows of branded products, most of which are so hermetically sealed in boxes, cans or plastic wrap you can't even tell there's food inside. Acres and acres of product, more like a sports arena than a grocery store. If we have to take the kids along, it's a nightmare battle of wills as they use every trick in *The Nag Factor*.

Then, too, millions of Americans live in poor areas where shopping for decent food is a virtual impossibility. There are neighborhoods in

New York City, for example, where the only "grocery store" is the corner deli or bodega, and the only "groceries" are some dusty, dented cans of tuna or black beans, half-hidden behind the racks of Slim Jims and bags of pork rinds.

I know middle- and upper-class people don't believe that. They think that poor folks could eat better if they just wanted to, that it's just laziness, ignorance and "cultural conditioning" that lead them to eat more fast food and bad food.

But think about this: There are typically three times as many supermarkets per capita in upper- and middle-income neighborhoods as there are in low-income neighborhoods. There are a lot of reasons the big chains don't build in the cities. One reason is our car culture—the chains like to build out where there are highways and freeways and space for them to create big parking lots. Real estate and transportation costs are higher in the cities, too. The chains worry about security in poorer neighborhoods. And because poorer people are on fixed or irregular incomes, the cash doesn't flow in as nice and smoothly the way it does out in the 'burbs.

Meanwhile, low-income households are six to seven times less likely to own cars, so even if they wanted to drive out to the suburbs to shop, they couldn't. They really are stuck with the lousy options of shopping at the corner store or the bodega. Or they could just eat out.

The evolution of the American grocery store into the supermarket has followed a familiar pattern: big, bigger, gargantuan . . . but not necessarily better. Before the twentieth century, when you went into a grocery store you'd read your shopping list to the grocer behind the counter, who'd pull your items for you. The first chain grocery store, the Great Atlantic & Pacific Tea Company, A&P, founded in 1859, still operated this way. Groceries in those days meant dry goods: flour, sugar, coffee, items like that. For meat you went to the butcher, for produce to the greengrocer, bread came from the baker and the milkman brought your dairy needs to your door in his horse-drawn cart.

In 1916, the first self-service grocery store, Piggly Wiggly, opened in Memphis. By 1940, there were almost 3,000 Piggly Wiggly locations nationwide. Safeway, A&P, King Kullen, Ralph's, Kroger's and the rest all followed suit. With their aisles of products all vying for the shopper's attention, these stores made brand names and packaging important for the first time. They also began the trend of one-stop food shopping as they added a meat counter, a fish counter and dairy and bakery sections. In short, they became "supermarkets." The frozen-food locker filled with Swanson TV dinners appeared in the early 1950s. By 1955, 60 percent of our food was bought in supermarkets.

Today, according to the Food Marketing Institute, there are almost 34,000 supermarkets (defined as grocery stores with $2 million or more in annual sales) in the United States, another 13,000 smaller grocery stores and about 1,000 of the giant wholesale clubs. (There are also, by the way, more than 130,000 convenience stores, like 7-Eleven, and about 21,000 gas stations that sell junk food and soda.)

And, wouldn't you know it, the rest of the world is racing to catch up with this American innovation. In Latin America, for instance, the supermarket phenomenon has grown as fast in the last ten years as it did in fifty years in the United States. Brazilians now do 75 percent of their food shopping in supermarkets. Mexicans now buy 30 percent of their food from a single chain, Wal-Mart. Meanwhile, in China the number of supermarkets exploded from zero to 6,000 within the last decade. Big supermarket chains are even starting to compete over South African townships like Soweto. (I wonder what Steve

Biko would think if he came back to earth and saw a ShopRite in the hood.)

As you push your squeaky cart down those miles and miles of super-market aisles, you're not just seeing boxes and cans of high-fat, high-sugar, processed goodness. You're also looking at the politics of food and the food industry. You're seeing favoritism, product placement, con-tractual obligations and piggyback partnerships in every single aisle. You're taking part in a world of advertising and target marketing, of psy-chological warfare and the impulse buy, without even realizing it.

Phil Lempert visits ten to fifteen supermarkets a week. He probably knows more than anyone alive about the supermarket shopping expe-rience and shares what he knows in books like *Being the Shopper,* on his website supermarketguru.com and on the *Today Show.* He walked me through a typical supermarket.

"The average American only spends twenty-two minutes on each shopping trip," he explained. "We go supermarket shopping 2.2 times a week. Now, in that twenty-two minutes, what that means is that each one of these products has one $\frac{1}{26}$th of a second to attract our attention. We're zooming up and down the isles."

Then again, he admits, when you've got two kids hanging from you, screaming for that cereal that's got the toy inside, it can be hard to stand there and read the label to see if that cereal's nutritious. And most of us won't know what we're reading anyway, unless we all get more education on nutrition.

Strolling down the cereal aisle—Lempert calls it "the parent's night-mare"—you can see all those billions of dollars the evil marketing ge-niuses throw into their cradle-to-grave strategies. Lempert said that "the cereal itself costs only about 15 percent of the price we pay for it." Half of the product's cost is in marketing and advertising.

And the supermarkets charge a premium to give your brand prime shelf space. "In a lot of supermarkets, you'll find breakfast cereals on one side of the aisle and candy on the other. That's not fair." Of course, the sugary kids' cereals are lower down, at the kids' eye level, while the healthier ones are up high.

That's why you also want to be careful with those big, gaudy displays they stick at the ends of the aisles, too, Lempert said. "This is what attracts most of our attention, but you always want to look at the price. Because only about 40 percent of what is in that end-aisle display is actually on sale. But because it's so bright and visual, we think it's all on sale."

Don't be fooled in the frozen-food section, either. I know a lot of people think that if they buy it at the store and heat it up at home, it's "homemade." Think again. It's the same processed crap, coming from the same scary meatpacking plants, injected with the same chemicals, supplied by the same wholesalers. Just because you heat it up at home doesn't mean it's any better for you.

One area of the supermarket where Lempert sees positive change is the produce department. As more of us Americans are getting hip, slowly, to the joys of fresh vegetables and salads, produce departments have been expanding both in size and in the variety of what they stock. It's not just iceberg lettuce and bags of carrots anymore. Still, you need to shop with care in this section, too.

"When it comes to produce, there are some serious issues," Lempert said. "Remember the Flavor Saver tomato of about twenty years ago? This was a product that was grown huge but had absolutely no flavor to it, and the good news is we didn't buy it. It disappeared very quickly. Now, in the age of genetic modification and biotechnology, the question is about food or feed. Do we want to just create a lot of feed, for a lot of people, in big sizes, and have them stuff their bellies? Or do we want food that tastes very good and is full of nutrition?"

When you're picking through veggies and fruit, Lempert advised, "Keep in mind that the closer produce is consumed to where it is grown, the more nutritious it is. A tomato that's grown 3,000 miles away and is brought on a truck for four or five days loses some taste and some nutrition."

In *Eat Here: Reclaiming Homegrown Pleasures in a Global Supermarket,* Brian Halweil of WorldWatch Institute explains that produce in the United States now travels an average 1,500 to 2,500 miles from the farm to your table—25 percent farther than twenty years ago. In the UK, the distance has increased 50 percent in the same period. Globally, the tonnage of food transported internationally has quadrupled over the last forty years.

The final trial for all supermarket shoppers is running the gauntlet on the way to checkout. First you pass the soda machines; then, flanking you as you wait to check out, there's all that candy and gum—the impulse buys. And lots of us give in to that impulse, don't we?

So what's the best way to shop in a supermarket?

First, Lempert says, make a shopping list and stick to it. Don't go when you're hungry. At the checkout, focus on the prices as they're being scanned, and ignore the candy.

My two cents on shopping: Never get sucked into the vortex that is the center of a grocery store. Do all your shopping around the perimeter of the store. That's where all the fresh food is—the produce, dairy, fresh meat and fish. The center is for boxed, frozen, processed, made-to-sit-on-your-shelf-for-months food. You have to ask yourself, "If this food is designed to sit in a box for month and months, what is it doing inside my body?" Nothing good, that's for sure.

And then there's organic food, which is increasingly available in normal supermarkets. Somehow the words "organic produce" and "Piggly Wiggly" or "Wal-Mart" just don't seem to go together, do they? I remember when the only place to go for organic was that hippie co-op just off the college campus.

"Organic" means farming and ranching without synthetic pesticides, chemical fertilizers, growth hormones or antibiotics. Organic farmers use frequent crop rotations and plant diversified crops (rather than chemical fertilizers) to replenish the soil, and beneficial insects to control the bad ones. They let livestock roam outdoors. And no genetically modified anything, or additives or preservatives. It can be just as productive and more profitable than corporate agri-techno-farming. Organic farms are home to a much wider diversity of insects, birds and wild plants than that chemically blasted agribusiness land. And, obviously, they aren't leaking deadly pesticides, antibiotics and supergerms into nearby waterways or building them up in our bodies.

The U.S. market for organic products has grown 20 percent or more every year since 1990. It's now around $10 billion. Not bad. The USDA says organic cropland doubled from 1992 to 1997, when it was at 1.3 million acres. In recent years the big supermarkets have caught on to the organic craze, and since 2000, more organic food is sold in supermarkets than anywhere else.

In 1990, Congress authorized the USDA to develop national standards for what gets to be labeled "organic" food. Apparently this was not a high priority for the Big Food execs occupying the department's offices on the revolving-door policy: It took the USDA *twelve years*, until fall 2002, to come up with them. By then, not coincidentally, organic farming had proven itself to be a viable enough enterprise that Big Food—General Mills, Smucker's, Heinz and others—had their own organic niche brands. The idea of Heinz selling organic ketchup at your local supermarket may fill you with suspicion, but Phil Lempert insists it's a good thing—the mainstreaming of organic food.

If you want to see how big and fast the organic food market has grown, just look at the Whole Foods Market chain. From a single outlet with nineteen employees in Austin, Texas, in 1980, one of maybe a half-dozen "natural-food supermarkets" around the country, by the end of 2004 it had grown to a national chain with 143 locations, plus Canada and the UK. (You can check their website, wholefoods.com, for store locations.) That makes it not only the largest natural-food chain in the country, but the fastest-growing company in the entire grocery industry. The Wild Oats Natural Marketplace chain (wildoats.com) now has stores in twenty-four states and British Columbia.

Still, I think the best place to shop for local and organic produce is at a local farmers' market. It comes closest to re-creating the old experiencing of "going to market." You can meet and talk to the actual people who grew the food you're buying, put it on a truck in the morning and drive it to the market. It doesn't get any fresher, unless you go out to the farm and pick it yourself. And because there's less overhead for them, it's almost always cheapest.

Throughout the United States and Canada, farmers' markets have seen explosive growth over the last decade. The website Local Harvest (www.localharvest.org) lists hundreds of farmers' markets around the country. The USDA has a similar list online (www.ams.usda.gov/farmersmarkets/map.htm). There's a great farmers' market within an easy walk of my apartment in Manhattan, at Union Square Park.

Farmers' markets have also been leading the way in bringing fresh produce, dairy and other foods into low-income, inner-city neighborhoods.

In Manhattan, the Washington Heights Greenmarket operates once a week at 175th Street and Broadway—call it Upper Harlem—an area where predominantly poor and working African Americans and

Dominican immigrants live, and where the usual food-shopping options are really lousy.

In the San Francisco Bay Area, there's Mandela Farmers' Market in West Oakland, a poor, predominantly African American area. Cooler still, there's the Mobile Market, a truck driven by area high school students that brings fresh produce to a lot of streets where there sure wasn't any available before. There's also a program under which fresh, local fruit and produce are being supplied to the sort of smaller neighborhood groceries and delis where you used to see maybe a half-dozen mealy old apples and some rotting onions. And they're bringing fresh goods from local farmers into some of the city's poorer senior centers and hospitals, too.

Fresh produce from local farms has even come to Compton, in South-Central Los Angeles. In 2004, ten Compton public elementary schools started augmenting the usual NSLP lunches with fresh fruit, vegetables and salads from California farms. The goal was to have all twenty-four elementary schools in Compton offering the fresh alternatives by 2005, and then to start adding high schools to the program.

According to *The Los Angeles Times*, it's a rousing success:

> In the cafeteria at Caldwell Elementary School in Compton one day recently, not a single child was in line for the standard lunch of corn-dogs and canned fruit. A few feet away, though, a dozen children stood waiting for the salad bar, where the line has gotten so long that an aide sometimes plays "Simon Says" to amuse the children while they wait. . . .
>
> More children are choosing salad than traditional school lunch. For example, at one campus the numbers were 266 versus 198 one day, and 257 versus 205 another day.
>
> The salad bars are part of a movement around the country called farm to school. Its advocates, including the federal government, say

they hope children will eat more healthful lunches and at the same time improve the health of small and medium-size farms by guaranteeing them customers.

Bear in mind, these are mainly desperately poor kids, some of them homeless. School lunches, lousy as they can be, are often the best meal they get in a day.

Interestingly, Tracie Thomas, the school nutritionist who started the Compton program, came to the school system after years in the fast-food industry. "I feel like my work is rewarding. I'm making a difference in kids' lives," she told the *L.A. Times.* "Before, I was contributing to the destruction of kids' lives."

Similar programs are now operating in Santa Monica, Berkeley and Davis schools.

And the feds are supporting this. Compton schools got a $2 million federal grant to start up the salad bars. The USDA's WIC program (Special Supplemental Nutrition Program for Women, Infants and Children) provides eligible low-income families and seniors with coupons they can redeem at farmers' markets for specific fresh fruits, veggies and herbs—one instance of the USDA actually doing the right thing.

In one of my favorite examples, the world-famous chef Alice Waters, creator of Chez Panisse Restaurant and Cafe in San Francisco, is also the founder and president of the Edible Schoolyard, an amazing program at the Martin Luther King Jr. Middle School in Berkeley, California. As a restaurateur and gourmet chef, Waters has always stressed the value of locally grown, organic foods, and has been extremely influential in supporting and organizing Bay Area organic farmers. In 1995, she began a collaboration with the King school to apply that knowledge and those principles. An abandoned lot next to the school was turned into an organic garden, where students grow food for their own lunches. The school's unused cafeteria was brought back to life. Students participate in and learn from every step of the process, from planting seeds to cooking and eating meals with their teachers to taking scraps and leftovers back out to the garden for composting.

Day 30 finally arrived. We had decided that for my Last McSupper, we'd throw a party. At McDonald's, of course. We invited friends, some with kids. Everyone who worked on the film came, plus some of the experts who appeared in the movie and now in this book. We had a cake. And a clown, Zoinks the Clown, instead of a Ronald. Zoinks was okay— not great, just okay. To get Ronald was five hundred bucks! Zoinks was a C-note. (What do you expect in NYC for a C-note?)

I knew I should be really excited—no more McDonald's for the rest of my life. *Woo hoo!* But by this stage, my body, my mind and my emotions were completely wrecked, and I think that says as much about the addictive qualities of this food as anything.

Over the last month, caffeine, sugar and fat had become my crack. And Alex had already told me she was going to make me go cold turkey—no soda, no sugar, nada—until my system was cleaned out and right again. I love coffee, but I wouldn't get any for two months. We had made a deal. My body had been mine to abuse for a month. Now it was hers for the next sixty days: my gut, my pimply face, my bloated and squishy liver. . . . I both was and wasn't looking forward to starting my detox the next morning.

I was remembering an exchange I'd had with Dr. Neal Barnard about food addiction.

"If someone is eating this food regularly," I asked, "and suddenly they go cold turkey, what are they going to feel?"

"With any addiction, the type of withdrawal you have varies dramatically," he replied. "With alcohol the withdrawals can be deadly; you can have seizures and so forth. For foods there's really no other withdrawal except you just crave that food. It can take several days for that to abate."

I was really hoping he was right.

And then, walking home through the Village after the party, feeling fat and worn out, I thought about how we had randomly surveyed 100 nutritionists from around the country, and forty-five of them had said you should never eat fast food. Of the remaining fifty-five, twenty-eight of them said you should only eat it about once a month. So, based on their recommendations, I'd eaten more McDonald's in a month than most nutritionists say you should eat in eight years!

And then, as I trudged home, visions of real food began to dance in my head. Asparagus, broccoli, cauliflower, radishes, beets. I wanted some collard greens, I wanted some okra, I wanted some green beans. Corn, lima beans, peas. Mashed potatoes, sweet potatoes, yams. Spinach. Real salads. (Mmmm, veggie delights.)

And that began to cheer me up.

On the Morning After, Day 31, I went for my final round of blood tests and checkups. The final reckoning of what damage I'd done to myself in just one month of a diet that's all too typically American.

My weight had topped out at 210 pounds. Remember, I was 185.5 when I started.

"You've gained a grand total of 24.5 pounds," Bridget announced.

Almost a pound for each day of my McDiet!

"That's 13 percent of your body weight, which is very significant," Bridget explained. "When you gain 10 percent of your body weight or lose 10 percent of your body weight, it causes a significant change in blood pressure, and there are other changes in biomarkers."

Bridget and I sat over a bunch of printouts, and she explained that the macronutrients (carbohydrates, fats, proteins) in my diet on a daily basis had usually far exceeded my needs, as estimated for someone of my height and weight. I was getting nearly double the calories, about 180 percent of the carbohydrates, one and a half times the protein and, on most days, at least twice the fat. Sure, I was meeting my RDA, which is the minimum recommended daily allowance for vitamins and minerals, thanks to the orange juice and enriched breads. I may have gotten enough vitamin C to prevent scurvy, but not nearly enough phytonutrients from whole foods to fight diseases such as heart disease and cancer. (Ever wonder why they say to eat five fruits and vegetables a day? Because that's where your body gets the compounds that protect you from illness, and I wasn't getting any of those.) Then we went over the totals of bad stuff I'd forced on my body over the month. All the sugar, all the fat. It was amazing.

I had been ingesting 450 grams of sugar every day—one pound of sugar a day. Thirty pounds of sugar—the equivalent of six of those five-pound bags you see at the supermarket—in a month.

When I asked Bridget how much sugar you should have in a month, she said "Choose sparingly. At the bottom line, it contributes to your carbohydrate intake. Carbohydrates should come from fruits, grains, bread, pasta, beans. Sugar can be a small percentage of that whole carbohydrate group."

The fats were just as bad.

"You're recommended to have about 80 grams of fat total, no more, per day," Bridget said. "You averaged about 184 grams, which is about 230 percent of what we would have wanted you to have. As far as saturated fat goes, it was around 240 percent of the recommended. You should have no more than 25 grams of saturated fat a day, and it ended up being about 60. Almost half a pound of fat everyday. That's approximately 12 to 15 pounds of fat in a month."

As my body tried to process all that fat, my cholesterol skyrocketed.

"It started at 165 and went up 65 points to 230, and then remained high up until the completion," she said. "It should be around 180. Your LDL, which is the bad cholestrol, went up significantly. The HDL increased a little bit, which is good, but the bad cholestrol went up more, so it was more damaging."

The blood tests showing what my McDiet had done to my liver were really scary. They were so bad that Dr. Ganjhu's first fear was that I had hepatitis A, which is a virus that can be contracted if somebody preparing your food has the disease and handles the food improperly. As it turned out, I didn't have hepatitis; my fast-food diet had simply deposited so much fat in my liver that it had become inflamed.

Elevated levels of two different enzymes in the blood, AST (aspartate aminotransferase) and ALT (alanine transaminase), are used to diagnose and track liver disease. My ALT should have been under 40. Before I began the project, it was at a very nice 17. It had shot up to 471 during the McMonth, presumably as my new diet had shocked the shit out of my liver, before settling down to a final level of 240. Six times what should be the maximum, and over 14 times where it had been when I started. The AST count similar shot up from 18 to a max of 171 before settling in at 86. It should have been under 37. (These tests, conducted by Dr. Lisa Chanwou, mirror those done by Dr. Isaccs and Dr. Siegel.)

Let me summarize that paragraph for you, just so we're clear: *In just one month of a fast-food diet, I was showing signs of liver disease.*

My liver had been in great shape before. Now it was damaged.

Think of how much fast food you eat—in a month, a year, over the course of your life. Think of what it could be doing to your liver. It's called cirrhosis.

The results of my uric acid test indicated that I was beginning to develop hyperuricemia, which can lead to gout and kidney stones.

Dr. Isaacs believed that those headaches I'd gotten, which I could only cure by eating more McFood, were either the result of hypertension, high blood pressure or hypoglycemia (low blood sugar). Dr. Siegel thought it was hypoglycemia as well. That would explain why all of Day 31, my first day of detoxing, the massive migraines started to come back. My body was screaming out for all those sugars I'd been ingesting for thirty straight days.

The chest pains remained a bit of a mystery. They might have been esophageal spasms. I sure did have plenty of heartburn during the month. And belching. But the pressure and pains seemed way beyond typical heartburn.

Many of the other things that had plagued me during the McMonth, the fatigue, weakness, depression, irritability, foggy brain and the total loss of libido, are all symptoms of hypothyroidism, a lack of sufficient thyroid hormone, which means your thyroid has trouble regulating your metabolism. Remember those studies suggesting that certain food substances can be addictive? The thyroid is thought to be a key player. Dr. Isaacs also said that in the long term, hypothyroidism might inhibit my ability to lose the weight I'd gained, and suggested taking a hormone supplement for a while until my body was back on track. (I opted to pass on the medication until I had completed Alex's detox diet.)

Basically, after one month on a McDonald's diet, I was a wreck.

I asked my health advisors if it would be okay with them if I continued the experiment for another month. They all looked at me like I was out of my mind.

"Of course not!" Dr. Isaacs laughed.

"What would you think would be the result if I would go back on the diet?" I pressed him.

"If you kept up the diet, you'd probably develop coronary heart disease in a greatly accelerated fashion. With the combination of high blood pressure and a high-cholesterol and high-fat diet, you'd develop heart disease in a more accelerated fashion than if you would have some other zingers like diabetes and cigarette smoking and family history."

With that sound advice, I ended my experiment, my month of being a fast-food lab rat. I gave myself up willingly to Alex's detox diet, and I can't tell you how wonderful it was to be eating real food again.

After two months, my cholesterol, liver function and blood pressure all returned to normal. I still wasn't exercising, just walking, and I lost 10 pounds. I believe this was all water weight; I'd been eating more than 6,000 mg of sodium a day during my McDiet—that's more than twice the recommended max (2,400 mg). Fast food is *loaded* with sodium.

After that, I went back to my normal, everyday, "eat what I want, but be sensible about it" diet. I started exercising, I stopped drinking soda for good, only having one every two months or so, and lost another 10 pounds in three months.

The last 4.5 pounds, though—those were the tough ones, the Yo-Yo pounds. It took me nine months to lose those pounds and keep them off. I would lose one and gain two, lose three and gain one, lose two and gain four. Up, down, up, down. I called my mom and told her how hard it was to lose these final pounds, and she said, "Congratulations, now you know how every woman in the world feels."

Thanks, Mom. I called Dr. Isaacs and asked him about it.

"Well, what you don't realize is that when you lose weight, those fat cells in your body, they never go away. They just get smaller."

That's a depressing thought. So now my body is filled with little skinny fat cells. They're just swimming around waiting for me to eat more calories than I expend, and they'll happily suck up the excess. Now I can gain 3 or 4 pounds in a weekend, lickity split, if I don't pay attention to what I'm putting in my body.

So now I pay attention to everything. I've become a very conscious consumer. What's in it? Where did it come from? What's it going to do to my body? I read the labels on everything now, which gets Alex very excited. "Look at you," she says, "reading a label!"

And no, I haven't been in a McDonald's since. Not even to pee.

FIFTEEN

THE GOLDEN HALOS

By the time this book is out, it will have been over two years since my McMonth in Hell. A lot has happened. Some of it good, some of it not so good and some of it just business as usual.

We spent the rest of 2003 finishing the movie—from shooting interviews and creating all the graphics and animation to weeks of editing. In the process, I got an invaluable education about food, nutrition, diet, schools, the corporate mentality, the courts, government. . . . an education that has continued every day, including lots that's in this book.

Our goal was to have the film done by January 2004, and we did it. It premiered at the Sundance Film Festival. Winning the festival's Best Director award for my first feature-length film, up against so many other great movies, was like when you were a kid and you dreamed of landing on Mars or winning the lottery. It felt like I was living someone else's life, somebody famous and successful. This was definitely some other guy's life. I kept waiting for him to tap me on the shoulder and take it back.

And then, when Big Food's hired attack dogs—Tech Central, CEI,

Center for Consumer Freedom, all of those characters—started yapping about the film before it had even gotten its theatrical release, I knew we were really on to something.

Super Size Me opened in the United States on May 7, 2004, in nine cities, on forty-one screens. Within two weeks that number had tripled. By May 19, it was the number-ten movie in the country. By midsummer it had grossed over $10 million—the third highest-grossing documentary in history!

The reviews poured in. Lots of raves and a few skeptical reactions. That's okay, I've realized that that comes with the turf. I was interviewed by the adorable Katie Couric, had a dream come true when I appeared on Letterman and then got to be on the funniest show on television, *The Daily Show*. Pretty soon my days were all media all the time.

All very weird for the boy from West Virginia.

The film opened outside the United States, and I began to travel around the world with it. Alex and I went to England—where, not surprisingly, it got a tremendous reception—Australia, New Zealand, Japan, South Korea, Germany, Austria, Switzerland, Spain, Holland, Sweden, Belgium . . . even Iceland. In all, we traveled to more than twenties countries in less than five months.

In Australia, the first country I went to, McDonald's unleashed a full-force anti–*Super Size Me* campaign. They put people in the lobbies of the theaters, handing out leaflets refuting everything the movie said. When I was interviewed on TV or radio, the CEO of McDonald's in Australia would be on the phone to the station minutes after I left the studio, demanding equal time. The friggin' CEO! This happened in other countries, too. Funny how when we were making the movie, absolutely no one from McDonald's would agree to talk. Now they were chasing me around like puppy dogs demanding attention.

They also rolled out a big new ad campaign that was supposed to show how "healthy" McFood is. The funniest was an ad that showed a

Granny Smith apple next to a McDonald's Baked Apple Pie, and said that their apple pies were only made with Granny Smiths.

On one level, this was a particularly hokey play to "Australian pride": the Granny Smith variety of apple was developed there in 1868, and has since become popular around the world because it's so hardy and takes so long to spoil. But it was the comparison itself that struck me—and a lot of Australians I spoke to—as completely ridiculous. On the one hand, you have this picture of a fresh, ripe, juicy, healthy, bright, shiny apple. On the other you have . . . this processed, industrial-strength dough sack filled with a goo of chemical preservatives and flavor enhancers, fat and sugar. Oh, and some pieces of something that look like they may have once been apples. There is no comparison between a real apple and a McDonald's apple pie. There's not even a comparison between a McDonald's apple pie and a real apple pie. You might as well be comparing that Granny Smith apple to a chair or a chainsaw. They have about that much in common.

In Japan, a very strange thing happened: No TV or radio station would interview me. Not one. Coincidence? I think not. In almost every country we went to, McDonald's reps threatened media outlets with the loss of significant ad revenue if they talked to me or did stories on the film. (How did I find out about this? The publicists and journalists told me themselves.) Japan is an even more obediently corporatized culture than we are, and its media are particularly subservient to advertisers. Just another rung in a tall ladder of media manipulation by a company that may only flip burgers and sell fries but still has the ability to influence what people see, hear and read. (Just think of what companies with real power are able to withhold from you in the news!) The sad thing is, Japan is one of the countries where the American fast-food diet has wreaked the worst havoc on traditional healthy eating habits.

In South Korea an environmental activist decided to copycat me and live on fast food for thirty days. But he only made it to Day 24 before

"doctors said he was risking his life" and made him stop. He did this before the movie even opened in South Korea. I swear I did not put him
up to it. (I wish I were that much of an evil marketing genius.)

"The toxic effect my eating had on my body was apparent, and doctors told me to abandon my experiment because it's too dangerous,"
the activist told an Asian news agency. "His liver was severely punished,
plus we found signs of heart problems," one of his doctors said.

You know what my favorite country may have been? Iceland. I loved
Iceland. An amazing place—an entire country built on volcanic rock,
where there are few trees and no forests. They still speak the oldest lan-
guage in the region, an ancient Norwegian dialect that's as close to
Viking talk as you'll get. Iceland's total population is only 280,000, yet
the capital city, Reykjavík, I'm sorry to say, is absolutely lousy with
American fast-food joints: KFC, McDonald's, Subway, Little Caesar's,
Burger King, Ruby Tuesday's, TGI Friday's . . .

On January 1, 2005, the highly respected and reputable medical publication
The Lancet published the results of a recent study that linked fast-food consumption to weight gain and insulin resistance (a key risk factor for type 2
diabetes). The study lasted fifteen years and involved more than 3,000 test
subjects (where *Super Size Me* only had one!). According to Dr. David Ludwig, one of the study's authors, individuals who ate fast food more than
twice a week over the fifteen-year period gained an extra ten pounds and
had a 200-percent increase in insulin resistance compared to those eating
fast food once a week or less. This relation remained even after taking into
account other factors that might affect body weight and diabetes risk, such
as socioeconomic level, exercise habits, amount of fat in the diet and so on.

To me, it was crucial to get the movie seen and discussed by as many
young people in the United States as possible. So even though I'd never

done public speaking before, I've been lecturing at colleges, high schools and junior high schools throughout the states. By the end of 2004 I'd done more than a hundred, and I'm sure it'll be a lot more by the time you read this. The response from students has been incredible. They offer phenomenal comments and ask really smart questions. They're hip to the problems and want to improve their diets and habits. They've given me hope for the future—that we really can turn this thing around. To help out, we developed a special reedited school version of the *Super Size Me* DVD, with teachers' guides, lesson plans and a whole bunch of additional information.

The regular DVD, by the way, came out in September 2004 and has been doing a great job of getting the news out to thousands of households and schools where folks didn't see the movie in the theaters.

Why didn't McDonald's feel it needed to throw around even more weight, legally and financially, against this one little low-budget documentary movie in America?

Because it wasn't just one little movie. The overwhelming groundswell of response to *Super Size Me* was just the latest proof of a growing awareness of just how bad fast food and junk food are, and what they're doing to us all. Even the Secretary of Health and Human Services at the time (before he stepped down) said, "It is important to pressure the food industry, the fast-food industry, the soft-drink society . . . getting them to offer healthier foods and put more things on the menu dealing with fruits and vegetables." By that point, Big Food had realized that it couldn't go on just denying and covering up and bullying its critics.

So, even while it's been doing that, the fast-food industry has gone into overdrive, coming up with all sorts of new ways to convince us all that fast food can be good, safe, healthy food. But don't be fooled. It's mostly just cosmetic changes and window-dressing, while they continue to flip the same old burgers.

No company's done more to give itself a shiny new image than McDonald's. By the second half of 2004, it was in the midst of what the *Times* of London called "the biggest rebranding exercise in corporate history." The *Times* quipped that McDonald's was "rushing upmarket faster than you can say 'hold the fries'. Their aim is to turn McDonald's into a combination of Pret A Manger and Starbucks, selling salads, barista cappuccinos and freshly made sandwiches."

All sorts of cosmetic changes were in the works. Besides the new "Premium" salads and all-breast-meat McNuggets, there were plans to introduce Subway-style made-to-order sandwiches, low-carb burgers and low-fat desserts, including fresh fruit. Internationally, the company has been testing lots of items that might add some local appeal to its menu, like white bean soup (*sopa de feijão blanco*) in Portugal. One of the goofier ideas was the redesign of numerous outlets into Starbucks-style "McCafes," with iced cappuccino, lounge furniture and wireless Internet access. None of which, *The Economist* pointed out, was a significant switch from McDonalds' core burger-flipping mission: ". . . [S]alads are sending a message to millions of customers: that it is now acceptable to eat at McDonald's again because the menu is 'healthier'—even though the vast majority still order a burger and fries."

Health by association again. You see, just by their selling salads, they get people thinking that magically, by veggie osmosis, everything else in the joint is better for you. *The Economist* article continued:

> *"There is no question that we make more money from selling hamburgers and cheeseburgers," says Matthew Paull, McDonald's chief financial officer. Sales growth is, he says, being driven by the "halo effect" of healthier food appearing on the menu. . . .*

The "halo effect." Another term for spin, for misdirection, for propaganda, meaning they aren't the angels you think they are.

Charlie Bell, that former CEO who lost his fight with colorectal cancer, put the halo on, too. In September 2004 he gave a remarkable interview to the reporter of that London *Times* article, in which he actually said, "We know we are not perfect, but we want to demonstrate that we are sincere about trying to do the right thing."

The article went on:

Asked about Spurlock's film (Super Size Me) *and Schlosser's hardhitting expose of the fast food business* (Fast Food Nation) *. . . he said: "These people have brought issues to the table around the world in varying ways. We don't necessarily agree with the way that they have done it, but we do want to be part of the solution. We have nothing to hide. We welcome criticism. We are on a learning curve."*

They welcome criticism! So speak up, everybody! Better yet, let your actions speak for you!

Other chains are racing Ronald upmarket. "The $144 billion fast-food industry, which serves almost a third of all American adults every day, is in the midst of a tectonic shift," *Fortune* magazine noted in August 2004. "Or so, at least, it appears. After all, two-thirds of American adults are now officially overweight, and the fast-food industry has been targeted as the primary villain in the obesity crisis. In the past few years it has been slapped with numerous lawsuits on behalf of overweight kids and has been the subject of powerful polemics in the media, such as the 2002 best seller *Fast Food Nation* and the recent documentary *Super Size Me. . . .*

"But it turns out to be awfully hard to devise healthier menu items that can work in a fast-food context. Fast food has to be, well, fast. It has to taste good. And it has to taste the same in California, Maine, and all points between. Just getting that much accomplished can be an operational nightmare—never mind whether the food is healthier or not."

Wendy's, for example, was testing a new item, mandarin orange slices. "Will customers actually order orange slices in place of French fries?" *Fortune* wondered. "Or will orange slices turn out to be just one more flop in the long history of healthy fast food that no one wanted?"

The article outlined some of history's highlights: There was the fast-food chain called D'Lites, which appeared in 1981, "offering lean burgers on multigrain buns and a big salad bar." Burger King was soon touting a low-sodium pickle, and McDonald's tested a Big Mac Lite.

D'Lites went belly up in 1987. McDonald's debuted the McLean Deluxe burger, "a 91% fat-free patty containing the seaweed derivative carra-geenan," in '91, and scrapped it in '96. Taco Bell launched its Border Lights menu in '95, killed it in '97. McDonald's introduced the horrible McSalad Shakers—aka the McTossers—in 2000, and killed them in 2003 (too late for me to avoid eating one), replacing them with its new "Premium" salad line. Wendy's and Burger King both offered new salad lines, too.

Having learned from past mistakes, *Fortune* noted, the fast-food industry often now simply offers items that "create the illusion of being healthier even though they aren't. And all the while it's continuing to peddle burgers, fries, and soda."

Fortune explained that

consumers often perceive an item that sounds higher quality as bet-ter for them, even if no mention is made of health or nutrition. That's why you see restaurants breathlessly shilling "applewood smoked bacon," even though it has the same amount of fat as plain old bacon. Kimberly Egan, a partner at the Center for Culinary De-velopment in San Francisco, which has done menu development for McDonald's, Burger King, and Wendy's, rattles off words that give "quality" cues: "slow-roasted," "tender," "grilled," "spicy," "fresh-cut." Fast-food companies use these words "to make people think that fast food is healthier for them," said Egan. Witness Burger

King's new Spicy TenderCrisp chicken sandwich, which is actually fried. (My emphasis.)

So you see what you're up against. These people aren't actually trying to make fast food healthier. They're just trying to make you think it's healthier.

It's all spin. All business as usual.

The one burger-flipping chain bucking the trend is Hardee's. While everyone else was rushing out their "healthier" lines, the geniuses at Hardee's figured, ah, screw it and went for broke, trundling out a new, bigger edition of their Thickburger—the aptly named Monster Thickburger, which the Associated Press described as "two 1/3-pound slabs of Angus beef, four strips of bacon, three slices of cheese and mayonnaise on a buttered sesame seed bun." It slams you with 1,420 calories and 107 grams of fat.

"Be afraid. Be very afraid," Hardee's self-parodying promotion for this thing declared.

And of course athletes were involved in promoting it—no less than ten "monstrous" NFL players, each working for two hours at a Hardee's drive-through, with proceeds from every Monster Thickburger sale going to the player's charity of choice. The Dishonor Roll included Kansas City Chief Will Shields, Minnesota Viking David Dixon, Jacksonville Jaguar Marcus Stroud, Carolina Panther Ricky Proehl, Tampa Bay Buccaneer Anthony McFarland, Indianapolis Colt Tarik Glenn and Tennessee Titan Brad Hopkins.

I hope the charities they gave to were the nearest children's hospitals—'cause that's where they're leading their young fans.

Executive director Michael Jacobson, of the Center for Science in the Public Interest, called the Thickburger "food porn," noting, "At a time of rampant heart disease and obesity, it is the height of corporate irresponsibility for a major chain to peddle a 1,420-calorie sandwich.

Eating one of these Thickburgers would be like eating two Big Macs or five McDonald's hamburgers. Add 600 calories' worth of Hardee's fries and you get more than the 2,000 calories that many people should eat in a whole day. If Hardee's persists in marketing this junk, it should at least list calories right up on the menu board."

Have you ever eaten at a Hardee's? My point exactly. Most of us don't, that's why they're not even in the top ten when it comes to fast-food restaurants. This was their attempt to get new business, to get attention. Believe me, you may go once, but I doubt you'll go back.

Undoubtedly the most despicable spin is the way these companies use their corporate charities to convince us all that they really care about kids.

Wendys' Dave Thomas Foundation helps orphaned kids find good homes. I'm not kidding. Burger King sponsors physical activity and fitness awards for kids at a bunch of schools around the country. I'm still not kidding. And KFC has its Colonel's Kids child-care charity. Even friggin' Outback Steakhouses support youth sports (though how kids who've just devoured a Bloomin' Onion are supposed to push themselves away from the table and go out to play sports is beyond me).

But by far the most repulsively phony attempt by any of these companies to improve its image and convince the world that it's a caring corporate citizen is McDonalds' annual World Children's Day, begun in 2002. Every November, this "worldwide fund-raiser" tries to guilt everyone who walks into a McDonald's into donating one dollar to the Children's Day fund. In addition, McDonald's earmarks some portion of the billions of dollars it earns making your kids fat and sick with its food. It then donates these ill-gotten gains to . . . the Ronald McDonald House Charities, of course.

All sorts of celebrities have lent their famous names to World Children's Day, from Céline Dion to Venus and Serena Williams to Jessica Simpson. Even worse, though, UN Director-General Kofi Annan and UNICEF actually gave their blessing to this thing when McDonald's began it in 2002. A group of health professionals wrote an open letter to UNICEF, saying in part:

> McDonald's is a global leader in the marketing of junk food that is creating soaring rates of childhood obesity and type 2 diabetes, and that is disrupting traditional ways of food preparation in families and cultures. It is truly a challenge to see how this partnership with McDonald's is consistent with UNICEF's claim to promote "good nutrition" to the world's children. As you know, McDonald's markets precisely the high-added-fat, high-added-sugar junk food that undermines good nutrition for the world's children.

In 2004, Ken Barun, who runs the Ronald McDonald House Charities, said, "We hope 2004 will be our most successful World Children's Day yet, and through increased fundraising, RMHC will be able to improve the health and well-being of even more children worldwide."

Let me repeat that: McDonald's was going to improve the health and well-being of children worldwide!

Man, that's one highly polished halo.

SIXTEEN

VOTE WITH
YOUR FORK

It's not just the fast-food chains that seem to be in a panic to improve their image. There have been big rumblings throughout the food industry. One of them is what's been going on with sugar.

In November 2004, the World Health Organization came out with its global health and diet recommendations. As NewsTarget summed it up: "The primary recommendations by the WHO report? Reduce the consumption of refined sugars (added sugars), processed foods, and salt, restrict the marketing of unhealthy foods to children, and enhance product labeling and health education so that people can make better informed decisions about foods. . . ."

At the Sugar Association, Andy Briscoe was continuing to insist that there were no links between refined sugar and diabetes or obesity, that it was all-natural, low in calories and good for you. "Sugar has an image problem—and we know it," he told USA Today. The association was gearing up for a big new ad campaign, its first in years, extolling the virtues of sugar.

No one seems to be listening. In what USA Today calls "a sea change in the national image of sugar," more and more consumers have been fleeing from refined sugar, reaching for low-sugar products at the supermarket and embracing new artificial sweeteners like Splenda.

In the last couple of years, food manufacturers have flooded the supermarket shelves with reduced-sugar versions of familiar brands. In 1999, *USA Today* says, just 36 new reduced-sugar products hit the market. In 2003, that skyrocketed to 607. In 2004, 948 were rushed out.

If you've been to the supermarket and shopped for cereal lately, you've seen the boom in new reduced-sugar products. Big cereal companies are working overtime to rebrand and reposition many of their best-known kids' cereals, from the "sugar-toasted" treats of old to "healthier," low-sugar versions. The boxes for brands like Trix and Cocoa Puffs, which used to shout at you about how much sugar they contained, are now shouting at you about how much sugar they've cut out. The box for the new reduced-sugar version of Trix, for instance, screams 75 PERCENT LESS SUGAR in letters that dwarf the Trix Rabbit, who's practically lurking in a corner. General Mills ran ads with mawkish sentiments like "75 percent less sugar. Because kids are sweet enough."

General Mills, which puts out Trix, also announced that it was going to switch all of its cereals—Trix, Cocoa Puffs, even Lucky Charms—to whole-grain. (Cheerios, Wheaties and Total were already whole-grain.)

"Kellogg's, meanwhile, is hyping Frosted Flakes and Froot Loops with 33% less sugar," *USA Today* reported. "There's even a version of Cap'n Crunch being tested with about one-third less sugar."

And it isn't just cereal. All sorts of popular drinks—Coke, Pepsi, Hawaiian Punch, even Red Bull—have come out with new reduced-sugar versions.

Even Krispy Kreme, seeing its sales and stock price drop in 2004, announced that it was coming out with a sugar-free doughnut.

Huh? If you look up the word "oxymoron" in the dictionary, there's a picture of a sugar-free Krispy Kreme doughnut next to it.

Trying to capitalize on the Atkins and South Beach diet fads, all sorts of food companies are now marketing "low-carb" products, too. As *Slate* commented,

> [W]e have taken this craze to its illogical extreme, creating all manner of low-carb products, including pastas, cereals, chocolate bars, brownies, and ice cream. In other words, instead of cutting out refined sugars and flours and moving toward more of a "whole foods" approach—which is what these diets implicitly (or explicitly) encourage—we have managed to spawn yet another generation of packaged, artificial foods. This is precisely what happened with the low-fat food boom in the '80s and '90s, which promised a dietetic alternative to every conceivable high-fat snack food and dessert. Indeed, many of the same physicians who tout the health benefits of low-carb diets worry that the sheer availability of low-carb options will confuse and mislead many dieters.

By the way, just because some cereal is now "low in sugar" doesn't mean it's good for your kids—at best it's just a little less bad for them. Just because the steak fajitas or the ice cream is "low-carb" doesn't mean you can gorge on it and still lose weight.

None of these companies is offering these new "improved" items because it cares about your health. They're just reacting to changes in the marketplace and competing as always with one another for your attention. Business as usual.

McDonalds' efforts to renovate its image seem to have been more successful in the United States than elsewhere. In the UK, that image has gotten so bad that the company actually rolled out a new advertising campaign in October 2004. In it, the universally recognized—and, in the UK, pretty universally despised—Golden Arches were replaced by . . . a Golden Question Mark.

The new tagline? "McDonald's. But not as you know it."

The website *Adrants* speculated that the company was "apparently attempting to distance itself from the association between the logo and clogged arteries. . . . Perhaps trying to distance itself from the recent 'Super Size Me' movie in which Morgan Spurlock eats McDonald's food exclusively for a month risking his death, the campaign will promote coffee, salads, fruits and, of course, calorie-laden bagels with cream cheese. Leo Burnett is behind the campaign and there's no doubt it's being considered for the U.S. as well."

Even in disguise, the company couldn't get a break in England. As the new ad campaign was being rolled out, the British tabloid *The Sun* got its hands on an internal memo from McDonald's to the casting company hiring actors for new TV commercials, which said: "Because this is McDonald's, it is important that all artists submitted to us are NOT FAT OR OVERWEIGHT in any way."

The article went on:

> A spokeswoman for McDonald's . . . insisted their original instructions had been changed.
>
> She said: "We are shocked that the brief has appeared embellished in this completely inappropriate way and are investigating.
>
> "We can only thank The Sun for bringing this to our attention."

Uh huh. We should *all* thank *The Sun*.

A director I know was hired to shoot a spot for McDonald's and was meeting with the corporation to talk about his top casting choices. One of them was a man who was just barely noticeably overweight. The corporation said, essentially, we like him, he's funny, but we've been having a bit of an image problem lately, so we'd rather not cast someone with a double chin. Apart from big purple Grimace, I've never seen a person of size in a McCommercial. Judging by their track record, I doubt I ever will.

In more good news from the UK, in 2004 the British government proposed a simple "traffic light" system of warning labels for foods: fatty, sugary foods would get a red label, good foods green. The government said the program would be voluntary on the part of food makers and supermarkets at first, but indicated that legislation would follow if they didn't comply. Parliament also proposed a ban on junk-food TV advertising before 9 p.m. This was done the same week that Hardee's launched the Monster Thickburger in the U.S. Can you see the difference of priorities and ideals here?

In Australia, I saw nutrition labels right on the wrappers for cheeseburgers. Which in my opinion is too late. Why? Because I've already bought it. So, not only are you going to take my money, you're going to make me feel bad afterward!

Which brings me back to the issue of legislation versus litigation. While I was making and then promoting my movie, Ashley Pelman and Jazlen Bradley, the Bronx teens whose lawsuit got me started on the whole thing, continued to pursue their case in court. After Judge Sweet ruled against their initial suit, their lawyer, Samuel Hirsch, filed an amended complaint. Judge Sweet ruled against that one, too.

But Hirsch was not to be dissuaded. In October 2004, he appealed to a higher court, this time arguing before the U.S. Second Circuit Court of Appeals. I guess the third time's a charm, because in late January of 2005, "A federal appeals court . . . revived part of the widely watched obesity suit" against McDonald's, according to Reuters, and "ruled that [Sweet] wrongfully threw out certain portions of the complaint in September 2003." Judge Sweet had done so because he said that the case didn't link the plaintiffs' injuries with eating McDonald's foods. The appeals court now says that link did not need to be established in the initial filing, but could have come later at the pretrial proceedings, so it was wrong of him to throw it out on that basis. So the case will now go back to Judge Sweet for further proceedings.

I guess it ain't over till the fat lady sings!

Attorney John Banzhaf says he continues to believe in the power of lawsuits like Ashley and Jazlen's to goad politicians into regulating the fast-food industry. But in March 2004, the House of Representatives overwhelmingly approved the so-called "Cheeseburger Bill"—officially the Personal Responsibility in Food Consumption Act. Which, Reuters explained, "would require courts to dismiss certain lawsuits filed against manufacturers and sellers of any food product as well as the trade associations that represent them. The bill would affect lawsuits seeking damages for injury resulting from weight gain, obesity, or any health condition associated with obesity as a result of consumption of these products."

In short, no more lawsuits like Ashley and Jazlen's, blaming the fast-food companies for making them sick.

This kind of "tort reform" tends to pit probusiness Republicans against Democrats, who like to see business be accountable for what it does to customers. They also pit industry lobbies against the Association of Trial Lawyers of America, both of whom put a lot of pressure on Congress and throw a lot of money into influencing votes on either side. Representative Ric Keller, an overweight Republican from Florida, was the Cheeseburger Bill's chief sponsor. As the website *Outside the Beltway* noted, Keller's district "is home to Darden Restaurants Inc., owner of the Olive Garden and Red Lobster chains."

"The gist of this legislation is there should be common sense in the food court, not blaming other people in the legal court," was Keller's often-repeated explanation for why he proposed the bill. The vast majority of Americans must agree; when polled, nine out of ten said they thought lawsuits like Ashley and Jazlen's should be forbidden.

As I write this, it's unclear how the Senate will vote on the issue in 2005. In the past, the Senate has shot down similar House bills, like one banning lawsuits against the gun industry and another forbidding asbestos sufferers from suing the building industry. But since the Republicans gained four Senate seats in the '04 elections, giving them a 55-44-1 majority, who knows?

Meanwhile, individual states weren't waiting on the federal government: By November 2004, twelve states had passed cheeseburger bills of their own, and a number of others are considering similar legislation.

Big Food's hired guns at fronts like the CCF and CEI have been crowing about how this legislation marks the triumph of "common sense" and "personal responsibility" over the food police and the nanny state, but I'm not sure they should be popping the cork on the champagne just yet.

Remember Big Tobacco. When the health-care costs from smoking-related illnesses became too crushing for states to bear, that's when the state attorneys general mobilized, tore a page from the "ambulance-chasers' " book and hauled the tobacco companies into court on the class-action suits that eventually yielded that massive $246 billion settlement.

Government is just beginning to wake up to the health-care burdens of obesity-related illnesses, to the tune of $117 billion annually. As the costs to states' health-care systems add up, those attorneys general may well look to Ronald McDonald et al. to help carry the load.

Personally, I still favor legislation over litigation. And I still think the best way things get changed is when we, as consumers, citizens, parents, teachers and school administrators, take matters into our own hands.

When we change our own habits and lifestyles, our own communities and schools. When we make change happen personally, and locally.

Marion Nestle has a great quote about this: "Every time you eat, you vote with your fork." I hope she doesn't mind my stealing it for the title of this chapter, but it's such a brilliant suggestion. Every time you put food into your mouth, you make a stand. You say, "Here's what I stand for. Here's what I believe in. Here's what I want for me, my family, my future."

And it's got to start with the kids. The kids are the ultimate victims here, the target market who are right in the bull's-eye of all those billions and billions of dollars of rapacious advertising and marketing schemes. We need to oppose all that "cradle-to-grave" marketing with some cradle-to-grave life strategies that promote healthy choices and smart habits.

That's why I've made a special effort to appear at schools and discuss these issues with students and teachers. That's a great place for change to start. It doesn't relieve parents from their responsibility to be good role models at the dinner table at home. But as surrogate parents who have our kids in their care for so much of their daily lives, teachers and school administrators have a heavy responsibility as well.

So I want to end this book with a few more examples of schools that have turned around their lunchrooms and emptied their vending machines of the sodas and candy. Every one of these schools is setting a great example for all of us:

At Aptos Middle School in San Francisco, parents worked with the staff and the administration to turn the lunchroom around. They threw out the pizzas and chips, the Slim Jims and BBQ wings, and replaced them with "fresh deli sandwiches, sushi, pasta, salads, homemade soups, and fajitas." As at other schools, teachers say the kids' behavior and academic performance have improved. And the new lunchroom is even making money.

In Sacramento County, the lunchrooms of the Folsom Cordova unified school district used to serve the same old junk and snacks. New food service director Al Schieder got rid of all that crap, and now kids can choose from "salads, lower fat pizza, sandwiches, pasta, wraps, rice and noodle bowls, and sushi." He also got rid of the stigmatizing system whereby low-income kids formed separate lines for their subsidized meals; now they all line up together, and pay by punching their student ID into a machine, "so no one has to know if or how much a student is paying for his or her lunch."

James Monroe High School in Los Angeles "had difficulty working within its existing beverage contract to eliminate sodas and other sugary beverages." They switched vendors and stocked vending machines with 100 percent juices and water. Students became the "Food Crew," taste-testing new menu choices. There's a new salad bar. Lunchroom revenue is up, and "teachers report that students are more focused in class and behavior has significantly improved, with a 74% reduction in violent suspensions and a 24% reduction in all suspensions since before the change in school foods and beverages."

Venice High School, also in L.A., proves that kids will choose healthier snacks over junk food, if they're given the opportunity. In fact, students themselves, "concerned about their school's food selections," spearheaded the change. "With the help of health teacher Jackie Domac, the students became nutrition advocates and began working on strengthening the school's food policy." Now the school vending machines are stocked with water, juices, soy milk and granola bars—and sales have doubled.

Across the country in Maine, funding from the state's Big Tobacco settlement helped Old Orchard Beach schools create a "Nutrition Team, consisting of members from food service, physical education, administration, and a school nurse. The team implemented Tulane University's CATCH nutrition education curriculum and wrote school vending policies that led to the removal of sodas and junk foods, and replaced them with water, 100% fruit juices, and healthier snack options."

In Minneapolis,

faced with alarming statistics about childhood overweight and obesity rates, Assistant Principal Bryan Bass of North Community High School re-evaluated the school's beverage vending practices. With the support of the administrative team, he contacted the district's Coca-Cola representative, who was willing to work with the school to provide healthier choices. As a result, the school increased the number of vending machines from four to 16, stocked 13 machines with water or 100 percent juice, two with sports drinks, and one with soda (which has limited hours of sale). They also instituted competitive pricing, selling water for $0.75, sports drinks and 100 percent juices for $1.00, and soda and fruit drinks for $1.25. The water machines were strategically placed in high-traffic areas and students were allowed to drink water in the classroom. Today, soda sales are down, but vending profits have increased by almost $4,000 a year and the total number of cases of beverages sold has more than doubled from the previous school year, with water being the best seller.

In Mississippi's McComb school district, teachers no longer use candy or snacks as classroom rewards. Vending machines have been removed from elementary schools; in higher schools, the Coke logos on machines have been removed, and they're stocked with water and real juice. Even faculty-lounge vending machines have been emptied of their junk-food items.

See Appendix 1 of this book for contact information about CSPI and other organizations that can tell you about other schools that are making similar changes.

And if you need more proof that parents can change what goes on in your kids' schools, check out the California group Parents Advocating School Accountability (PASA) at their website (pasaorg.tripod. com). From the website you can download brief, no-nonsense publications full of proven, firsthand advice—from Aptos Middle School and elsewhere—on banning sodas and junk food from schools, how to organize fundraisers and other topics.

What else can I say? You are what you eat. If you continue to eat bad food, you'll continue to suffer bad health. If you want things to change, remember that change starts with you. Your own life, your own family.

Get aware. Get active. Parents, you are your children's primary role models. What they see you do, they'll imitate. Take charge of your kids' diets, their attitudes about food, their daily physical activity, their schools. Take them shopping at your local farmers' market and organic greengrocer. Make the buying, preparing and enjoying of good, wholesome food a cherished family activity again. You don't have to completely stop eating burgers and fries—I know I haven't—but you can stop buying them processed and chemically infused from fast-food joints, and patronize a real sandwich shop that makes you a real burger and real fries right there when you order. Stop driving yourself and your kids everywhere from door to door. Get out and walk or ride a bike with them. Plant some veggies with them in your backyard. I promise you'll remember how fun it is and how good it makes you feel. And you'll be teaching your kids invaluable life habits.

Teachers, you are your students' surrogate parents during all that time they spend with you in school. If you surround them with healthy messages about nutrition and health, you'll support the guidance of their parents. You should be doing everything you can to promote smart habits—in the classroom, the lunchroom and the gym. Don't use candy bars as rewards! Don't serve junk food for lunch!

And all of us can let our elected political representatives, on every level of government, know where we stand on the issues—from legislation like those cheeseburger bills to food safety to nutritional labeling to vending machines in public buildings. The giant corporations of

Big Food have all those lobbies, spending all that money to influence politicians the wrong way. We have to be our own lobby, a lobby of consumers and citizens and parents, showing them that we've got a lot of money at our disposal, too.

And we're prepared to vote with our forks.

ACKNOWLEDGMENTS

This book would not have been possible without the assistance and help of the following groups and individuals. Very special thanks to:

At the Center for Science in the Public Interest (CSPI): Joy Johanson, Melissa Osborn and Margo Wootan.

At the Physicians Committee for Responsible Medicine (PCRM): Neal Barnard, Daria Karetnikov, Amy Lanou, Mindy Kursban and Jen Reilly.

At Cornell University: Larry Robinson, Colin Campbell, Betsy Bihn, Chang Lee and Susan Brown.

At Worldwatch Institute: Brian Halweil, Danielle Nierenberg and Erik Assadourian.

At Johns Hopkins University School of Public Health: Lance Price, Jay Graham and Ellen Silbergeld.

To Carole Morrison—for not being afraid to tell the truth.

And to these invaluable, irreplaceable people: Marion Nestle, Lisa Young, Jeremy Chilnick, Antonia Demas (founder of Food Studies Institute; see school appendix), Marzena and Marcin Stawiccy (Poland), Sermet Yuce (Turkey), Margareta Brilioth, Lars Kjellström (Sweden), Guillaume Garoff (France), Jennifer Lady, Susan Linn, John Banzhaf, Eric Schlosser, Greg Critser, Kelly Brownell, Phil Lempert, Bridget Bennett, Lisa Ganjhu, Steve Siegel, Daryl Isaacs, Paul Stitt, Phil Lawler, Deb Larson, Greg Bretthauer (Dean of Students at Appleton Alternative School), Vanessa Ruddy (parent who spearheaded organic foods program in Olympia, Washington), Paul Flock (child nutrition supervisor for Olympia school district), Harold Goldstein (California Center for Public Health Advocacy), Michelle Smith (Texas Action for Healthy Kids), Brian Wimer, everybody at McSpotlight.org, Senator Tom Harkin, Derek Miller, Billy Ingram of TVparty.com, Bob Wallace, Elyse Cheney, Jennifer Hershey and, last, John Strausbaugh and Karen Pelland—you guys are the greatest.

APPENDIX 1

IMPROVING YOUR CHILD'S SCHOOL LUNCH PROGRAM

Here is contact information for some parents, administrators and school nutritionists who've successfully reduced or eliminated fast food and junk food in their schools.

Aptos Middle School PTSA
San Francisco, California
Contact: Ericka Lovrin, Principal
Phone: 415-469-4520

Folsom Cordova Unified School District
Sacramento County, California
Contact: Al Schieder, Food Service Director
Phone: 916-355-1180
E-mail: aschied@fcusd.k12.ca.us

James Monroe High School
Los Angeles, California
Contact: Lisa Jones, Grants Coordinator
Phone: 818-892-4311
E-mail: lrath1@lausd.k12.ca.us

Venice High School
Los Angeles Unified School District, California
Contact: Jacqueline Domac, Teacher and Education Policy Specialist
Phone: 310-713-7070
E-mail: info@nojunkfood.org
www.nojunkfood.org

Old Orchard Beach Schools
Old Orchard Beach, Maine
Contact: Jacki Tselikis, RN, School Health Coordinator
Phone: 207-934-4461
E-mail: jackiet@oobschools.org

North Community High School
Minneapolis, Minnesota
Contact: Bryan Bass, Assistant Principal
Phone: 612-668-1726

McComb School District
McComb, Mississippi
Superintendent: Dr. Pat Cooper
Contact: Child Nutrition Director
Phone: 601-684-4661

Olympia, Washington, School District
Contact: Paul Flock, Child Nutrition
Supervisor
Phone: 360-596-7007
E-mail: pflock@osd.wendet.edu
or
Vanessa Ruddy (parent who spearheaded
Olympia organic program)
E-mail: vanessaruddy27@hotmail.com

Perspectives Charter School
Chicago, Illinois
Contact: Debbie O'Connor, Food
Services Manager, Chef
Phone: 312-604-2132
E-mail: doconnor@perspectivescs.org

Natural Ovens Bakery, Inc.
Contact: Paul A. Stitt, Founder and Re-
search Director
P. O. Box 730
4300 County Trunk CR
Manitowoc, WI 54221-0730
Phone: 920-758-2500
Fax: 920-758-2594
E-mail: paul.stitt@naturalovens.com
www.naturalovens.com

Nutritional Resource Foundation
Contact: Melissa Luedtke
P.O. Box 730
Manitowoc, WI 54221-0730
Phone: 920-758-2500 x131
E-mail: nrf@naturalovens.com

The Edible Schoolyard
Martin Luther King Jr. Middle School
1781 Rose Street
Berkeley, CA 94703
Phone: 510-558-1335
Fax: 510-558-1334
E-mail: info@edibleschoolyard.org
www.edibleschoolyard.org

The following websites offer a lot of useful information as well:

http://www.cspinet.org/nutritionpolicy/get_involved.html
The website for the Center for Science in the Public Interest (CSPI) includes excellent links.

http://www.cspinet.org/schoolfood
CSPI's School Foods Tool Kit for parents, teachers and administrators.

http://www.actionforhealthykids.org
A comprehensive site with a great "How You Can Take Action" section. Action for Healthy Kids, founded by former U.S. Surgeon General David Satcher, is a nationwide nonprofit initiative with fifty-one state teams dedicated to each state's individual needs and situation. Find out what's happening in your state and how you can get involved.

http://www.cfpa.net
California Food Policy Advocates (CFPA) is a statewide public policy and advocacy organization dedicated to improving the health and well-being of low-income Californians by increasing their access to nutritious and affordable food. It's located in San Francisco; the telephone number 415-777-4422. The website contains all sorts of helpful information on how to communicate with your elected officials, write op-eds in your local newspapers, etc.

http://www.choiceusa.net
Citizens for Healthy Options in Children's Education (CHOICE) was launched in 1994 by a group of concerned parents to promote wholesome plant-based meals and nutrition education in our nation's schools. It is supported entirely by individual contributions. CHOICE produces and distributes teaching materials, supports parents working for change in their schools, assists school administrators and food-service providers in developing healthier meals, encourages students to select healthier food choices and reports on similar efforts throughout the United States. The site has a great "Effecting Change" section to help you get involved. Call 1-877-6CHOICE, or e-mail info@choiceuse.net.

http://www.nojunkfood.org
This website was designed as a resource for those who wish to create a healthier learning environment for kids. Despite the lobbying efforts of big soda and junk-food companies, a tremendous wave of healthier alternatives in school vending machines and cafeterias is sweeping the nation. Legislators, community activists, teachers, parents, vendors, administrators and, most important, students, are stepping up to the plate and creating change.

http://www.foodstudies.org
The Food Studies Institute is a nonprofit, educational and charitable organization dedicated to improving the long-term health and education of children. Founder and President Antonia Demas, PhD, has won several awards for her creativity and effectiveness in teaching children in schools about plant-based nutrition and cooking. She's worked with over 300 schools nationwide, creating programs where kids learn not only about growing their own food (by doing it) but also about the cultural and historic significance of the meals the children create. By making cooking and food a fun group project for thirty plus years, Antonia has found children's responses overwhelming. E-mail or call for more information on how to bring Antonia's unique learning program to your school. Call 607-387-6884, or e-mail antoniad8@yahoo.com.

APPENDIX 2
McDONALD'S FOOD TESTING RESULTS

Originally, I had intended to list the name of the independent lab that performed the tests and provided the results below. The lab that I chose to use was recommended by a nationally recognized nutritionist as one that is reliable and frequently used by journalists when they have tests performed for publication in major national papers. When I asked for permission to reproduce these results and give credit to the lab, they refused me permission to use the name of their lab in associaton with the results they'd provided.

Items tested: Quarter Pounder w/cheese, Filet-O-Fish, Fiesta Salad w/Salsa Dressing, french fries (medium), Chicken McNuggets (six pieces), Fruit 'N Yogurt Parfait (small).

In order to make direct comparisons between the results from items we purchased at a McDonald's in midtown New York and the nutritional information provided on the McDonald's website, we have to calculate the content of 100 gram serving sizes for each. This is because the servings we provided to the lab were predominantly larger than those listed on the website. For instance, the website says a medium serving of fries weighs 114 grams and contains 350 calories. But the medium fries we brought to the lab weighed 123 grams and contained 430 calories.

Obviously, you're getting a lot more calories than you expected, simply because you're getting more fries, but the test results *also* show that the 100 gram serving of fries we bought yielded 352 calories, but on the McDonald's website it says 307. That means that the number of calories we discovered in the french fries is actually 15 percent higher than McDonald's is telling us. This has a double whammy effect—not only are you getting more fries than you think, but even if you knew you were getting more fries, the calorie information on McDonald's website is flawed beyond any reasonable margin of error (plus or minus 10 percent), making it impossible for someone to accurately count calories.

Following are the results in detail:

	FULL ITEM		100g SERVING	
FRENCH FRIES (medium)	LAB (123g)	WEBSITE (114g)	LAB	WEBSITE*
Calories	430	350 (23% more)	352	307 (15% more)
Total Fat	23g	17g (35% more)	19g	15g (26% more)
Saturated Fat	5g	3g (67% more)	4g	2.6g (54% more)
Sodium	220mg	430mg (95% more)	350mg	193mg (81% more)
Sugars	1g	0g	.5g	0
Dietary Fiber	2g	4g (half as much!)	1.7g	3.5g (half as much!)

Here, all categories for both serving sizes were telling, some more than others. Not only were all the bad things underreported on the website, the amount of dietary fiber, which is a *good* thing, was *overreported* on the McDonald's website by a factor of two. Also, the McDonald's website claims there is no sugar in the fries, yet the lab detected 1 gram, which makes sense since the website lists "dextrose" in the fries ingredients.

	FULL ITEM		100g SERVING	
FIESTA SALAD with Newman's Own Salsa Dressing	LAB (435g)	WEBSITE (369g)	LAB	WEBSITE*
Calories	510	390 (31% more)	118	106 (11% more)
Total Fat	30g	22g (36% more)	6g	6.83g (14% more)
Saturated Fat	13g	10g (30% more)	2.7g	3g (11% more)
Sodium	1,090mg	870mg (25% more)	250mg	236mg (6% more)
Sugars	4g	2g (twice!)		

This item did not have particularly egregious inaccuracies in the "per 100 gram serving" comparisons of data (though still outside a 10 percent margin of error), but the actual size of the item was nearly 18 percent larger and yielded significantly higher levels of nutritional content. This is significant not only because it is the item McDonald's rolled out as part of the Go Active! Happy Meal to adults this past spring, but it's a *salad*, for Pete's sake.

	FULL ITEM		**100g SERVING**	
CHICKEN MCNUGGETS (six pieces)	LAB (102g)	WEBSITE (96g)	LAB	WEBSITE*
Calories	320	250 (28% more)	316	260g (21.5% more)
Total Fat	21g	15g (40% more)	20.5g	15.6g (31.4% more)
Saturated Fat	5g	3g (67% more)	4.7g	3.13g (50% more)
Sodium	770mg	670mg (15% more)	750mg	698mg (7% more)

This item was only 6 percent larger in the lab than on the website, but the percentage by which the lab results were higher than the website data was significant, both in full serving and 100 gram serving comparisons.

	FULL ITEM		**100g SERVING**	
FRUIT 'N YOGURT PARFAIT (small, without granola)	LAB (186g)	WEBSITE (142g)	LAB	WEBSITE*
Calories	170	130 (30% more)	92	90
Sugars	25g	19g (32% more)	13.5g	13g

This item we bought was 31 percent larger than is indicated on the McDonald's website; therefore it would follow that the calories and sugar content were higher by the same percentage. So there appears to be no flaw in the way McDonald's analyzes nutritional data here, but rather in the portions it doles out to customers.

	FULL ITEM		**100g SERVING**	
QUARTER POUNDER WITH CHEESE	LAB (184g)	WEBSITE (199g)	LAB	WEBSITE*
Calories	550	540	298	271 (okay, 9%)
Total Fat	32g	29g (10% more)	17.5g	14.5g (20.6% more)
Saturated Fat	16g	13g (23% more)	8.6g	6.5g (32% more)

This is interesting because the portion size we got was actually *smaller* than what McDonald's lists on the website . . . and *still*, the calories and fat were much higher in the lab, as indicated by the "per 100g serving" results.

FULL ITEM			100g SERVING	
FILET-O-FISH	LAB (132g)	WEBSITE (141g)	LAB	WEBSITE*
Calories	390	410	297	290
Total Fat	21g	20g	16g	14g (14% more)
Saturated Fat	5g	4g (25% more)	3.68g	2.84g (29% more)

Nothing noteworthy here except that the fat is outside a 10 percent margin of error.

*McDonald's does not provide nutritional information for 100 gram servings on their website. These numbers are based on my calculations from the information provided on the McDonald's website.

**Our lab report stated that their reports apply only to samples tested and that they made no guarantee that this sample is representative of the product lot.

***McDonald's website claims, "While the ingredient information is based on standard product formulations, variations may occur depending on the local supplier, the region of the country and the season of the year. Further, product formulations change periodically. Serving sizes may vary from quantity upon which the analysis was conducted." The information used in this appendix was drawn from what was available on the website in September 2004.

APPENDIX 3

YOU ARE WHAT YOU . . . SMOKE?

Sure, you'd never knowingly give your money to a big, bad tobacco company like Philip Morris. But you may be doing just that, without realizing it.

Go to the website of Altria—the vague, innocent-sounding name Philip Morris goes by now (http://www.altria.com). Look at all the different food products that come under that one gigantic corporate umbrella. See any products here you buy?

Kraft Foods North America Brands

Coffee

General Foods
Gevalia
International Coffees
Maxim
Maxwell House
Sanka
Starbucks*
Yuban

Frozen Treats

Kool-Aid Slushies

Powdered Soft Drinks

Country Time
Crystal Light
Kool-Aid
Tang

Ready-to-Drink

Capri Sun†
Country Time

*Starbucks is a registered trademark of Starbucks U.S. Brands Corporation.
†Capri Sun is a registered trademark of Rudolf Wild GmbH & Co. KG, used under license.

Crystal Light
Kool-Aid Bursts

Bacon

Louis Rich
Oscar Mayer

Cold Cuts

Louis Rich
Oscar Mayer

Dinner Kits

Taco Bell*

Frozen Pizza

California Pizza Kitchen†
DiGiorno
Jack's
Tombstone

Hot Dogs

Oscar Mayer

Lunch Combinations

Oscar Mayer Lunchables

Macaroni & Cheese Dinners

It's Pasta Anytime
Kraft
Kraft Easy Mac
Velveeta

Meat Alternatives

Boca

Meat Snacks

Tombstone

Pastas and Sauces

DiGiorno

Cookies

Barnum's Animals
Biscos
Café Crème
Cameo
Chips Ahoy!
Crispin (Puerto Rico only)
Dad's
Danish (Puerto Rico only)
Family Favorites
Famous Chocolate Wafers
Hony Bran (Puerto Rico only)
Konitos (Puerto Rico only)
Lorna Doone
Mallomars
Marshmellow Twirls
Nabisco (Puerto Rico only)
National Arrowroot
Newtons
Nilla
Nutter Butter
Old Fashioned Ginger Snaps
Oreo
Peak Freans
Pecan Passion
Pecanz
Pinwheels
SnackWell's
Social Tea
Stella D'oro
Sweetie Pie (Puerto Rico only)
Teddy Grahams
Wild Thornberry's**

*Taco Bell is a registered trademark owned and licensed by Taco Bell Corporation.
†California Pizza Kitchen is a trademark owned and licensed by California Pizza Kitchen, Inc.
**Nickelodeon and all related titles, characters and logos are trademarks owned and licensed by Viacom International Inc. All rights reserved.

Crackers

Air Crisps
Better Cheddars
Cheese Nips
Club Social (Puerto Rico only)
Crown Pilot
Doo Dad
Flavor Crisps
Harvest Crisps
Honey Maid
Nabisco Grahams
Nabs
Premium
Ritz
Royal Lunch
SnackWell's
Sportz (Puerto Rico only)
Stoned Wheat Thins
Sultana (Puerto Rico only)
Triscuit
Uneeda
Waverly
Wheatsworth
Wheat Thins
Zwieback

Ice Cream Cones

Comet Cups

Packaged Food Combinations

Handi-Snacks
Lunchables

Refrigerated Ready-to-Eat Desserts

Handi-Snacks
Jell-O

Snack Nuts

Corn Nuts
PB Crisps
Planters

Sugar Confectionery

Altoids
Callard & Bowser
CremeSavers Hard Candy
CremeSavers Soft Candy
Jet-Puffed
Kraft Caramels
Life Savers
Milka L'il Scoops
Nabisco Fun Fruits
Terry's
Toblerone
Trolli

Cold Pack Cheese

Woody's

Cottage Cheese

Breakstone's
Knudsen
Light n' Lively

Cream Cheese

Philadelphia
Temp-tee

Grated Cheese

Kraft

Natural Cheese

Athenos
Churny
Cracker Barrel
DiGiorno
Handi-Snacks
Harvest Moon
Hoffman's
Kraft
Polly-O

Process Cheese Loaves
Kraft Deluxe
Old English
Velveeta

Process Cheese Sauce
Cheez Whiz

Process Cheese Slices
Kraft Deli Deluxe
Kraft Free Singles
Kraft Singles
Kraft 2% Milk Singles
Velveeta

Process Cheese Spread
Easy Cheese

Baking Chocolate/Coconut
Baker's

Baking Powder
Calumet

Barbecue Sauce
Bull's-Eye
Kraft

Breakfast Beverage
Postum

Coating Mix
Oven Fry
Shake 'n Bake

Condiments
Grey Poupon
Kraft
Sauceworks

Cooked Cereal
Cream of Wheat

Cereal Bars
Nabisco

Dips
Kraft

Dog Biscuits
Milk-Bone

Dry Packaged Desserts
Dream Whip
D-Zerta
Jell-O
Knox Gelatin
Minute

Energy Bars
Balance

Fruit Preservatives
Ever Fresh

Frozen Whipped Topping
Cool Whip

Ice Cream Topping
Kraft

Margarine
Parkay (Puerto Rico only)

Pasta Salads
Kraft

Pectins
Certo
Sure-Jell

Pickles/Sauerkraut
Claussen

Pie Crusts
Honey Maid
Nilla
Oreo

Ready-to-Eat Cereals
- Alpha-Bits
- Banana Nut Crunch
- Blueberry Morning
- Cinna-Cluster Raisin Bran
- Cranberry Almond Crunch
- Frosted Shredded Wheat
- Fruit & Fibre
- Golden Crisp
- Grape-Nuts
- Great Grains
- Honey Bunches of Oats
- Honeycomb
- Nabisco (Puerto Rico only)
- Natural Bran Flakes
- Oreo O's
- Pebbles*
- Raisin Bran
- Shredded Wheat
- Shredded Wheat 'n Bran
- Spoon Size Shredded Wheat
- Toasties
- Waffle Crisp
- 100% Bran

Rice
- Minute

Salad Dressings
- Good Seasons
- Kraft
- Seven Seas

Sour Cream
- Breakstone's
- Knudsen

Spoonable Dressing
- Kraft Mayo
- Miracle Whip

Steak Sauce, Marinade, Worcestershire
- A. 1.

Stuffing Mix
- Stove Top

Toaster Pastries
- Kool Stuf

Yogurt
- Breyers†
- Jell-O
- Light n' Lively

Kraft Foods International Brands

Confectionary
- Bis
- Côte d'Or
- Daim
- Freia
- Gallito
- Laka
- Marabou
- Milka
- Prince Polo & Siesta
- Shot
- Sonho de Valsa
- Suchard
- Sugus
- Terry's Chocolate Orange
- Toblerone
- 3-Bit

*Pebbles is a registered trademark of Hanna-Barbera Productions, Inc. Licensed by Hanna-Barbera Productions, Inc.
†Breyers is a registered trademark owned and licensed by Unilever, N.V.

Biscuits

Chips Ahoy!
Club Social
Express
Kraker/Hony/Aveny Bran
Lucky
OREO
Ritz
Trakinas

Salted Snacks

Estrella
Lux
Maarud

Coffee

Blendy
Carte Noire
Gevalia
Jacobs
Jacques Vabre
Kaffee HAG
Kenco
Maxim
Maxwell House
Saimaza

Refreshment Beverages

Clight
Fresh
Frisco
Kool-Aid
Q-Refres-Ko
Tang
Verao

Cheese

Cheez Whiz
Dairylea
Eden
El Caserio
Kingdom
Kraft Singles
Kraft Sottilette
Philadelphia

Convenient Meals

Kraft Macaroni & Cheese
Lunchables
Mirácoli Dinners

Desserts

Bird's Angel Delight
Bird's Custard
Dream Whip
Royal

Enhancers

Ketchup & Sauces
Kraft Mayonnaise
Kraft Pourable Dressings
Miracle Whip
Vegemite

Cereals

Post CocoBall
Post Corn Flight

NOTES

Chapter One

2 . . . *over a billion people in the world are smokers . . . five million people died in 2000:* World Health Organization, Tobacco Free Initiative, http://www.who.int/tobacco.

2 *Smoking kills 440,000 Americans every year:* "The Health Consequences of Smoking," A Report of the Surgeon General, 2004.

3 . . . *overall rates of smoking began to decrease:* Centers for Disease Control and Prevention, "Percentage of Adults 18 Years and Older Who Were Current, Former, or Never Smokers," National Health Interview Surveys, selected years, United States 1965–2000, http://www.cdc.gov/tobacco/research_data/adults_prev/adstat1.htm.

3 . . . *from 36 percent of high school kids in 1997:* Centers for Disease Control and Prevention, "Cigarette Use Among High School Students, United States, 1991–2003," *Morbidity and Mortality Weekly Report*, June 18, 2004.

3 *The number of adults who have never smoked:* Centers for Disease Control and Prevention, "Number of Adults 18 Years and Older Who Were Current, Former, or Never Smokers," National Health Interview Surveys, selected years, United States 1965–2000, http://www.cdc.gov/tobacco/research_data/adults_prev/tab_3.htm.

4 . . . *four out of five current smokers are in developing countries:* U.S. Department of Health and Human Services, GlobalHealth.gov, http://www.globalhealth.gov/tobacco.shtml.

4 . . . *the big tobacco companies agreed:* Campaign for Tobacco-Free Kids, "Special Report: State Tobacco Settlement," http://www.tobaccofreekids.org/reports/settlements/.

5 . . . *auto industry spent $18.2 billion:* Jean Halliday, "Auto Industry Slashes Q1 Ad

Spending; Big 3 Explore Ad Alternatives, Incentives, Await New Models," *Advertising Age*, April 5, 2004.

5   . . . more cars than drivers: Department of Transportation, National Household Travel Survey, 2001.

5   *We drive everywhere now:* Department of Transportation, National Household Travel Survey, 2001.

6   *In 2002, the retail industry in this country spent $13.5 billion: Advertising Age*, http://aamedia.chaffee.com/page.cms?pageID=4.

6   . . . *in 2003 we spent nearly $8 trillion:* Department of Commerce, "Personal Consumption Expenditures by Major Type of Product and Expenditure," Bureau of Economic Analysis: 2003 Comprehensive Revision of the National Income and Product Accounts.

6   *We spend more . . . gross national product: World Development Indicators Database*, World Bank, September 2004.

6   . . . *the food industry spends around $33 billion:* Marion Nestle, *Food Politics: How the Food Industry Influences Nutrition and Health* (Berkeley: University of California Press, 2002).

6   *Antidepressant use in the U.S. nearly* tripled: Centers for Disease Control and Prevention, "Health, United States, 2004," National Center for Health Statistics report, September 2004.

6   . . . *we Americans spent $227 billion on medications:* Department of Commerce, "Personal Consumption Expenditures by Major Type of Product and Expenditure," Bureau of Economic Analysis: 2003 Comprehensive Revision of the National Income and Product Accounts.

Chapter Two

9   *Sixty-five percent of American adults are overweight; 30 percent are obese:* Centers for Disease Control and Prevention, "Prevalence of Overweight Among Adults: United States, 1999–2002," National Center for Health Statistics report.

9   . . . *127 million Americans are overweight:* American Obesity Association Fact Sheet, http://www.obesity.org/subs/fastfacts/obesity_US.shtml.

9   . . . *obesity figures ballooned . . . from 12 percent . . . to 21 percent:* Centers for Disease Control and Prevention, "Prevalence of Obesity Among U.S. Adults, by Characteristics, 1991–2001," National Center for Chronic Disease Prevention and Health Promotion.

9   *Over 20 percent of the adults in forty-one states plus Washington, D.C., are obese:* "F as in Fat: How Obesity Policies Are Failing in America," Trust for America's Health report, October 2004, healthyamericans.org.

9   *In November 2004, the Associated Press reported:* Daniel Yee, "Feds Say Obesity Epidemic Weighing Down Planes, Pushing Up Fuel Costs," Associated Press, November 4, 2004.

10   *So many of us are obese that we've created a market:* J. M. Hirsch, "Obesity Epidemic Spurs Market for Oversized Furniture," Associated Press, September 4, 2004.

10   *16 percent of active-duty troops are obese:* "F as in Fat: How Obesity Policies Are Failing in America," Trust for America's Health report, October 2004, healthy americans.org.

11   *Obesity rates in children:* Centers for Disease Control and Prevention, "Prevalence of Overweight Among Children and Adolescents: United States, 1999–2002," National Center for Health Statistics.

11   *. . . nine million American kids:* "Preventing Childhood Obesity: Health in the Balance," Institute of Medicine, September 30, 2004.

11   *. . . 77 percent of . . . women and 61 percent of African American men are overweight:* "Prevalence and Trends in Obesity Among U.S. Adults, 1999–2000," *Journal of the American Medical Association* 288, no. 14 (October 9, 2002).

11   *. . . Mexican American women are 1.5 times more likely:* "Health Problems in Hispanic American/Latina Women," Department of Health and Human Services, National Women's Health Information Center, May 2003.

11   *The Seattle Post-Intelligencer says:* Julie Davidow, "The Obesity Crisis: A Healthy Diet Often Beyond the Means of Poor, Hungry," *Seattle Post-Intelligencer,* September 9, 2004.

12   *. . . obesity rates decline as the level of education increases:* "Prevalence of Obesity Among U.S. Adults, by Characteristics, 1991–2001," Centers for Disease Control and Prevention, National Center for Chronic Disease Prevention and Health Promotion.

12   *The USDA reports that the cost of vegetables and fruit rose:* Davidow, "The Obesity Crisis."

13   *. . . sticking to the Atkins diet:* Davidow, "The Obesity Crisis."

13   *. . . families who rely on government assistance:* Dennis O'Brien, "Alarm Sounded on Child Obesity," *The Baltimore Sun,* October 1, 2004.

13   *Obesity-related illnesses will kill around 400,000 Americans:* "Actual Causes of Death in the United States, 2000," *Journal of the American Medical Association* 291, no. 10 (March 10, 2004).

13   *"The epidemic of childhood obesity":* Tom Farley and Deborah Cohen, "Fixing a Fat Nation: Why Diets and Gyms Won't Save the Obesity Epidemic," *The Washington Monthly,* December 2001.

13   *The United States spends about $117 billion:* The Surgeon General's Call to Action to Prevent and Decrease Overweight and Obesity, December 13, 2001.

14   *The prevalence of diabetes has skyrocketed:* Centers for Disease Control and Prevention, National Center for Chronic Disease Prevention and Health Promotion, 2003 National Diabetes Fact Sheet.

14   *Larry Axmaker:* Larry Axmaker, "Excess Weight, Diet, Inactivity Linked to Half of All Cancer," Online Wellness Center, Vanderbilt University, January 2004, http://vanderbiltowc.wellsource.com/dh/Content.asp?ID=1508.

15 . . . *because up to 60 percent of cancers may be prevented:* American Cancer Society, http://cme.amcancersoc.org/misc/About_ACS.shtml.

15 . . . *less likely that very overweight people will have children:* Marilynn Marcione, "Size May Matter When It Comes to Sperm," Associated Press, October 22, 2004.

15 *One in four cats and dogs in America is obese:* Cynthia Hubert, "When Pets Get Pudgy, UC Davis Program Helps Animals Beat Obesity," *The Sacramento Bee*, August 28, 2004.

16 . . . *"obesity gene":* "Obesity Gene Pinpointed," BBC News, August 12, 2001.

16 *Between 1971 and 2000, the daily caloric intake:* Centers for Disease Control and Prevention, National Health and Nutrition Examination Surveys, United States, 1971–2000.

17 *An extra 10 calories a day:* Amy D. Otto and John M. Jakicic, "Effective Weight Management," American College of Sports Medicine, Fit Society Page Newsletter, Summer 2004.

18 . . . *Greg Critser cites:* Greg Critser, *Fat Land: How Americans Became the Fattest People in the World* (Boston: Houghton Mifflin, 2003).

19 *In 1970, there were around 70,000 fast-food establishments:* National Restaurant Association, 2004 Restaurant Industry Forecast.

19 . . . *Americans spent $6.2 billion:* National Restaurant Association, 2004 Restaurant Industry Forecast.

19 . . . *the percentage of fast-food calories in the American diet:* Jason P. Block, Richard A. Scribner, and Karen B. DeSalvo, "Fast Food, Race/Ethnicity, and Income: A Geographic Analysis," *American Journal of Preventive Medicine* 27, no. 3 (October 2004).

22 . . . *Del Taco was offering a "Macho" meal that weighed four pounds:* Critser, *Fat Land*.

22 . . . *NYU study that compared the portion sizes:* Lisa R. Young and Marion Nestle, "The Contribution of Expanding Portion Sizes to the U.S. Obesity Epidemic," *American Journal of Public Health* 92, no. 2 (February 2002).

22 . . . *a Cornell professor has proved it:* Amber Smith, "Is it Possible to Eat Healthy at McDonald's?," *Syracuse Post-Standard*, July 5, 2004.

23 . . . *"Women of McDonald's" pictorial:* Parija Bhatnagar, "McDonald's Gals in Playboy Display," CNN, November 16, 2004.

23 *A recent study showed that the average American dinner at home:* Samara J. Nielson and Barry McPopkin, "Patterns and Trends in Food Portion Sizes, 1977–1998," *Journal of the American Medical Association* 289, no. 4 (January 22, 2003).

23 *A study done at Penn State:* "Dubious Value Meals: Bigger Is Not Better," April 2003, http://www.psu.edu/ur/2003/valuemeals.html.

23 *A University of Illinois study:* "Do Larger Packages Increase Usage? The More You See, The More You Eat," 2003, http://www.foodpsychology.com/newsreleases/dolargerpackagesin.htm.

24 . . . *30 pounds of french fries annually:* Eric Schlosser, *Fast Food Nation: The Dark Side of the All-American Meal* (Boston: Houghton Mifflin, 2001).

24   *Soft-drink consumption in the United States:* Samara Joy Nielsen and Barry M. Popkin, "Changes in Beverage Intake between 1977 and 2001," *American Journal of Preventive Medicine* 27, no. 3 (October 2004).

25   *. . . boys consumed more than twice as much milk . . . the average American teen drinks two or more 12-ounce sodas a day:* Michael F. Jacobson, "Liquid Candy: How Soft Drinks Are Harming Americans' Health," Center for Science in the Public Interest Study, 1998.

25   *Between 40 and 60 percent of peak bone mass:* Grace Wyshak, "Osteoporosis Prevention: A Pediatric Challenge," *Archives of Pediatrics and Adolescent Medicine* 154, no. 6 (June 2000).

25   *. . . health researcher David Ludwig:* "Childhood Obesity, Soft Drinks Linked; First Long Term Study Targets Sweet Beverages," *Detroit Free Press*, February 16, 2001.

Chapter Three

27   *. . . almost 60 percent of Americans exercise rarely or never:* "Obesity Epidemic Threatens Health in Exercise Deprived Societies," Earth Policy Institute Alert, December 19, 2000.

28   *Physical activity declined 13 percent among adolescents:* "Health Trends in Adolescents Over the Past 20 Years," an analysis of federal health data by Lisa Sutherland, University of North Carolina, April 2003.

28   *"[I]f a person drives instead of walks":* Tom Farley and Deborah Cohen, "Fixing a Fat Nation: Why Diets and Gyms Won't Save the Obesity Epidemic," *The Washington Monthly*, December 2001.

31   *. . . Suzanne Somers coos:* Suzanne Somers, *Get Skinny on Fabulous Food* (New York: Crown Publishing Group, 1999). Suzanne Somers, *Somersize Desserts* (New York: Crown Publishing Group, 2001). Suzanne Somers, *Eat, Cheat, and Melt the Fat Away* (New York: Crown Publishing Group, 2001).

31   *. . . Dr. Atkins declared:* Dr. Robert Atkins, *Dr. Atkins' New Diet Revolution* (New York: Avon Books, 1996).

32   *. . . The Abs Diet:* David Zinczenko and Ted Spiker, *The Abs Diet: The Six-Week Plan to Flatten Your Stomach and Keep You Lean for Life* (Emmaus, PA: Rodale, 2004).

33   *It has a brochure:* "Red Flag: Bogus Weight Loss Claims: A Reference Guide for Media on Bogus Weight Loss Claim Detection," Federal Trade Commission, Bureau of Consumer Protection, 2003.

34   *As The New York Times later joked:* Tom Kuntz, "Bubba Can't Bypass the Past," *New York Times*, September 12, 2004.

35   *Then take Jim Cantalupo:* "McDonald's Chairman and CEO Jim Cantalupo Passes Away," McDonald's press release, April 19, 2004.

35   *The man who instantly replaced Cantalupo:* Delroy Alexander, "McDonald's Taps Rising Star as CEO; Cantalupo's Death Shocks Company," *Chicago Tribune*, April 20, 2004.

35 *Well, a week later he held a press conference:* John Schmeltzer, "McDonald's Chief Has Cancer," *Chicago Tribune*, May 6, 2004.

35 *". . . totally unrelated acts of God":* Anna Cock, "Cancer-Hit Big Mac Chief Back at Work," *Queensland Courier Mail*, May 22, 2004.

35 *. . . Bell stepped down:* "Charlie Bell Steps Down; Board Elects Jim Skinner CEO and Mike Roberts President & COO," McDonald's press release, November 22, 2004.

Chapter Four

37 *. . . a couple of teens in the Bronx:* Marc Santora, "Teenagers' Suit Says McDonald's Made Them Obese," *New York Times*, November 21, 2002.

38 *When is hot coffee just too frickin' hot?:* Andrea Gerlin, "A Matter of Degree: How a Jury Decided That a Coffee Spill Is Worth $2.9 Million," *Wall Street Journal*, September 1, 1994.

39 *. . . also representing a guy named Caesar Barber:* Victorino Matus, "Dollar-Menu Death Wish; Fast Food Giants Are Faced with Another Lawsuit Claiming Their Food Is-Gasp-Unhealthy," *The Daily Standard*, December 3, 2002.

40 *. . . "physically and psychologically addictive":* Jonathan Wald, "McDonald's Obesity Suit Tossed," CNN Money, January 22, 2003.

47 *Dr. Erik Steele:* Erik Steele, "Big Food Is Acting Like Big Tobacco," *Bangor Daily News*, August 31, 2004.

48 *. . . "a science project conducted by the class clown":* Peter Rainer, "Where's the Beef?" *New York*, May 10, 2004.

48 *. . . "Heavy Users":* FindLaw.com, Judge Sweet's September 3, 2003, decision on amended complaint in Pelman v. McDonald's, http://news.findlaw.com/cnn/docs/mcdonalds/pelmanmcd90403opn.pdf.

50 *McDonald's said very little:* "McDonald's Response to Super Size Me Movie," McDonald's press release, April 29, 2004.

50 *An article . . . in the* Washington Monthly: Nicholas Confessore, "Meet the Press: How James Glassman Reinvented Journalism—as Lobbying," *The Washington Monthly*, December 2003.

51 *It calls itself "a non-profit, non-partisan public policy group":* Competitive Enterprise Institute, http://www.cei.org. See also Disinfopedia, http://www.disinfopedia.org/.

51 *. . . a woman named Soso Whaley:* www.cei.org. See also http://www.disinfopedia.org/wiki.phtml?title=Soso_Whaley.

52 *. . . Center for Consumer Freedom . . . PR Watch:* Sheldon Rampton and John Stauber, "Berman & Co.: Non-Profit Hustlers for the Food and Booze Biz," *PR Watch* 8, no. 1 (2001); Sheldon Rampton and John Stauber, "Tobacco Money Takes on Activists' Cash," *PR Watch* 9, no. 1 (2002).

53 *. . . claiming that the entire obesity epidemic was a scam created by the diet-pill makers!:* "CDC Admits Obesity Stats Flawed, Other Serious Errors Documented in CCF Report," Center for Consumer Freedom press release, November 23, 2004. Also see

"More Big Fat Lies: Obesity Statistics Are as Bogus as Weight-Loss Scams, Says the Center for Consumer Freedom," November 10, 2004, www.consumerfreedom.org.

53   ... *"Anyone who criticizes tobacco":* "ActivistCash.com/Center for Consumer Freedom," PR Watch's Impropaganda Review, http://www.prwatch.org/improp/ddam.html.

54   *The American Dietetic Association, for example, calls itself:* www.eatright.org (ADA website).

54   *But really, the ADA serves its corporate sponsors:* "Who Is the Dairy Coalition?" *PR Watch* 7, no. 4 (2000).

55   *Big American Dietetic Association funders ($100,000 plus) have included:* "Non-Profit Organizations Receiving Corporate Funding," Center for Science in the Public Interest (CSPI), Integrity in Science Project, http://www.cspinet.org/integrity/nonprofits/american_dietetic_association.html.

55   *American Cancer Society's major donors:* "Non-Profit Organizations Receiving Corporate Funding," Center for Science in the Public Interest (CSPI), Integrity in Science Project, http://www.cspinet.org/integrity/nonprofits/american_cancer_society.html.

56   *In a sixty-five-page ruling, Judge Sweet:* [Feb. 2003]: Jonathan Wald, "McDonald's Obesity Suit Tossed," CNN, January 22, 2003; and http://news.findlaw.com/cnn/docs/mcdonalds/plmnmcd12203opn.pdf.

Chapter Five

60   ... *"serving" 46 million people a day worldwide:* http://www.mcdonalds.com.

60   *Every day, one in four Americans eats fast food:* Eric Schlosser, *Fast Food Nation* (Boston: Houghton Mifflin, 2001).

60   ... *about 43 percent of them at a McDonald's:* Judge Sweet, "Pelman v. McDonald's Corporation," *New York Law Journal*, January 28, 2003.

60   *The first McDonald's arrived in New York City:* "Largest Metropolitan McDonald's in America Makes Its Debut on Broadway and 42nd Street," McDonald's press release, September 25, 2002.

60   ... *city health-code inspectors:* Independent study conducted by the author on August 17, 2004, using New York City's Department of Health and Mental Hygiene website, http://www.nyc.gov/html/doh/html/rii/.

61   *At travel destinations around the globe:* "Fascinating McFacts About McDonald's International," http://www.licenseenews.com/news/news167.html.

61   *There's even a McDonald's ... near the Dachau:* Schlosser, *Fast Food Nation;* and Timothy W. Ryback, *Ghost Town: The Last Survivor* (New York: Pantheon Books, 1999).

61   *McDonald's ... in South Africa:* http://www.mcdonalds.co.za.

61   ... *drastic changes in the eating habits of South Africans:* "Super Size South Africa," August 27, 2004, http://www.iafrica.com.

61   *And obesity is spreading there rapidly:* Andrew Donaldson, "Junk Food May Be as Addictive as Heroin," *The Sunday Times* (South Africa), July 20, 2003.

62 *There are now over 600 McDonald's in China:* Liz Clarke, "McDonald's Goes for Gold with Olympic Sponsorships," *Washington Post,* August 17, 2004.

62 *. . . the rapid spread of obesity in China:* "Chinese See Rise in Obesity as They Adopt Western Diets," News Target Network, November 10, 2004; "200 Million Chinese Are Overweight," Associated Press, October 14, 2004.

63 *"As India struggles":* Michael Morain, "Urban Indians Growing Fatter Along with Westernized World; Heart Attacks, Diabetes on the Rise," Associated Press, November 8, 2004.

63 *"American-style fast food was unknown in the Philippines":* Danielle Nierenberg, "Factory Farming in the Developing World," *World Watch,* May/June 2003.

63 *In China . . . no such thing as birthdays:* James Watson, ed., *Golden Arches East: McDonald's in East Asia* (Stanford, CA: Stanford University Press, 1997).

64 *. . . more McDonald's than public libraries:* National Center for Education Statistics, "Public Libraries in the United States, Fiscal Year 2001."

64 *. . . more McDonald's than . . . hospitals:* American Hospital Association, Fast Facts from AHA Hospital Statistics, October 2004.

64 *On opening day in Kuwait City:* Brian Halweil, "The Global Spread of Food Uniformity," Worldwatch Institute, 2004, http://www.worldwatch.org/pubs/goodstuff/fastfood.

64 *The opening of the first McDonald's in Moscow's Pushkin Square:* Vincent J. Schodolski, "Muscovites Stand in Line for a 'Beeg Mek' Attack," *The Chicago Tribune,* February 1, 1990.

65 *A young couple in Poland:* Marzena and Marcin Stawiccy, Lodz, Poland.

65 *A friend in Turkey:* Sermet Yuce, Istanbul, Turkey.

66 *More than a billion adults worldwide are now overweight:* World Health Organization, "Obesity and Overweight Fact Sheet, 2004."

66 *"The global epidemic of obesity":* Ania Lichtarowicz, "Obesity Epidemic Out of Control," BBC News World Service, October 31, 2004.

67 *There are over 1,200 of them now: The UK Franchise Directory,* nineteenth edition, http://www.theukfranchisedirectory.net/franchises/McDonalds_Restaurants_Limited.htm.

67 *Obesity levels in England have tripled:* Sam Lister, "Rising Obesity Will Condemn One in Ten Britons to Diabetes by 2010," (London) *Times,* October 7, 2004.

67 *The British rock star Morrissey:* John Robertson, ed. *Morrissey: In His Own Words* (London: Omnibus Press, 2001).

67 *Charles, the Prince of Wales, is famously opposed:* Caroline Davies, " 'Slow Food' Feast Proves Prince Is a Man of Taste," *Daily Telegraph,* October 25, 2004.

67 *The [Slow Food] movement started in 1986:* http://www.slowfood.com.

67 *In 1990, McDonald's took advantage:* McSpotlight.org, http://www.mcspotlight.org/case/index.html.

68 *. . . World Anti-McDonald's Day:* McSpotlight.org, http://www.mcspotlight.org media/press/releases/msc2008041.html.

68   *McDonald's pretax profits:* Jonathan Prynn, "McDonald's Profits Dive," *Evening Standard*, September 28, 2004.

69   *In 2004, the Scottish government urged:* Stuart MacDonald, "Time to Mac Big Changes; Super Portions Face the Axe," *The Mirror*, August 9, 2004.

69   *The Swedes have done a lot:* Jeff Rosenblum, "McDonald's Sweden: A Case Study," *The Natural Step*, http://www.naturalstep.org.

69   *Margareta, a young mother in Sweden:* Margareta Brilioth, Nacka, Sweden.

70   *Since the first Mac Shack opened in France:* "Delicious Irony: A Nation of Burger Munchers," *The Economist*, April 25, 2002.

70   *It has over a thousand now:* Adam Sage, "How France Keeps Children Out of McDonald's," (London) *Times*, October 24, 2004.

70   *A friend of mine named Guillaume:* Guillaume Garoff, Paris, France.

71   *. . . chef Dominique Valadier abandoned his career:* "How France Keeps Children Out of McDonald's," (London) *Times*, October 24, 2004.

72   *. . . McDonald's took tremendous flak:* "Putting on Pounds in India," Associated Press, November 14, 2004.

Chapter Six

77   *In his book* Cigarettes Are Sublime: Richard Klein, *Cigarettes Are Sublime* (Durham, NC: Duke University Press, 1995).

80   *The typical American gobbles three burgers:* Eric Schlosser, *Fast Food Nation* (Boston: Houghton Mifflin, 2001).

81   *Since a Big Mac packs 560 calories total:* http://www.mcdonalds.com.

81   *. . . color-coded labels . . . on packaged foods:* David Derbyshire, "Shoppers Support 'Danger Food' Logos," *The Daily Telegraph*, November 26, 2004.

82   *. . . "Outback Steakhouse does not make nutritional claims":* http://dietfacts.com.

82   *A Burger King Whopper [nutritional info]:* http://www.bk.com.

82   *A Quarter Pounder with cheese [nutritional info]:* http:www.mcdonalds.com.

82   *A KFC extra crispy chicken thigh [nutritional info]:* http://www.kfc.com.

82   *In May 2004, Cathy Kapica:* "McDonald's Corporation Announces Worldwide Nutrition Director," McDonald's press release, October 8, 2003.

83   *Wendy's Taco Supremo Salad:* http://www.wendys.com.

83   *McDonald's Fiesta Salad:* http://www.mcdonalds.com.

84   *. . . the British magazine* New Scientist *reported:* Diane Martindale, "Burgers on the Brain," *New Scientist* 177, no. 2380 (February 1, 2003).

85   *. . . Harvard Medical School nutritionists:* Alberto Ascherio, Meir J. Stampfer, and Walter C. Willet, "Trans Fatty Acids and Coronary Heart Disease," Harvard School of Public Health and Brigham and Women's Hospital joint study, 1999.

86   *At their peak use . . . almost 40 percent of the prepared foods:* "The Skinny on Bad Fat," *Newsweek*, December 1, 2003.

86   *"In Europe [food companies] hired chemists and took trans fats out":* Judith Weinraub, "Getting the Fat Out," *Washington Post*, November 12, 2003.

87 *McDonald's USA announced:* "McDonald's USA Announces Significant Reduction of Trans Fatty Acids with Improved Cooking Oil," McDonald's press release, September 3, 2002.

88 *In* Fortune *magazine:* Matthew Boyle, "Can You Really Make Fast Food Healthy?" *Fortune,* August 9, 2004.

89 *McDonald's quietly released:* "McDonald's TFA Reduction Timeframe Extended," McDonald's press release, February 28, 2003.

89 *Ban Trans Fats filed a class-action lawsuit against McDonald's:* Dan Ackman, "McDonald's Plaintiff Not Your Average McFatso," *Forbes,* July 12, 2004, http://www.bantransfat.com.

89 *They ran a full-page ad in* The New York Times: "McDonald's Panned for 'Broken McPromise' on Trans Fat," Center for Science in the Public Interest press release, September 24, 2004; http://cspinet.org/new/pdf/broken_mcpromise_final.pdf.

90 *In February 2005, McDonald's agreed to . . . paying out $8.5 million:* "McDonald's Settles Suit Over Trans Fats in Oils," *Los Angeles Times,* February 12, 2005.

90 *. . . publish notices to enlighten us patrons:* "McDonald's TFA Settlement Announcement," McDonald's press release, February 9, 2005.

90 *. . . Ban Trans Fats sued the giant Kraft Foods:* http://www.bantransfat.com/oreo.htm.

90 *Kraft sent out a detailed press release:* "Kraft Foods Announces Global Initiatives to Help Address Rise in Obesity," Kraft Foods press release, July 1, 2003.

91 *. . . new and improved Reduced Fat Oreo:* "Oreo Takes On a New Twist with New Varieties That Contain Zero Grams of Trans Fat Per Serving," Kraft Foods press release, April 6, 2004.

91 *. . . Kraft still hasn't gotten rid of trans fat in regular Oreos:* Pallavi Gogoi, "The Heat in Kraft's Kitchen," *BusinessWeek,* August 4, 2003, http://www.kraftfoods.com/main.aspx?m=contact_us/contact_us&q=trans%20fat.

92 *. . . Kraft had reduced trans fat in only "about 5% of its North American product volume":* Delroy Alexander, "Kraft Won't Shrink Portions; Clearer Nutrition Labeling Instead," *Chicago Tribune,* June 2, 2004.

92 *Some scientists believe . . . "Eating energy-dense foods:* Diane Martindale, "Burgers on the Brain," *New Scientist* 177, no. 2380 (February 1, 2003).

93 *. . . food does seem to be addictive:* Neal Barnard, MD, *Breaking the Food Seduction: The Hidden Reasons Behind Food Cravings* (New York: St. Martin's Griffin, 2003).

94 *. . . there's sugar in everything:* Greg Critser, *Fat Land: How Americans Became the Fattest People in the World* (Boston: Houghton Mifflin, 2003).

95 *. . . the typical American consumes between 120 and 150 pounds of refined sugar:* David and Anne Frahm, *Healthy Habits: 20 Simple Ways to Improve Your Health* (New York: Tarcher, 1998).

95 *. . . excessive sugar consumption is believed:* Paulette Millis, "The Dangers of Sugar," *Wholife-Wholeness and Wellness Journal of Saskatchewan* 10, no. 1 (May/June 2004).

97   *Some critics believe HFCS is a major player:* Kim Severson, "Sugar Coated: We're Drowning in High Fructose Corn Syrup. Do the Risks Go Beyond Our Waistline?" *San Francisco Chronicle,* February 18, 2004.

97   *. . . let's consider artificial sweeteners:* Food and Drug Administration, *FDA Consumer,* November–December 1999; Nexus 2, no. 28 (October–November 1995) and 3, no. 1 (December 1995–January 1996); "CSPI's Guide to Food Additives," Center for Science in the Public Interest, http://www.cspinet.org/reports/chemcuisine.htm #Additives%20rated; "Nutrasweet Is Suspected in Rise in Brain Tumors," *Minneapolis–St. Paul Star-Tribune,* November 5, 1996; Mercola, "The Potential Dangers of Sucralose," December 2000, http://www.mercola.com/2000/dec/3/sucralose_dangers. htm#.

Chapter Seven

101   *The USDA says we eat 1 million animals an hour:* Dr. Neal Barnard, Physicians Committee on Responsible Medicine, in interview conducted by the author, 2003.

101   *Take the cattle industry:* "Progress for US Beef, But Safety Issues Linger," *Christian Science Monitor,* November 23, 2004.

102   *. . . 200,000 cows at a time stand around:* Eric Schlosser, *Fast Food Nation* (Boston: Houghton Mifflin, 2001).

102   *. . . countries in the European Union won't let us export beef:* George Raino, "Staging a Comeback; Reopening of Japanese Markets Vital for State's Cattlemen," *San Francisco Chronicle,* January 11, 2005.

102   *. . . the first case of mad cow in the United States:* Brad Knickerbocker, "Progress for U.S. Beef, But Safety Issues Linger," *Christian Science Monitor,* November 23, 2004.

102   *. . . if humans eat the meat of cows suffering from BSE:* USDA, Food Safety and Inspection Service Division.

102   *By the end of 2003, 143 official cases:* USDA, Food Safety and Inspection Service Division.

102   *. . . a Florida woman died of it in 2004:* Ashley Fantz, "Mad Cow Disease Kills Broward Woman," *The Miami Herald,* June 22, 2004.

102   *. . . Oprah Winfrey did a show on mad cow:* John Stauber and Sheldon Rampton, *Mad Cow USA: Could the Nightmare Happen Here?* (Monroe, ME: Common Courage Press, 1997). Also see Howard Lyman, http://www.madcowboy.com.

103   *. . . as many as 400 cows:* Walter Nicholls and Candy Sagon, "The American Burger: How Safe Is It?" *Washington Post,* December 31, 2003.

103   *. . . hundreds or even thousands of animals . . . [in] a single burger":* "Modern Meat," *PBS Frontline,* interview with Dr. Robert Tauxe of the Centers for Disease Control, April 18, 2002.

103   *. . . as much as 78 percent of ground beef contains microbes:* Schlosser, *Fast Food Nation.*

103   . . . *feedlot production has grown from 2 million hogs per year:* Danielle Nierenberg, "Factory Farming in the Developing World," *World Watch*, May/June 2003.

104   . . . *in what are called "factory farms":* Michigan State University, Detroit College of Law, Animal, Legal and Historical Web Center, "Legal Protections of the Domestic Chicken in the U.S. and Europe," 2003, http://www.animallaw.info/articles/dduschick.htm#1.

104   . . . *there's a new super-strain of salmonella:* Amy Ellis Nutt, "Antibiotic-Resistant Germs: In Soil, Water, Food, Air," *Newark Star Ledger*, December 8, 2003.

104   *E. coli 0157:H7:* Centers for Disease Control and Prevention, Center for Bacterial and Mycotic Diseases, 2004, http://www.cdc.gov/ncidod/dbmd.

105   . . . *feeding all sorts of animals to the animals they feed to us:* Stephanie Simon, "Mad Cow Case Casts Light on Beef Uses," *Los Angeles Times*, January 4, 2004.

105   *Oh, and they do the same with roadkill:* Simon, "Mad Cow Case Casts Light."

106   . . . *the giant meat corporations have been expanding:* Danielle Nierenberg, "Factory Farming in the Developing World," *World Watch*, May/June 2003.

107   *Today, Americans spend about 90 percent of their food budget on processed foods:* Schlosser, *Fast Food Nation*.

108   *Fast-food companies purchase frozen fries:* Schlosser, *Fast Food Nation*.

109   *They were called NewLeaf potatoes:* Michael Pollan, *The Botany of Desire: A Plant's Eye View of the World* (New York: Random House, 2001).

110   *Although they were also used in Pringles:* Scott Kilman, "McDonald's, Other Fast Food Chains Pull Monsanto's Bio-Engineered Potato," *Wall Street Journal*, April 28, 2000.

110   . . . *the NewLeaf was discontinued:* Scott Kilman, "Monsanto's Genetically Modified Potatoes Find Slim Market, Despite Repelling Bugs," *Wall Street Journal*, March 29, 2001.

110   . . . *Monsanto claimed "that it has thoroughly examined":* Michael Pollan, "Playing God in the Garden," *New York Times*, October 25, 1998.

110   *Pollan visited a potato farmer:* Pollan, *The Botany of Desire*.

111   . . . *water, modified cornstarch, salt [Chicken McNuggets ingredients]:* http://www.mcdonalds.com.

112   . . . *about 75 percent had any nutritional data available to customers:* http://www.mcdonalds.com.

112   . . . *only about 50 percent of American households . . . hooked up to the Internet:* "A Nation Online: How Americans Are Expanding Their Use of the Internet," United States Department of Commerce, National Telecommunications Infrastructure Administration, February 2002.

114   . . . *the most eaten vegetable is the french fry:* National Restaurant Association Menu Analysis Survey, 1997.

114   *Potatoes, partially hydrogenated [french fries ingredients]:* http://www.mcdonalds.com.

Chapter Eight

119   *"This is a game of hysteria"*: Johanna Newman, "Obesity Fuels Their Fervor," *Los Angeles Times*, July 26, 2004.

122   *The average man weighing 150 pounds*: http://www.coolnurse.com/calories _burned.htm; http://www.nutristrategy.com/activitylist.htm.

125   Today's grandparents are more active: American Council for Fitness & Nutrition, "Health Trends in U.S. Adolescents over the Past Twenty Years"; National Association for Sport & Physical Education, "Shape of Our Nation's Children," http://www. actionforhealthykids.org/docs/fs_naspe.pdf.

126   *... the presence of PE has sharply declined*: National Association for Sport & Physical Education, "Shape of Our Nation's Children."

126   *The CDC reports that in 1991*: "Physical Activity Levels Among Children Aged 9–13 Years—United States, 2002," *CDC Weekly*, August 22, 2003; "Physical Activity and the Health of Young People;" http://www.cdc.gov/healthyyouth/physical activity/pdf/facts.pdf.

127   *"Increasing physical education instruction"*: "Rand Study Finds Modest Increase in Physical Education Can Help Cut Number of Overweight Young Girls," RAND Corporation press release, August 27, 2004.

128   *According to a 2004 survey*: "Bally Total Fitness: Americans' Embarrassment About Nation's Obesity Rate Not Leading to Action," *Club Industry*, February 1, 2004.

Chapter Nine

133   *... eating trans fats ... impairs memory and learning*: "Study: Eating Trans Fat Inhibits Learning," United Press International, October 26, 2004.

134   *... thirteen-year-old Justin Fletcher*: Martin Yvonne, "Fast Food Equals Slow Brain, Teen Finds," *Christchurch Press*, February 3, 2004.

136   *... Department of Health and Human Services has said [aspartame] ... troubling side effects*: "Report on All Adverse Reactions in the Adverse Reaction Monitoring System," Department of Health and Human Services, February 1994.

136   *There was a hilarious moment during that McLibel trial*: McSpotlight.org, trial transcripts, Day 046, November 4 1994, p. 45.

138   *[Downey, California, McDonald's] ... is actually registered with the National Trust*: http://www.nationaltrust.org/11most/list.asp?i=103.

139   *... Ray Kroc, a salesman*: http://www.mcdonalds.com.

139   *Now, the last really successful new meal*: "Big Mac's Makeover," *The Economist*, October 14, 2004.

140   *By 2001, Subway had passed McDonald's*: Ruby Millington, "Fred Deluca's Sandwich Chain Is Taking a Huge Bite of the UK Market," *The Express*, October 8, 2004; and "Big Mac's Makeover," *The Economist*, October 14, 2004.

140   *... the first Subway opened in Tikrit*: "Army & Air Force Exchange Service Opens First Subway Shop in Iraq," *Dallas Business Journal*, September 15, 2004.

141   *According to Subway's own website [Subway nutritional information]*: http://www.subway.com.

141   *The 12-inch Double Meat Meatball Marinara Sub whacks you*: "Hardee's Hails Burger as 'Monument to Decadence,'" *USA Today*, November 15, 2004.

141   *One British paper dubbed him*: Millington, "Fred Deluca's Sandwich Chain."

144   *Partly because of competitors . . . the worst in the history of McDonaldland*: John Arlidge, "Fat, Dumb and Happy," (London) *Times*, September 26, 2004.

145   *. . . a McDonald's spokesman called their reporting "bullshit" . . . "corrupt" and "a scandal sheet"*: David Leonhardt, "McDonald's: Can It Regain Its Golden Touch?" *BusinessWeek*, March 9, 1998.

145   *. . . the company has been showing signs of bouncing back*: Arlidge, "Fat, Dumb and Happy."

Chapter Ten

148   *. . . Houston had the dubious honor*: "America's Fattest and Fittest Cities," *Men's Fitness*, February 2004.

149   *"We have living proof"*: Karen Stabirer, "Get 'Em While They're Young," *Los Angeles Times*, August 15, 1993.

150   *In the summer of 2004 alone*: Mrk Graser, "Downsizing a Super-Sized Deal," *Variety*, June 28–July 11, 2004.

150   *According to Marion Nestle*: Marion Nestle, *Food Politics: How the Food Industry Influences Nutrition and Health* (Berkeley: University of California Press, 2002).

150   *In her book* Consuming Kids: Susan Linn, *Consuming Kids: The Hostile Takeover of Childhood* (New York: The New Press, 2004).

151   *It's called the "nag factor"*: Jenny Deam, "Targeting Kid Consumers," *The Denver Post*, July 23, 2002.

152   *You can see some egregious examples*: TV Party, http://www.tvparty.com/vault comsat.html.

153   *. . . Kellogg stuffed something like 25 million Muppet*: Muppet Central, http://www.muppetcentral.com/news/1999/120899.shtml.

153   *In 2002, General Mills went so far*: "Stars Wars and General Mills Join Forces," press release, August 8, 2002, http://www.starwars.com.

154   *. . . "the American Heart Association (AHA)"*: Nestle, *Food Politics*.

156   *"Now, Light wants to turn"*: "Marketing in the 'the Age of I,'" *BusinessWeek Online*, July 12, 2004.

156   *Its magazine* National Geographic Kids *is*: Center for Science in the Public Interest press release, July 19, 2004.

157   *Television advertising accounts*: Linn, Television Bureau of Advertising.

157   *. . . around 40,000 TV commercials . . . have a very hard time distinguishing advertisements from reality*: Report of the American Psychological Association Task Force on Advertising and Children, February 20, 2004.

157   . . . *Federal Trade Commission proposed a rule to ban:* "Pestering Parents: How Food Companies Market Obesity to Children," Center for Science in the Public Interest, November 2003.

158   *It began on the BBC:* "PBS Should Protect Children by Taking Teletubbies Off the Air, Coalition Says," Commercial Alert press release, Wednesday, March 22, 2000.

158   . . . *"merchandising was never, ever a consideration":* Gloria Goodale, "Entertainment's Message: 'Buy Me!' " *The Christian Science Monitor,* June 12, 1998.

159   *Neopets.com is the most popular:* http://www.Neopets.com.

160   . . . *"McDonald's wants to be integrated":* Daren Fonda, "Pitching It to Kids; On Sites Like Neopets.com, Brands Are Embedded in the Game. Is Children's Marketing Going Too Far?" *Time,* June 28, 2004.

160   . . . *Neopets toys in Happy Meals:* "From the Virtual World of Neopia to McDonald's, Happy Meals to Feature Neopets," McDonald's press release, May 24, 2004.

160   *McDonald's also teamed up with* . . . *Electronic Arts:* Daren Fonda, "Pitching It to Kids."

161   *Of course, your friends in government:* "Pestering Parents: How Food Companies Market Obesity to Children," Center for Science in the Public Interest, November 2003.

161   *McDonald's has been an Olympic sponsor:* "McDonald's Announces Worldwide Olympic Partnership Through 2012 Games," McDonald's press release, February 26, 2004.

161   . . . *McDonald's employees from thirty-five countries:* "McDonald's Announces Global Olympic Champion Crew Team for 2004 Athens Olympic Games," McDonald's press release, July 9, 2004.

162   . . . *Carly Patterson* . . . *"I couldn't even tell you":* Mike Beradino, "One of the Top U.S. Hopes for Gold, Patterson Says There's Time for Usual Teen Stuff After Games," *Fort Lauderdale Sun-Sentinel,* August 13, 2004.

162   *"It's fruit and yogurt. It's good for you":* Liz Clark, "McDonald's Goes for Gold with Olympic Sponsorships," *Washington Post,* August 17, 2004.

163   *At the Athens Games:* Mark Franchetti, "Pepsi's a Crime at the Sponsor Mad Olympics," (London) *Times,* August 8, 2004.

163   . . . *Euro 2004 Football Championships:* "McDonald's Defends Football Links," *Marketing,* June 23, 2004, http://www.brandrepublic.com.

164   . . . *American Youth Soccer Organization:* "McDonald's Teams with American Youth Soccer Organization to Promote a Balanced, Active Lifestyle for Southland Youth," McDonald's press release, September 4, 2004.

164   . . . *University of Miami Hurricanes:* Miami Hurricanes press release, September 22, 2004.

164   . . . *The Lancet called the practice "especially bizarre":* "Celebrity Junk Food Ads Attacked," BBC News, November 14, 2003.

165 *Every year, tons of Hollywood celebrities:* Deborah Cameron, "In Japan, the Ad Stars Rise in the West," *The Age,* December 4, 2004.

165 *Beyonce Knowles and Destiny's Child:* "Beyonce Knowles Loves McDonald's," November 4, 2004. www.imdb.com/news/wenn/2004_11_04.

166 *"I love her voice," Bjork told an interviewer:* George Rush and Joanna Molloy, "Beyonce's Buggin' Bjork," *New York Daily News,* November 5, 2004.

166 *. . . McDonald's signed Mary-Kate and Ashley Olsen:* Devin Gordon, Nicki Gostin, and Joe Clebatoris, *Newsweek,* September 27, 2004.

166 *. . . Center for Individual Freedom ranted:* "More Anti-American Images Found at German Subway Stores," Cybercast News Service, August 4, 2004, http://www.cfif.org.

168 *. . . "It was an inexpensive, imaginative way":* Eric Schlosser, *Fast Food Nation* (Boston: Houghton Mifflin, 2001).

168 *Thus the Ronald McDonald House Charities:* http://www.mcdonalds.com.

168 *It is ridiculous to call this an industry:* http://www.rotten.com/library/crime/corporate/mcdonalds/.

168 *McDonald's currently operates something like 8,000 "Playlands":* Schlosser, *Fast Food Nation.*

169 *Burger King has about 3,200:* Julie Vallese, "Burger King to Replace Netting in Play Areas," CNN, June 12, 2001.

169 *. . . Chuck E. Cheese's that took this concept all the way:* http://www.chuckecheese.com.

169 *By 2003, Happy Meals accounted for about 20 percent:* Sandra Eckstein, "Playing with Food," *Atlanta Journal Constitution,* April 29, 2004.

169 *And let's not forget the Mighty Kids Meal:* http://www.mcdonalds.com.

170 *Recently, Advertising Age cited Ronald McDonald:* David Klein and Scott Donatos, *Advertising Age, The Advertising Century.*

Chapter Eleven

175 *Through the National School Lunch Program:* Marion Nestle, *Food Politics* (Berkeley: University of California Press, 2002).

175 *An encyclopedia (Wikipedia) definition of the USDA:* http://www.wikipedia.org.

176 *Some critics call it "USDA Inc.,":* Philip Mattera, "USDA Inc.: How Agribusiness Has Hijacked Regulatory Policy at the U.S. Department of Agriculture," report released at the Food and Agricultural Conference of the Organization of Competitive Markets, Omaha, Nebraska, July 23, 2004.

176 *. . . something like forty-five of the top offices of the USDA:* Mattera, "USDA Inc."

178 *. . . how to revise and update both the Guidelines and the Pyramid:* Amy Lanou and Patrick Sullivan, "Recipe for Disaster: Scientists with Industry Ties Dominate Dietary Guidelines Advisory Committee," September 23, 2003, http://www.tompaine.com.

178 *Private citizens were allowed to write to the panel:* USDA website, http://www.usda.gov/cnpp/pyramid-update/Comments/index.html.

179   *The Food Pyramid got the USDA into trouble:* Neal Barnard, M.D., "U.S. Dietary Guidelines: Victory in Court," PCRM *Magazine,* Winter 2001.

179   *Big Sugar has lobbied:* "OUCH!: Congressional Candyland," *Alternet,* June 20, 2000; Cindi Ross Scoppe, "How Sweet It Is to Manipulate Government Diet Guidelines," *The Slate,* September 14, 2004, http:www.slate.com.

179   . . .The New York Times *reported . . . that the new guidelines:* "Added Sugars, Less Urgency? Fine Print and the Guidelines," Marion Burros, *The New York Times,* August 25, 2004.

180   *The sugar lobby also tried to throw:* "Sugar Lobbyists Sour on Study," Associated Press, April 23, 2003; "Big Sugar's 'Thuggish' Tactics Come Under Fire," Center for Science in the Public Interest press release, April 21, 2003; Sarah Baseley, "Sugar Industry Threatens to Scupper WHO," *The Guardian,* April 21, 2003.

180   *The dairy lobby is also celebrating:* Nicholas Zamisko, "How Milk Got a Major Boost," *Wall Street Journal,* August 30, 2004.

181   *Actually, the "Got Milk?" ad campaign:* http://www.beefboard.org, Frequently Asked Questions About National Checkoff Programs. See also USDA's Agricultural Marketing Service, http://www.ams.usda.gov; Pork Promotion, Research and Consumer Information Order, http://www.ams.usda.gov; "New Milk at McDonald's Fact Sheet," Dairy Management, Inc. press release, May 25, 2004, http://www.dairycheck off.com/ news/release-mcdonaldsfacts.asp.

181   . . . *Pork Board paid McDonald's thousands of dollars to help create and promote:* Physicians Committee for Responsible Medicine provided the author with internal Pork Board documents requested through the Freedom of Information Act; *Pork Leader* newsletter 23, no. 5 (March 7, 2003).

182   . . . *U.S. Supreme Court declared the mushroom checkoff:* "Mushroom Checkoff Declared Unconstitutional by Nation's Highest Court," *In Motion Magazine,* July 5, 2001.

182   . . . *beef producers are awaiting:* Troy Marshall, "Beef Checkoff Case Now Before the Supreme Court," *Beef,* December 13, 2004.

182   . . . *pork checkoff has been flopping:* Farmers Legal Action Group (FLAG), http://www.flaginc.org/news/Checkoff/checkoff.htm.

182   *How did the USDA get in the business:* Nestle, *Food Politics.*

183   *"The meat industry has used the NSLP":* "Congress: Stop Fattening Kids with Giant Meat and Cheese Subsidies, Say Doctors," Physicians Committee for Responsible Medicine press release, October 6, 2003.

Chapter Twelve

185   . . . *operating virtual franchises inside many schools:* "Foods Sold in Competition with USDA School Meal Programs," Center for Science in the Public Interest report to Congress, January 12, 2001.

185   *Some 23,000 of our public schools:* "School Foods Tool Kit: A Guide to Improving School Foods & Beverages," Center for Science in the Public Interest, September 2003.

185 . . . *cafeterias actually became licensed fast-food franchises:* "Expelling the Corporate Bucks," *Mothering*, July 1, 1999; Shawn Cox, "Doing Business with Schools; Partnerships Can Benefit Students, Corporate World," *Richmond Times Dispatch*, March 4, 2003; and Piper Henriques, "Lunch Is Served; While Pizza and Anything Chicken Reign as the Must-Have Dishes of the Cafeteria, Schools Strive to Offer Varieties with a Balanced Diet," *Richmond Times Dispatch*, January 16, 2002.

185 *Attorney John Banzhaf put it bluntly:* Testimony before the House Judiciary Subcommittee regarding HR 339, Personal Responsibility and Food Consumption Act, June 19, 2003.

186 . . . *nine out of ten high schools . . . have soda and snack vending machines:* "School Foods Tool Kit: A Guide to Improving School Foods & Beverages," Center for Science in the Public Interest, September 2003.

186 . . . *American schools have become "7-Elevens with books":* Anne Underwood, "Nutrition: How to Flunk Lunch," *Newsweek*, September 16, 2002.

186 *A study conducted in some 250 schools:* "Dispensing Junk: How School Vending Undermines Efforts to Feed Children Well," Center for Science in the Public Interest, May 2004.

186 . . . *New York City . . . got a cool $166 million for awarding Snapple:* Marian Burros, "The Snapple Deal: How Sweet It Is," *New York Times*, September 17, 2003.

187 *In 2004, Illinois Governor Rod Blagojevich:* "Official Business," *New York Times*, September 23, 2004.

188 *"Not all families own television sets":* Marion Nestle, *Food Politics: How the Food Industry Influences Nutrition and Health* (Berkeley: University of California Press, 2002).

188 *Some corporate-sponsored education materials:* "Pestering Parents: How Food Companies Market Obesity to Children," Center for Science in the Public Interest, November 2003.

189 . . . *"Krispy Kreme stores will give":* "Krispy Kreme to Reward Florida Students with Doughnuts for Good Grades," Associated Press, August 25, 2004.

189 *No wonder McDonald's has been rumored:* "Analyst Says Krispy Kreme May Be in Line to Be Bought," *Winston-Salem Journal*, September 28, 2004.

190 *In Arkansas, a new law "requires schools":* "Confusion over Candy in Classes Clarified," Associated Press, November 8, 2004.

190 . . . *Channel One debuted TV in classrooms:* Nestle, *Food Politics*; Linda Reid and Alberto Gedissman, "Required TV Program In Schools Encourages Poor Lifestyle Choices," *AAP News*, November 2000; Mark Walsh, "Commercials in the Classroom," *UNESCO Courier*, April 2000.

191 *"There's only one way to increase customers":* Catherine Seipp, "Marketing the Mouse," *National Review*, July 7, 2004.

191 *The Boston Globe explains:* Raja Mishra, "School Lunch Bill Targets Obesity," *Boston Globe*, October 25, 2004.

192 *In 2004, the Seattle school board . . . Fayette County public schools:* "School Foods

Tool Kit: A Guide to Improving School Foods & Beverages," Center for Science in the Public Interest, September 2003.

193   . . . *Senator Tom Harkin of Iowa:* Marguerite Higgins, "Bill Seeks Healthy Choices for Students," *Washington Times,* May 11, 2004; see also http://www.harkin.senate.gov.

194   *Sweden, Norway [and other countries that have banned marketing to children]:* Susan Linn, *Consuming Kids: The Hostile Takeover of Childhood* (New York: The New Press, 2004).

194   *The 120 students at Appleton Central Alternative Chapter School:* "School Foods Tool Kit: A Guide to Improving School Foods and Beverages," Center for Science in the Public Interest, September 2003.

196   *Browne Junior High School in Washington, D.C.:* School Foods Tool Kit.

197   *In Montana, Whitefish Middle School switched from selling:* School Foods Tool Kit.

197   *But watch out. Big Food sees which way the wind is blowing:* Nichola Groom, "School Food Companies Seek Profits from Health," *Reuters,* July 11, 2004.

Chapter Thirteen

200   *Americans spend more than $40 billion:* National Eating Disorders Association, http://www.nationaleatingdisorders.org/p.asp?WebPage_ID=286&Profile_ID=41138.

201   . . . *"Miracle diets come and go":* "Carbo-Phobia: Zoning Out on the New Diet Books," *Nutrition Action Health Letter,* Center for Science in the Public Interest, July/August 1996.

201   *Apparently, though, weird diet plans . . . William the Conqueror . . . vinegar diet . . . Horace Fletcher . . . grapefruit diet:* Martha Brockenbrough, "The Skinny on Fat and Fad Diets," MSN Encarta website, http:www.encarta.msn.com.

202   *Sylvester Graham . . . William Banting:* Stephanie Schorow, "You Can't Eat *That* . . . History Shows Fad Diets Are Nothing New," *Boston Herald,* April 13, 2004.

203   . . . *"most of the weight a person loses":* "Frequently Asked Questions About Weight Loss," U.S. Department of Health and Human Services, National Women's Health Information Center, January 2002.

204   *Recent studies suggest that the Atkins:* Kathy Goodwin, "The Atkins Diet—A Comprehensive Analysis," The Diet Channel, August 9, 2004, http:www.thedietchannel. com.

204   *And remember Fen-Phen:* "Health Risks and Dangers of Weight Loss Pills," Weight Loss Information, http://www.weight-loss-i.com/health-risks-weight-loss-pills.htm.

205   *Meridia weight-loss pills:* "Meridia Weight Loss Is No Gain," Consumer Justice Group, http://www.consumerjusticegroup.com/meridiawholearticle.htm.

205   *In 2000, the FDA issued a warning about the use of phenylpropanolamine:* Kevin Sack and Alicia Mundy, "Over the Counter Peril; A Dose of Denial; How Drug Makers Sought to Keep Popular Cold and Diet Remedies on Store Shelves After Their Own Study Linked Them to Strokes," *Los Angeles Times,* March 28, 2004.

205   *In 2004, the FDA banned ephedra . . . Baltimore Orioles pitcher Steve Bechler died:*

David Ginsburg, "Loved Ones Reflect on Bechler's Death," Associated Press, February 16, 2004.

210   *It's called bariatric surgery . . . 25,000 . . . performed in 1998; in 2004, it was 144,000:* Thomas H. Maugh II, "Major Benefits Seen in Weight-Loss Surgeries," *Los Angeles Times,* October 13, 2004.

212   *Bariatric surgeons seem reluctant to publish detailed:* Gina Kolata, "Weight Loss Surgery May Soon Be Paid by Medicare," *New York Times,* September 30, 2004.

212   *. . . "more than a quarter of the phenomenal growth in health care spending":* Ceci Connolly, "Obesity Gets Part of Blame for Care Costs," *Washington Post,* October 20, 2004.

212   *Fewer than one out of four American employers:* Eric Berger, "While Doctors Say a Bariatric Operation May Be the Only Hope for Some Severely Overweight Kids, Many Insurance Firms Contend They Need More Evidence of Procedure's Benefits to Offer Coverage," *Houston Chronicle,* October 10, 2004.

213   *Blue Cross and Blue Shield of Florida . . . Cigna HealthCare also dropped:* Liz Freeman, "Stomach-Stapling Surgery Now Increasingly Popular," *Naples Daily News,* August 1, 2004.

213   *"Gastric bypass surgery is an extremely risky procedure":* Mark Sherman, "Medicare Seeks Weight Loss Plans That Work," Associated Press, July 20, 2004.

213   *. . . "insurance companies feel threatened by the rising costs":* Berger, "While Doctors Say a Bariatric Operation."

213   *Then again, Blue Cross and Blue Shield of North Carolina:* Jean P. Fisher, "Blue Cross to Fund Fight Against Fat," *Raleigh News & Observer,* October 13, 2004.

213   *The federal government added to the confusion:* "Fat May Soon Be No. 1 Cause of Preventable Deaths in U.S.," *Mercury News,* March 10, 2004; Ceci Connolly, "Medicare Changes Policy on Obesity," *Washington Post,* July 16, 2004.

214   *. . . bariatric surgery is now being performed more often on obese children:* Shari Roan, "Obese Children Turn to Surgery," *The Scotsman,* November 1, 2004; Marc Santora, "Shedding 'Baby Fat' Through Surgery," *New York Times,* November 26, 2004.

214   *"At least half a dozen major hospitals in the New York City area":* Marc Santora, "Teenagers Turn to Surgery to Shrink Their Stomachs," *New York Times,* November 26, 2004.

215   *. . . Brandon Bennett:* "Private Facility to Fund Gastric Bypass Surgery for Teen," Associated Press, October 14, 2004.

216   *For one thing, the American medical establishment has never focused on nutrition:* Mike Adams, "Health Illiteracy Is Widespread," *News Target,* November 23, 2004.

216   *. . . "Nutrition is essential to medical education":* Dr. Allan W. Walker, speech given at the Sixth Annual Post Graduate Nutrition Symposium at Harvard Medical School, 2002, http://www.hms.harvard.edu/nutrition/education/edu_nut_symp_sum.html.

216 *As of 2003, a nutrition course was required:* LuAnn Soliah, "A Survey of Nutrition in Medical School Curricula," *Today's Dietician* 6, no. 2 (February 2004).

217 *. . . childhood obesity is underdiagnosed:* Dr. Ihuomi Eneli, "Childhood Obesity Under-Diagnosed in Doctors' Offices and Urgent Care Facilities," Michigan State University report presented at the annual meeting of the Pediatric Academy Sciences, Seattle, May 2003.

217 *In response, Brown University has developed:* Kim M. Gans, Elizabeth Ross, Claudia W. Barner, Judith Wylie-Rosett, Jerome McMurtay, and Charles Eaton, "REAP and WAVE: New Tools to Rapidly Assess/Discuss Nutrition with Patients," American Society of Nutritional Sciences, February 2003, http://www.nutrition.org.

217 *Also, the Department of Health and Human Services has produced:* "Combatting Childhood Obesity," Agency for Healthcare Research and Quality, http://www.ahrq.gov/child/dvdobesity.htm.

218 *. . . about 19 million Americans a year are diagnosed:* "America's Mental Health Survey 2001," National Mental Health Association, May 2001, http://www.nmha.org/pdfdocs/mentalhealthreport2001.pdf.

218 *Their symptoms are treated with drugs:* http://www.antidepressantsandchildsuicide.com.

218 *LCTS, or low-carb tunnel syndrome:* Mike Adams, "Doctor Reveals New Risk for Low-carb Dieters," *News Targets*, May 9, 2004, http://www.emediawire.com/releases/2004/5/emw124561.htm.

219 *. . . FDA is rife with conflicts of interest:* (part one), Dennis Cauchon, "FDA Advisers Tied to Industry," *USA Today*, September 25, 2000; and (part two), Dennis Cauchon, "Number of Drug Experts Available Is Limited," *USA Today*, September 25, 2000.

219 *There's been a McDonald's at Texas Children's:* Marc Santora, "If the Hospital Cafeteria Is a McDonald's, Is Fast Food Still Unhealthy?" *New York Times*, October 26, 2004.

220 *"The doctors liked McDonald's":* "Burgers for the Health Professional," *New York Times*, October 26, 2004.

220 *Which Happy Meals:* [Happy Meal nutritional info]: http://www.mcdonalds.com.

220 *A 2002 University of Michigan survey:* University of Michigan Health System, "Nation's Leading Hospitals Serving Up Fast Food," June 12, 2002, http://www.med.umich.edu/opm/newspage/2002/fastfood.htm.

221 *. . . Harlem Hospital Center booted:* "Big Mac Attack," *Crain's New York Business*, August 3, 2004.

221 *Cleveland Clinic CEO Dr. Toby Cosgrove:* Michael McIntyre, Mike Tobin, and Rich Exner, "McDonald's Digs in to Hold Spot at Clinic," *The Plain Dealer* (Cleveland), November 22, 2004.

222 *The Academy of the Sierras:* Pallavi Gogoi, "A Hogwarts for Obese Kids," *BusinessWeek Online*, October 27, 2004, http://www.businessweek.com/bwdaily/dnflash/oct2004/nf20041027_5868_db-92.htm.

222   *Having declared obesity a national crisis:* Pallavi Gogoi, "Federal Funds Fight the Fat," *BusinessWeek Online,* October 27, 2004, http://www.businessweek.com/bwdaily/dnflash/oct2004/nf20041027_5537_db-92.htm.

Chapter Fourteen

226   *It has been said that the main causes of obesity's spread:* Gerald Schluter and Chinkook Lee, "Changing Food Consumption Patterns: Their Effect on the US Food System, 1972–1992," *Food Review,* January–April 1999.

228   *This international anti–fast food movement:* http://www.slowfoodusa.org.

230   *There are typically three times as many supermarkets:* "Transportation and Food: The Importance of Access," Urban and Environmental Policy Institute Center for Food and Justice, October 2002.

230   *The evolution of the American grocery store:* Groceteria, http://www.groceteria.net; Food Marketing Institute, http://www.fmi.org.

231   *. . . there are almost 34,000 supermarkets:* Food Marketing Institute, Supermarket Facts Industry Overview, 2003, http://www.fmi.org/facts_figs/superfact.htm.

231   *. . . the rest of the world is racing to catch up:* Stefania Bianchi, "Supermarkets Booming in Developing Countries," Inter Press Service, July 24, 2004.

234   *. . . produce in the United States travels an average 1,500 to 2,500 miles:* Brian Halweil, *Eat Here: Reclaiming Homegrown Pleasures in a Global Supermarket* (Washington, D.C.: World-Watch Institute Books, 2004).

234   *"Organic" means farming:* "New Organic Standards to Hit U.S. Shelves on October 21, 2002," World-Watch Institute press release, October 9, 2002.

235   *The U.S. market for organic products:* Carolyn Dimitri and Catherine Greene, "Recent Growth Patterns in the U.S. Organic Foods Market," USDA Economic Research Science Agriculture Information Bulletin #777, September 2002.

235   *In 1990, Congress authorized:* Gwen Schoen, "Stamp of Approval, What's Organic? Government Hopes New Rules on Labeling Will End the Confusion," *Sacramento Bee,* October 16, 2002.

235   *. . . the Whole Foods Market chain:* Julia Boostin, "Natural Selection," *Unlimited,* November 1, 2003; http://www.wholefoods.com.

236   *The Wild Oats Natural Marketplace chain:* http://www.wildoats.com.

236   *. . . farmers' markets have seen explosive growth:* http://www.localharvest.org; USDA, http://www.ams.usda.gov/farmersmarkets.

236   *In Manhattan, the Washington Heights Greenmarket:* "Farmers' Markets," World Hunger Year Food Security Learning Center, http://www.worldhungeryear.org.

237   *In the San Francisco Bay Area:* Tara Duggan, "Bringing Healthy Produce to Poor Neighborhoods," *The San Francisco Chronicle,* July 16, 2004.

237   *Fresh produce from local farms has even come to Compton:* Mary MacVean, "If You Build It, Children Will Come to the Salad Bar," *Los Angeles Times,* November 4, 2004.

238   *Alice Waters . . . the Edible Schoolyard:* http://www.edibleschoolyard.com; Leslie Crawford, "Alice Waters," November 16, 1999, http://www.salon.com/people/bc /1999/11/16/waters.

Chapter Fifteen

247   *In South Korea an environmental activist:* "South Korean Activist Ends Risky Diet of Junk Food," Agence France Presse, November 11, 2004.

248   *. . . The Lancet published the results of a study:* M. A. Pereira, A. I. Kartashov, C. B. Ebbeling, L. Van Horn, M. L. Slattery, D. R. Jacobs, and D. S. Ludwig, "Fast-Food Habits, Weight Gain, and Insulin Resistance (The CARDIA study): 15-Year Prospective Analysis," *The Lancet,* January 1, 2005.

249   *. . . "It is important to pressure the food industry":* Dr. Manoj Jain, "Hospitals Can Lead Attack on Obesity," *Memphis Commercial Appeal,* November 15, 2004.

250   *No company's done more to give itself a shiny new image:* John Arlidge, "Fat, Dumb and Happy," (London) *Times,* September 26, 2004.

250   *. . . white bean soup (sopa de feijão blanco) in Portugal:* "McDonald's Portugal Offers Local Dishes," Associated Press, November 13, 2004.

250   *. . . McDonald's core burger-flipping mission:* "Big Mac's Makeover," *The Economist,* October 14, 2004.

251   *Charlie Bell, that former CEO:* Arlidge, "Fat, Dumb and Happy."

251   *"The $144 billion fast-food industry":* Matthew Boyle, "Can You Really Make Fast Food Healthy?" *Fortune,* August 9, 2004.

253   *. . . the aptly named Monster Thickburger:* "Hardee's Introduces New Mega-Calorie Monster Thickburger," Associated Press, November 16, 2004.

253   *Executive director Michael Jacobson:* "Hardee's Monster Thickburger More Porno Than Ever," Center for Science in the Public Interest press release, November 16, 2004.

254   *Wendys' Dave Thomas Foundation:* http://www.wendys.com; http://www.bk. com; http://www.outback.com.

254   *. . . McDonalds' annual World Children's Day:* "McDonald's World Children's Day Kick-off Features All-Star Line-Up," McDonald's press release, November 9, 2004.

255   *A group of health professionals wrote an open letter to UNICEF:* William MacDougal, "World Children's Day: McDonald's, Cheeseburgers and Charity," *ZNet,* November 15, 2003, http://www.zmagsite.zmag.org/Jan2004/macdougal-1-4.htm.

255   *In 2004, Ken Barun, who runs the Ronald McDonald House:* "McDonald's World Children's Day."

Chapter Sixteen

257   *In November 2004, the World Health Organization:* NewsTarget, "World Health Organization Adopts Global Health and Diet Recommendations: Reduce Sugars,

Processed Foods, Soft Drinks, and Junk Food Advertising," February 13, 2005, www.newstarget.com.

257 *At the Sugar Association, Andy Briscoe:* "Sugar Business Sours as U.S. Goes Diet Crazy," *USA Today*, October 4, 2004.

258 *General Mills, which puts out Trix:* Bruce Horovitz, "General Mills Cereals Go Totally Whole Grain," *USA Today*, September 30, 2004.

258 *Even Krispy Kreme:* Jeff Clabaugh, "Krispy Kreme Debuts in District," *Washington Business Journal*, August 24, 2004.

259 [W]e have taken this craze: Amanda Schaffer, "A Carb Is a Carb Is a Carb," *Slate.com*, November 9, 2004, http://www.slate.com.com/id/2109384.

260 *. . . a Golden Question Mark:* "McDonald's Launches Push in Britain with Health Theme," *Chicago Tribune*, October 14, 2004; http://www.adrants.com, October 13, 2004.

260 *. . . the casting company hiring actors:* Clodagh Hartley, "Small Mac and Skinny Fries, Please," *The Sun*, November 5, 2004.

261 *. . . the British government proposed a simple "traffic light" system:* Gaby Hinsliff, J. Revidl, and Dennis Campbell, "Junk Food Ads Banned to Fight Fat Epidemic," *The Observer*, November 14, 2004.

262 *. . . the so-called "Cheeseburger Bill":* "House Passes 'Cheeseburger Bill,' " Fox News, March 11, 2004; "US Approves 'Cheeseburger Bill,' " BBC News, March 12, 2004.

262 *. . . Keller's district "is home to Darden Restaurants Inc.":* James Joyner, "Cheeseburger Bill," March 13, 2004, http://www.outsidethebeltway.com/archives/005371. html.

264 *. . . examples of schools that have turned around their lunchrooms:* "School Foods Tool Kit," Center for Science in the Public Interest, http://cspinet.org/schoolfood /index.html.

266 *. . . Parents Advocating School Accountability (PASA):* http://pasaorg.tripod.com.

ABOUT THE AUTHOR

Morgan Spurlock is an award-winning writer, producer and director. Originally from West Virginia, he graduated from New York University's Tisch School of the Arts in 1993.

In 2004, Morgan's debut feature film, *Super Size Me*, became the third-highest-grossing documentary of all time. He won the best director prizes at both the Sundance and Edinburgh film festivals. The movie was named to more than thirty-five year-end top ten lists and was a National Board of Review and Critic's Choice best documentary nominee. New York Film Critics Online named it the best documentary of 2004.

Don't Eat This Book is Morgan's first book and picks up where the movie left off, diving even deeper into the psyche of a super-sized nation.

He currently lives in the East Village in New York City with his vegan fiancé, Alexandra Jamieson, and their manly cat, Sue.